Monty Waldin

BIODYNAMIC
GARDENING

 Penguin
Random
House

Senior Editor Helen Fewster
Senior Art Editor Sonia Moore
Senior Designer Alison Gardner
Design Assistant Amy Keast
Jacket Designer Sonia Moore
DK Picture Library Claire Cordier
Senior Producer Ché Creasey
Preproduction Producer Andy Hilliard
Managing Editor Penny Warren
Publisher Mary Ling
Art Director Jane Bull

North American Consultant Jim Fullmer
US Editor Kate Johnsen
US Senior Editor Shannon Beatty

Biodynamic Shoot Consultant Briony Young
Lead Photographer Will Heap

First American edition, 2015
Published in the United States by DK Publishing,
345 Hudson Street, New York, New York 10014
A Penguin Random House Company

15 16 17 18 19 20   10 9 8 7 6 5 4 3 2 1
001–259425–March/2015
Copyright © 2015 Dorling Kindersley Limited.

Published in Great Britain by
Dorling Kindersley Limited.

A catalog record for this book is available from the
Library of Congress.

ISBN 978-1-4654-2986-5

DK books are available at special discounts when
purchased in bulk for sales promotions, premiums,
fund-raising, or educational use. For details,
contact: DK Publishing Special Markets,
345 Hudson Street, New York, New York 10014 or
SpecialSales@dk.com.

Printed and bound in China by Hung Hing.

A WORLD OF IDEAS:
SEE ALL THERE IS TO KNOW

www.dk.com

Contents

What is biodynamic gardening?

Biodynamics offers a simple way to nurture the soil beneath your feet and reconnect with seasonal cycles and natural rhythms. It is a sustainable way of growing tasty, high-quality food that is good for your body and soul, and puts more back into the soil than it takes out. Initially, some of the methods may seem a little strange, but overall, biodynamics has an unbeatable logic based on old-fashioned farming values familiar to many who are already gardening organically: healthy soil, self-sufficiency, putting more back into the soil than you take out, and working with nature rather than against it. The difference lies in the use of the biodynamic preparations—nine remedies based on plants and minerals that bring vitality to your soil and garden—that are unique to biodynamics. Best of all, connecting the natural cycles of the sky above your head with the natural cycles beneath your feet costs nothing and makes for better gardening.

The organic way

Know your garden

Deciding what you want to grow is one thing, but knowing what the garden is capable of growing is another. The key to success is balancing the potential of what will grow in your plot with your own needs. To put it another way, concentrate on crops that will naturally thrive with minimal work, cost, and intervention.

Deciding what to grow

Growing the crops you like to eat goes without saying, but it is essential to learn what grows best in your garden. As a starting point, ask your neighbors which crops work well for them, and which do not. Don't take everything they say as the final word, since their gardens may offer different conditions from yours. The next step is then to assess the growing conditions your site offers, which will shape the crops you choose to grow. All crops need looking after, and most require daily care, so it's important to grow those that you will have time to maintain. If you have a lot of spare time, you can almost grow what you like. If you don't, consider growing perennial vegetables and herbs, and fruit bushes and trees that need only minimal day-to-day care.

Assessing your growing conditions

The direction your garden faces, how air flows across it, and where and when light falls throughout the day all influence the crops you can grow. An essential thing to know is its latitude—its distance from the equator. Latitude affects how long the days and seasons are through the year, and the duration and quality of sunlight. It also determines when the first and last frosts occur each year. This directly impacts on the growing season of tender crops, such as tomatoes, that may need to be started, or grown entirely, under cover. It is also important to hardy perennial crops, such as fruit trees that only crop if they flower after the last spring frost, and winter brassicas that taste much better after winter chill. When planning your planting, check your garden for frost pockets—usually low areas, or where the ground dips.

When deciding which crops to grow, also consider how much rain typically falls in your area, and when. Where rain is unreliable in summer, thirsty crops such as spinach will require very regular watering. If you know when to expect rain, plan to collect and store as much as possible for dryer times of year. In areas where there are prolonged periods of heavy rainfall, bare soil can be damaged. In such places, again, plan ahead and protect exposed soil by sowing either crops or green manures (*see p.19*). In addition to the general climate, your garden will also have microclimates, specific areas that are warmer or colder, which may only be a few paces apart. Take note of these, and plant according to the conditions they offer.

Assessing your soil

The type of soil you have determines the crops you can grow. However, since healthy soil contains decomposed plant matter, what you grow influences the type of soil you have. Soil also contains clay, sand, and rocks, and their relative proportions affect how well it drains water and retains nutrients. The ideal soil has a balance of clay and sand, and is known as loam. Loam drains steadily, giving plants time to absorb water and food, without becoming waterlogged. In contrast, sandy and rocky soils drain well but allow nutrients to wash away quickly, while nutrient-rich clay soil drains slowly and is prone to waterlogging.

You can assess how well your soil drains by digging holes around your plot to see how quickly buckets of water drain away. Alternatively, for a more accurate assessment of its structure, fill a large glass jar with a water, add a trowel scoop of soil, shake, then let it settle overnight. If the jar is more than half-filled with sand and rocks, the soil is sandy; if the water stays cloudy or the jar is over half full of very fine sediment, the soil is rich in clay.

Understanding your soil

To improve sandy and rocky soils, dig in generous amounts of compost, or sow soil-building green manures, to make them more earthy. Clay soil is also improved by digging in compost, which breaks up its dense structure, allowing water to drain more freely while still retaining nutrients. Adding compost to your soil increases its levels of organic matter, which holds the soil together. It also helps sustain worms and soil organisms that create tiny tunnels and galleries in the soil, through which air, water, and nutrients pass. The compost itself helps plants find more of the food they need because it provides all-important humus. Humus is like concentrated soil, and holds and releases the nutrients plants need.

Even if your soil is fertile, your crop's ability to absorb nutrients is affected by its pH, or acidity. Soil pH affects how soluble many nutrients, and especially micronutrients, are—and therefore whether these nutrients are easily available to your plants. The ideal pH for most crops is about pH 7, meaning neutral; a low pH suits acid lovers; a higher one suits plants that like alkaline conditions. You can use a kit to test your soil pH, or simply look out for pH sensitive weeds, such as acid-loving dandelions and plantain, or alkaline-loving scarlet pimpernel and Queen Anne's lace (wild carrot). You can also refer to weeds to assess other aspects of your soil. Creeping buttercups suggest waterlogging, grasses thrive on compacted soil, while many other weeds indicate the presence or lack of certain nutrients.

Planning a new garden

When planning a new garden, the first step is to map out the existing plot and to draw a rough map. On it, first include permanent or semipermanent features, such as ponds, raised beds, sheds, paths, and whether the site slopes. An existing shed may be a useful windbreak, while the side of a sunny slope could be planted with fruit trees, and use the base as the site for a pond. Then add aspects that will affect what you grow, including frost pockets, hot spots, and the prevailing wind direction. Finally, mark on natural boundaries or fixed areas, such as walls and fences that will provide shelter.

Preparing your plan

The aim when designing a garden is to ensure it suits you, what you want to grow, and is laid out to enable the plot to be worked efficiently. First, start with laying out the pathways needed to give access across the garden and to important areas, such as the shed, greenhouse, compost pile, house, or gate. These are arteries through which you and any green waste, tools, compost, and crops should be able to move around as effortlessly as possible. Then divide the garden into areas for preparing, growing, and storing crops, keeping tools, composting, and harvesting water. Areas needed for raising seedlings include greenhouses and hotbeds for sowing, and cold frames for hardening off. If you have a greenhouse and a hotbed, site them closely together, and position any cold frames where they will experience a full range of weather conditions so that plants harden off successfully.

Existing walls in the garden are ideal for positioning raised beds, cold frames, pergolas, and even chicken runs against.

• Include storage in your plan
Storage is important for tools, equipment, and produce, so include as much as you can. Garden tools should be kept under cover, out of the elements, and secure from opportunists. A lockable garden shed is ideal.

Many crops also require storage space, and need particular conditions. Onions and pumpkins need somewhere airy, while potatoes, carrots, turnips, and other roots prefer somewhere cool and dark, such as a root cellar or storage box. Apples and pears store best kept in conditions somewhere in-between.

Saved seeds also need the right environment where they can be sorted, cleaned, dried, and stored, so leave space for that. Finally, find a partly shaded spot to store your biodynamic preparations, whether they were made onsite or purchased (*see pp.120–121*).

• Allow space for wildlife To attract wildlife, create corridors of flowering plants of different heights, shapes, and colors throughout the garden. The sight, sound, and smell of these floral arteries will increase biodiversity in the garden and inspire your work. A wildlife pond can provide a real focal point for your plot, and will act as a draw for a multitude of beneficial insects and amphibians. Ensure it is safe for children, and find a way to keep it filled up with captured rainwater. Also, install a solar-powered pump to keep the water oxygenated and healthy. Where space allows, leave quiet areas for wildlife habitats, and plant a selection of native plants to attract them.

• Make life easier Garden lighting is well worth designing into your plans, to allow you to work into the evening when required. It will also help prevent accidents, since you can see what you're doing and where you are walking. To make life easier, locate several portable trash cans in the garden to avoid constant trips to the compost pile or back to the house with recyclables. On larger plots, consider installing spigots connected to the main water supply for easier watering, or lay seep hoses across your beds.

• Leave space for yourself Above all things, create a space for you, your friends, and family to share, where you can sit and watch the whole garden and sky above. Observation is the greatest and most cost-effective tool for learning that any biodynamic gardener can wish for.

Making use of raised beds

The best way to grow a constant supply of fresh vegetables without heavy digging, the minimum of weeding, and mud-free shoes, is in raised beds—they are ideal for smaller urban gardens.

The idea for raised beds first evolved in late 19th-century Paris. Needing to dispose of the increasing amounts of manure left in the street by horses pulling carriages, Parisians started piling the manure up in their back gardens. After a while it composted down into lowish mounds of fertile soil, around which people could walk while sowing seeds and planting vegetables. The pile was occasionally topped off with fresh manure, and there was no need to dig. Because the soil was so fertile, crops could be planted closer together than normal, while giving high yields and quality. This became known as the French intensive system.

• **Prepare the site** A modern raised bed is simply a pile of rich earth and compost held in place above the ground by edging the sides and ends. Common choices for this are naturally treated wooden edging boards or railroad ties, held in place by stakes. Rocks, bricks, and pavers can also be used.

Before building the bed, level the ground to ensure it will be stable. Dig out perennial weeds, discourage them with weed peppers and teas, or smother them with mulch. If there are a lot of weeds, cover the whole area with thick weed barrier, which will prevent them from emerging in the paths between your beds.

• **Building the bed** For the best crops, position the beds for maximum light, and trim back any nearby trees and shrubs that might cause unwanted shade. Ideally, make the beds at least 18in (45cm) deep, or higher if you have trouble bending. The center should be within an arm's reach from either side to allow you to tend the bed without treading on the soil. You can make the bed as long as you like, although bear in mind that if it is too long, it will be a chore to walk around. As a variation of a conventional raised bed, if there is a sturdy wall in the garden, set a three-sided bed against it to make the most of the available space.

Before filling, check the bed is level using a bubble level and adjust if necessary. Fill the bed with biodynamic compost mixed with high quality topsoil, patting it down lightly every so often.

• **Making best use of your bed**
When using the beds for growing vegetables, crop rotation is easier if you have multiples of four beds—for potatoes, legumes, brassicas, and roots. If you have fewer, or just one bed, crops can still be rotated as long as you remember what grew where. To maintain soil fertility, topdress the bed with fresh compost when required. Since it is never trodden on, the soil should remain light and open enough to work with hand tools, such as a trowel.

Before building your raised beds, choose the best site to suit the crops you want to grow, whether in full sun for heat-lovers, or light shade for leafy crops. Be sure to leave good access around them.

To make tending your beds easier, try to position sheds, storage, and preparation areas nearby. You will find having a convenient water source and compost pile especially helpful.

When filled with rich compost, watered well, and regularly fed, raised beds can be more productive than conventional vegetable patches. They are certainly easier to tend and maintain.

Making compost

One of the aims of the biodynamic garden is to maintain the circle of fertility as plants absorb, release, then absorb nutrients again with each season. Making compost is essential to this—all organic waste is recycled as compost, never thrown away. Fallen leaves, weeds, grass clippings, and prunings decompose naturally back into what they began life as: rich, dark, living earth.

Good compost requires a balance of soft and woody ingredients.

The basic principles

Kitchen scraps, garden waste, and animal manure will take 2–6 months to compost, although the exact length of time depends on how the compost pile is made, and the weather. Composting starts with bacteria that first break down the different ingredients in the pile. At this stage the pile becomes hot, between 104–131°F (40–55°C), which is sufficient to kill most weed seeds. After the hot phase the pile cools down as the bacteria die off and fungi take over. Helped by compost worms, they restructure the degraded organic matter into the darker, earthier-smelling material rich in humus, otherwise known as compost.

Site and preparation

Composting requires plenty of worms, so choose a site that suits them—one that is shady and sheltered with well-drained soil. It should also be easy to get to, so that regular trips to the pile with materials from the garden and kitchen do not become a chore. If you haven't got space for a compost pile, a worm bin no bigger than a small fish tank is the best way to compost kitchen scraps. The worms will digest all food scraps, including meat, producing crumbly, earthy "casts" and liquid manure.

Building the pile

Clear away any weeds and position your compost directly on the soil, so worms have easy access. If you have a lot of material to compost and plenty of space, simply create an open pile, between waist- and chest-height, and as wide as you need. Smaller, lower piles struggle to heat up adequately, so if you have less material to compost, use a compost bin. There are many types to use, including slatted wooden ones, plastic bins with lids and open bases, or "tumbler" bins that allow for easy turning and quicker composting. You should ideally have three bins or compost piles: one for fresh material, one that is active, and one ready to use. Alternatively, make a single pile and keep adding material to it until compost forms at the base (*see p.125*).

The right ingredients

Good compost needs the right balance of woody, carbon-rich materials—like straw, finely chopped wood prunings, or sawdust—and softer green materials, rich in nitrogen, such as barnyard manure, leaves, grass clippings, and kitchen peelings. Manure from farm animals, especially cows, is the best ingredient to add due to the powerful, regenerative effect the animal's digestive system had on the grass it ate. Adding just a small bucket of cow manure to the pile gives it "cow power." Dilute a handful of manure in a bucket of water and steep prunings and other dry compost materials in it before they go on the pile. Biodynamic gardeners also add six special preparations to the heap to help it compost faster (*see pp.86–119, and 138–139*).

Caring for your compost pile

Good compost needs the right amount of air, water, and warmth, depending on what the pile contains. If compacted and too wet, the compost stays cool, airless, slimy, and smelly, which can happen if grass clippings are layered too thickly. Aerate or turn the pile completely with a fork, breaking up any lumpy areas. Piles that get too hot will end up dry and powdery, especially if built with thick layers of loose, dry straw and not much else. Sprinkle water on dry piles or rebuild by adding thin layers of manure-steeped shredded hay, interspersed with sprinklings of soil, fresh weeds, and old comfrey, nettle, or tree leaves. Finished compost should be a dark, earthy-smelling material that can be squeezed without either crumbling to dust or dripping water.

Making your own potting mix

Fine potting mix can be made by composting grass clumps pulled in fall from beds intended for planting the following spring. Layer the clumps, including the leaves, roots, and soil, with alternate layers of manure and hay, steeped in manure liquid. Pat the pile down gently to avoid any air gaps, and insert a set of biodynamic compost preparations (*see pp.86–119, and 138–139*). By next spring this will have rotted down into very fine, dark soil that can be used as a high-quality potting mix.

Growing green manures

Soil suffers if left bare to the elements, since nutrients and humus are washed out and weeds take over. However, by using green manures, which are sown directly, you can avoid these problems. Green manures add nutrients to the soil, and allow it to rest and recover. When dug in or left as mulch, they also add organic matter. This improves soil texture, how well it drains and retains nutrients, and encourages beneficial soil organisms. Green manures also protect the soil, explaining their other name, cover crops.

Nitrogen-fixing legumes are the most commonly used green manures. The plants are cut before they flower, and are either dug in or left as a mulch for worms to incorporate. To boost nitrogen in your soil, grow clovers, vetches, lupines, or alfalfa, sown in fall or spring. Vetches and lupines are the hardiest, holy clover is best for alkaline soils, and black medick can be sown in fall.

Oats and barley produce dense, fine roots that channel water and air into the soil, encourage worms, and suppress weeds. They are hardy, and can be sown in fall to overwinter until dug in during spring. They are ideal for improving sandy soil and stabilizing slopes.

Green manures can also be used to break up compacted soils. Before installing a raised bed, for example, sow alfalfa in spring or fall, letting it grow for 1–2 years. Its roots can reach down 22ft (7m), breaking up the soil and drawing nutrients nearer the surface. This topsoil will then become a nutrient-rich and worm-friendly base for the raised bed positioned above it.

Red clover is a legume that adds nitrogen to the soil. Cut it down as its flowers start setting seed, and dig in the roots.

Water wisely

Where water is concerned, plants and humans have something in common— our bodies are mostly made of it, and we couldn't survive without it. Having a plentiful and a convenient supply of water is essential in the garden. It falls freely from the sky, so it makes sense to collect and store as much as you can.

Preparing water for plants

Plants get a small amount of the water they need from the atmosphere via their leaves, but most is absorbed by their roots from the soil. The soil receives most of its natural water as rainfall, although some comes from the water table. In dry spells, tapwater is commonly used to irrigate plants, which contains chlorine and fluoride. Chlorine is added to make water safe for us to drink, while fluoride is used to reduce tooth decay.

Plants and soil organisms in the garden prefer water that is free from additives, and rainfall is best. However, there are times when tapwater may need to be used, and although you cannot remove the fluoride, you can reduce its level of chlorine. Passing it through a hose with a sprinkler head attached aerates the water and helps to drive off the chlorine as gas. Another way of removing chlorine is to run water into a container in the morning, aerating it by splashing it as much as possible, then leaving it uncovered until the evening when it can be used. The biodynamic technique of stirring or dynamizing the water in a longer, more rhythmical way is another good way of aerating water (*see pp.60–61*).

Collecting rainwater

Tapwater costs money but capturing rainwater is free. The most obvious source is from the roof of your home, although there are points to consider, especially if you live in an urban area. The first is to allow the rain to clean the roof of any pollution residues or impurities before starting to collect it. Even if the roof is clean, still wait 5–10 minutes before letting rainwater run into the barrel to avoid impurities. For the safety of children, pets, and even wildlife, cover any collected water with a lid. This will also stop midges, gnats, mosquitoes, and algae from taking up residence.

Watering in the morning ensures the soil is moist, ready for the plants as they stir back into growth.

Ensure the water you apply goes where it is most needed. Create watering pits around thirsty crops to act as a reservoir.

Mulching prevents evaporation and keeps the soil surface cool, helping to retain soil moisture. Water the soil before applying mulches.

How often and much to water

Water your crops generously at regular intervals, rather than with a constant stream of light daily sprinklings. Less water is lost to evaporation this way, and some plants benefit by being stressed slightly during the dry period. It also encourages plants to root more deeply in search of water, exposing them to a greater range of micronutrients—especially if the soil has been regularly fed with compost and biodynamic sprays. This tougher approach gets plants used to fending for themselves a little more. Assess how dry the soil is before watering by poking a finger in. If it comes out with soil stuck to it, it is still moist enough.

Certain annual crops, especially leaf crops like lettuce and spinach, prefer soil that is kept moist. If they become dry, they take it as a sign that they are about to die of thirst. In response, they stop producing leaves, and instead grow upward, or bolt, forming a flowering stem. No plant wants to break the first rule of evolution—to die without leaving any offspring behind. Bolting means the plant is about to die, and the crops will taste bitter. Dry soil also affects root crops, such as carrots, which can split as their roots swell again after dry periods, spoiling them.

The speed at which soil in the garden dries out depends on the weather, the season, and on latitude—how near the garden is to the equator. However, it mainly it depends on your soil type. Sandy soils dry out quickest, while those rich in clay hold plenty of water. Unfortunately, with clay soil, it is prone to becoming compacted if walked on or worked while wet, which keeps water from soaking into it. The ideal soil is a loam (*see p.15*), which has a balance of water-retaining clay particles and water-filtering sand. Keeping soils topped off with good compost helps both sandy and clay soils acquire and retain loamlike qualities.

When to water

The best times to water are early morning or late evening. Using harvested rainwater has the advantage of it being roughly the same temperature as the soil, whatever time of day it is. This is perfect for heat-loving plants, such as tomatoes and eggplant, whose sensitive roots can become stressed if the soil temperature changes rapidly. Avoid watering during the heat of the day, because although some water will penetrate the soil, most will simply evaporate. The crops miss out on a vital drink, and the water evaporating off the soil makes it easier for diseases, like downy mildew and gray mold (*Botrytis*), to spread.

Using water carefully

Regular watering can become a chore, and if you are using tapwater, it can also be expensive. You should, therefore, try to water efficiently by reducing the amount you need, only watering when necessary, and by reducing waste.

If you live in a drier area, avoid growing plants that need constant moisture, such as spinach. Instead, try alternatives that cope with dryer conditions, like New Zealand spinach. Thirstier crops, including lettuce and basil, can also be planted in part shade, below a tree for example, or interplanted between taller, equally thirsty crops, like tomatoes, eggplant, and sweet corn.

To ensure the water you apply reaches down to the roots of your thirstiest plants, insert homemade funnels into the soil next to them to direct it downward. Be sure to direct water onto the soil where it is needed, rather than wetting the leaves, which also encourages disease. Mulching crops with straw or compost after watering them helps to prevent evaporation, keeping as much moisture in the soil as possible.

Welcoming wildlife

Biodiversity and balance go hand in hand: a biodiverse garden is a balanced garden, encompassing every part from soil to sky. It starts with healthy soil alive with worms, fungi, and other organisms, which are all vital for plant health. Above the ground, pollinating insects and beneficial predators all play essential roles. Not every creature works in your favor, but they are all necessary for a harmonious biodynamic garden.

Attracting pollinators

Most flowering plants rely on bees and other insects to pollinate their flowers. Without them, flowers would not be fertilized, fruit would not form—meaning no harvest—and there would be no seeds to collect and sow. A healthy population of pollinating insects is essential in the biodynamic garden, resulting in better crops, higher yields, and better quality seeds to collect.

Installing beehives is a surefire way to welcome bees into your garden, although maintaining them takes skill and commitment. Instead, place bee hotels around your garden to provide homes for a wide range of bee species—all good pollinators—that will fend for themselves. You can also encourage pollinators, including bees, by growing colorful flowers rich in nectar. Choose plants with simple open blooms such as poppies, and sow or plant a diverse range to attract as many insects as possible.

Garden birds

Birds can be viewed as a problem in the garden, attacking newly planted brassicas, snatching fruits and seeds, and plucking worms from the soil. However, they also do a valuable job in consuming the larvae and pupae of pests, especially of those lying in wait over winter in the soil, ready to attack new crops in spring. Birds save far more crops from potential ruin than they eat themselves. They are also part of the ecosystem, so should be encouraged to promote balance in the garden.

The best way to attract birds is to install nesting boxes and bird feeders. Nesting boxes are best positioned away from wind and full sun, with a direct line of sight to trees and shrubs, where birds can perch. Place them high enough off the ground on walls and in trees, where cats cannot disturb them. Before birds nest in them each spring, take the boxes down and clean them thoroughly to reduce the risk of disease.

Bird feeders are a magnet for birds; be careful to position them where cats cannot spring an attack. Provide a mix of fruit, nuts, seeds, and fats, and avoid feeding them milk or bread, which can make them sick. Clear away uneaten food daily, and ensure the stations are clean to prevent the spread of bird diseases. Also, be sure to put out clean water every day for birds to drink and bathe in.

Creating habitats

The best way to encourage biodiversity in your garden is to provide suitable habitats. This means places where wildlife can sleep, breed, and hibernate, and find all the food and water they require. These areas do not have to be large but the more types you can include, the greater diversity you will attract.

• **Garden ponds** are one of the richest habitats you can include in your garden. They provide homes for amphibians that readily feed on garden pests—especially slugs—and also attract other beneficial creatures looking for a drink, such as hedgehogs and birds. Ensure the pond is safe for children, pets, and wildlife, and keep it natural by not adding goldfish that happily devour tadpoles.

• **Flowering and fruiting plants** provide nectar and food for insects, birds, and mammals. Grow a variety of plants that flower and fruit throughout the year to keep the kitchen well stocked with natural products.

• **Wild, untended areas**, where wildlife can set up home and live undisturbed, will soon be colonized by a wide range of creatures. Choose a quiet corner or edge, and avoid neatening it up. Provide piles of logs for beetles, which are voracious consumers of slug eggs, potato beetles, and cutworms. Wait to cut back shrubs until after leaf fall; collect the leaves and pile them up at the base of hedges or in quiet corners of the garden to encourage hibernating hedgehogs.

• **Position bird feeders** and bee hotels in suitable places around your garden. Any habitat is valuable to wildlife—and it doesn't have to be totally natural.

Leave part of the garden as a wild zone, either sown with wildflowers or left to develop its own natural character.

Place bee hotels in sheltered corners, near a ready supply of nectar-rich flowers.

Nesting boxes encourage birds to make a home in your garden year after year.

Domestic animals

All gardens can be improved by the presence of farm animals, as long as you have the time and space. Whether you raise them for profit or for pleasure, depending on what you have, these animals provide manure, tend the soil, and can help control pests. All must be well cared for, however, and it is essential they are kept secure, safe from predators, and in good health—which can be expensive and time consuming. Keeping animals is best left to the more experienced biodynamic gardener.

Your natural allies

Companion planting

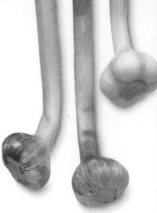

Your crops are a little like people in terms of the company they like to keep—or avoid. Some plants are good companions that help crops to thrive and to stay healthy; others are nothing special but are fine to hang out with all the same; then there are those to avoid altogether because of the negative effects they may have. Choosing the right companions for your plants will help to deter pests, and can even enhance the flavor of certain crops.

Sap-sucking aphids can be repelled from a wide range of garden plants by growing garlic as a companion.

Using crops for good space efficiency

Certain crops can be grown together to help make the best the use of your space, and to take full advantage of the growing season. These combinations are effective because the plants either encourage and support each other's growth, or because their different growth rates give each the opportunity to thrive. Planting vegetables in this way is especially useful for smaller plots and raised beds where every inch counts. They are also worthwhile in larger plots to maximize your harvests.

The three sisters

This classic example of companion planting was devised by the Native Americans. Sweet corn and runner beans are sown next to each other, so the corn supports the beans. In return, the beans feed the corn via their nitrogen-fixing roots. The third sister, a pumpkin or squash, trails over the ground, suppressing weeds and shading the soil, keeping it moist for the other two sister crops.

Catch cropping

Quick-growing leafy greens, like spinach, arugula, and lettuce, can be sown directly alongside slow starters, such as beans, cabbage, and Brussels sprouts, which are all also planted widely apart. The leafy crops develop while the slow-starters gradually establish, providing an extra crop and suppressing weeds at the same time. Leafy greens are less aggressively competitive than weeds—meaning that the slow-starters can develop the strong root systems that they need to thrive.

Using companion plants to defend your crops

Plants that repel pests

Growing companion plants is an effective way to control pests in your garden. Many are also valuable crops, providing a line of defense across your vegetable garden.

Marigold

- **Tansy** repels cabbage white butterflies.
- **Nasturtiums** stop woolly aphids from attacking apple trees and deter whiteflies from tomatoes.
- **Lemon basil** also deters whiteflies from tomatoes.
- **Strong scented herbs**, such as rosemary, lavender, and mint protect eggplant and brassica crops from repeated flea beetle attacks.
- **Wormwood** also deters flea beetles—but remember that it cannot be planted near brassicas, because they are intolerant to it.
- **Marigold roots** release compounds in the soil that flush out soilborne pests.
- **Garlic, onions, leeks, and chives** all release odorous compounds into the soil, which drive away soil pests.
- **Onion, leek, and chive leaves** release a scent that repels carrot rust flies from carrot crops.
- **Carrots**, in reply, give off an odor from their leaves that repels onion flies and the leek moths.

Chives

Plants that attract predators

In addition to repelling pests, plants can be used to attract predators that feed on them instead. Ladybugs feast avidly on aphids, and can be attracted to the garden by planting stinging nettles, dandelions, and yarrow, where the adults can lay their eggs and the young can hatch. Pots planted with tansy—which ladybugs love—can also be placed strategically near aphid-prone crops, such as broad beans.

To attract lacewings, minute pirate bugs, and hoverflies, grow flowering herbs, such as fennel, dill, parsley, sage, and cilantro. These plants also attract parasitic wasps, which feed on their pollen and lay their eggs in the caterpillars of cabbage white butterflies, preventing them from attacking your crops.

Saving your own seeds, and allowing crops to flower, is another good way to attract many beneficial insects.

Yarrow

Tansy

Marigolds

Lavender and rosemary

Fleabane

Buddleja

Green manures as companions

Some green manures release compounds from their roots that help deter weeds and noxious soilborne pests, or at least stop them from building to dangerous levels. Examples include oats, rye, and mustard. These can all be sown in fall, then cut and turned in during spring. Sunflowers have the same beneficial effect but are sown in late spring for harvest in late summer. Green manures, such as buckwheat (*right*) and phacelia, can also help to reduce pests by attracting predatory insects. To prevent reseeding, however, dig them in before they set seed.

Better brassicas

To encourage balanced growth, plant brassica crops near strongly aromatic plants, like tansy and other herbs. Brassicas also benefit from growing near plants that flower very freely, such as daisy fleabane and buddleja.

Seed saving

Saving seeds from crops growing in your garden to sow the following year is the most simple and cost-effective first step toward creating a self-sustaining cycle of fertility. Seed saving, in fact, is a core part of the biodynamic approach, because every garden, personal or community, should become, as far as possible, a self-sustaining living organism. Saving seeds also saves money—and by collecting seeds from your best plants it allows you to improve your crops.

Garden fennel seed heads

Bok choy
gone to seed

Understanding seeds

Most vegetable seeds on sale are "F1 hybrids" that have been bred for intensive growing and bear crops with uniform shapes and colors that consistently ripen at a precise time. Although seed can be collected from them, their offspring perform poorly and are less fertile, producing lower yields with unpredictable shapes, colors, and tastes. As a result, F1 seeds must be bought new every year—hardly the biodynamic way.

The alternative is to sow open-pollinated seed that results from natural pollination between crops of the same type. Unlike F1s, these are intrinsically adapted to low-input organic and biodynamic gardening. If enough plants are left to flower, the seeds you collect will produce true crops every year. This means that although open-pollinated seeds are initially more expensive, you can collect your own thereafter, and only need to buy them once. Plus, you can swap spare ones with your friends.

Open-pollinated seeds are also known as heritage seeds: they descend from crops our ancestors may have sown in their own gardens before farming became industrialized after the 1940s. Only three percent of the heritage vegetables grown at the start of the 20th century survive today.

Why save your own seeds

An obvious advantage of saving your own seeds is financial. Seeds are expensive, and by saving your own, and trading them with your friends, you can acquire all you need without spending a penny. Another important benefit is that by saving seed from the plants that perform best, you can develop a strain that is specifically adapted to the growing conditions in your garden, with resistance to localized pests and diseases. Over successive generations, your crops will evolve to suit your garden, making them easier to grow, and giving consistently reliable, high-quality crops.

Selecting seeds from the best plants also allows you to concentrate on the qualities that you particularly like, such as size, flavor, texture, and how well a crop stores.

Pea seeds

Seed-saving techniques

The first step to saving seeds is to let the plants flower. Although this is normal practice for fruiting crops like tomatoes, leaf and root crops are usually harvested long before flowers ever form. This means leaving a number of plants in the ground unharvested—consider this an investment in your garden's future.

Easy and reliable crops to start saving seeds from include tomatoes, squash, pumpkins, melons, beans, and peas. Being annuals, they produce seeds in their first year. Grow them in the normal way from open-pollinated seed, not F1 hybrids, and collect their seeds at end of the growing season—when they would be harvested anyway. For annual flowers grown to attract pollinators, such as nasturtiums and poppies, save the seeds once the flowers have wilted. Collect their seeds by tapping the dried flower heads into a paper bag.

For tomatoes and other soft-fruiting crops, like melons, cucumbers, or squash, squeeze or scrape the seeds out, remove any pulp, rinse and dry them thoroughly on a paper towel, old rag, newspaper, or in an airing cupboard. Improperly dried seed of any type does not store well.

Saving seed from biennial plants like onions, rutabagas, turnips, and parsnips means sowing them in the normal way. They can either be left in the ground over winter to flower the following year, or if frost tender, they can be lifted, stored, and replanted in spring. If biennials flower or bolt in their first year, do not collect their seeds because they will be of poor quality.

To prevent cross-pollination, which causes variation between parent plant and offspring, avoid growing two or more varieties of the same crop that flower at the same time. Brassicas, for example, all set seed in late spring, and there is the risk that insects may transfer pollen between different family members, such as cabbage and Brussels sprouts. To stop this from happening, only allow the plants you want to collect seeds from to flower. Remove the flowers from other related plants, cover them with paper bags, or cover the plants with fine nets to keep pollinating insects away.

To collect seed from fruiting crops, such as squash, leave the fruit to develop to maturity.

Pod-forming crops, such as peas and beans, should be allowed to develop and dry on the plants.

Crops must flower to produce seeds. Annuals flower in their first year but biennials like onions won't set seed until their second year.

Seeds must be fully developed and dry before they are stored. Beans and peas can be laid out on drying racks outside in the sun, or under cover if necessary.

Thoroughly clean seeds from fruiting crops like tomatoes. Remove any flesh and rinse under running water.

Covering flowering crops with garden fabric is an effective way of preventing cross-pollination. Peg it down firmly.

🫖 *Natural remedies*

Using plants to cure plants

Simple, plant-based sprays are an effective way to keep the garden healthy—better still, you can grow your own cures. Teas, decoctions, and liquid manures boost the natural self-defense mechanism of the treated plants, help keep disease spores from germinating, and provide an easy-to-apply source of food that stimulates growth.

How to make plant teas

Teas act in a subtle way, and are not intended to be very extractive. To make an herb tea for the garden, place the leaves, shoots, flowers, and sometimes even the roots of the plant in freshly boiled rainwater, or pour the boiling water over the plant material.

1. Collect the appropriate part of the plant. Here, stinging nettle leaves are gathered to make a tea that is packed with nutrients. It helps garden plants grow strongly—which means they become less attractive to pests.

2. Add freshly boiled water and leave it to infuse for the set time, usually just a few minutes, or until the water cools.

3. Strain the tea, squeezing out all the liquid, and compost the vegetable matter. Dilute the tea in the appropriate amount of water, and apply as a spray.

Making plant decoctions

Tough, woody, spiny plant material that does not loosen up in boiled water is best made as a decoction—a plant tea that is actually boiled. Place the bark, shoots, leaves, or flowers of the medicinal plant in cold water, bring it to a boil, and simmer for the appropriate time to extract the desired substances.

1. Chop the plant material into small pieces—or grate it. This makes the beneficial substances easier to extract. Here, horseradish root is used to make a powerful fungicide to treat fruit trees, such as plums, at risk of brown fruit rot.

2. Place the chopped material in a pan, add cold water, and bring to a boil. Simmer for the appropriate time, usually 10–60 minutes. Keep the lid on the pan to prevent the extracted plant substances from evaporating into the air.

3. Remove from the heat. Leaving the lid firmly in place, allow the decoction to cool completely. Strain off the liquid and compost the plant residue. Dilute the concentrate before applying it as a spray.

Making plant fertilizers and liquid manures

Liquid manure, or slurry, provides your plants and the soil with a source of readily accessible nutrients in a form they find easy to digest. It is particularly good for container plants and heavy feeders that may not find the range or quantity of nutrients they need in the soil, but you can also use the liquid manure directly on the soil, where it has a softening effect. To make it, leave nutrient-rich plants like stinging nettle or comfrey to decompose in water, releasing their nutrients into the liquid as they break down.

1. Collect the leaves and stems from established plants (here, comfrey).

2. Pack the leaves into a watertight container; the more you can push in, the more nutritious the manure will be. Weigh the leaves down with rocks. Add water, and leave it to ferment for about 10 days.

3. Strain the liquid and dilute it with the appropriate amount of rainwater before applying it to your plants or soil.

Biodynamic gardeners can make liquid manures even better using additives that help plants break down (*see pp.136–137*).

Achillea millefolium

Yarrow

Attracting beneficial insects to the rest of the garden, yarrow is a significant biodynamic plant (*see pp.86–91*). Use the sulfur-rich flowers to make a tea that discourages fungal diseases including powdery mildew, which affects ornamentals like roses, as well as a number of edible plants. Yarrow tea also strengthens fruiting crops from within, helping plants such as tomatoes, zucchini, strawberries, and tree fruit prepare for the next flowering period, and maintain balanced, high-quality yields.

Methods and applications

• **Infuse a handful of yarrow flowers** in 1¾ pints (1 liter) of hot water for 10 minutes. Strain, then dilute 1 part yarrow tea in 10 parts water. Apply as a spray to all parts of the plant, especially to the upper leaves, which are most susceptible to fungal infection.

• **Apply yarrow tea to fruiting crops** in the mornings around flowering time to strengthen them. Give your fruiting crops a further boost with a second application when the fruit is just starting to ripen—so when strawberries or tomatoes are changing from unripe green to riper red. Yarrow makes this transition smoother: both the fruit and the stems it hangs from become a little firmer as a result of the spray.

• **Combine yarrow with stinging nettle tea** to make an all-around preventive spray. Yarrow regulates attack from fungal diseases; nettle controls insect activity, notably mites. Use 2oz (50g) of yarrow flowers in 1 gallon (5 liters) of cold water, and bring to a boil. Add 2oz (50g) of stinging nettles to the water, then remove from the heat. Strain, and dilute 1 part concentrate in 10 parts water. Apply as a general spray to all crops.

Allium sativum

Garlic

In the garden garlic has many uses as a companion plant, but you can also use it to make a natural fungicide, insect repellent, and insecticide. Outside of the garden garlic is a plant that divides opinion—it is either something we should eat every day because it makes us healthier, or it is something we should avoid if we want to keep our friends within speaking and breathing distance.

Methods and applications

• **To make a fungicide** against gray mold (*Botrytis*), soak 3 or 4 chopped garlic cloves in 1¾–3½ pints (1–2 liters) of cold water for a couple of days. Strain and spray without diluting.

• **To tackle aphids, codling moths, and deter snails or slugs**, crush 2 garlic cloves and macerate in a cup of olive oil for 2 days. Decant the oil into a bottle of warm water to emulsify out the garlic, and shake well. Keep it out of direct light for 2 days. To use, dilute 1 part garlic in 20 parts water and stir for 20 minutes before spraying the leaves of the affected plants, and the surrounding soil.

Allium schoenoprasum
Chives

Like garlic, chives should be ever-present in the garden, both as a food and as a tool to help keep the rest of your plants free of pests and diseases. Make a liquid manure to ward off carrot rust flies, and infusions to deter aphids, cabbage flies, and mites.

Methods and applications

• **To make liquid manure**, soak a few handfuls of chopped chive stems in 1¾–3½ pints (1–2 liters) of water in a small bucket for a week. Then drain and spray as a concentrate, without diluting.

• **Treat areas around the carrot patch** with chive liquid manure before you thin or harvest carrot crops. The manure masks the scent released when carrots are moved, which is what attracts carrot rust flies.

• **Use a chive infusion** to tackle aphids, mites, and cabbage flies, in the garden. Chop 1oz (25g) chives and infuse in 1¾ pints (1 liter) of tepid water for 24 hours. Avoid spraying leaf crops like lettuce when they are about to be harvested because they are liable to taste and smell "oniony."

Artemisia absinthium
Absinthe

Absinthe—or wormwood—is perhaps best known for the bitter green oil used to make the addictive alcoholic beverage popular in France in the late 19th century. In the garden the smell of absinthe can repel ants, slugs, and the black bean aphid. It can also help deter red spider mites from attacking the leaves of fruit trees that are stressed by a lack of water in hot weather.

Method and application

• **Make the decoction** by adding 2–4oz (50–100g) of dried or fresh flowers, stems, and leaves to 1¾–3½ pints (1–2 liters) of water. Allow this to soak overnight then bring it to a boil and simmer for 15–30 minutes. Strain, then dilute 1 part absinthe in 10 parts water.

• **Apply the spray** 2 or 3 times over a 1-week period to deter mites on fruit and woody plants, fruit flies on cherries, and aphids on beans.

• **Keep the residue from absinthe tea** on one side, out of reach of children, and let it decompose in the sun. Do not add it to the compost heap: the repellent effect is so potent that microorganisms stop working, which is detrimental to the pile.

⚠ Absinthe contains the toxin thujone, which can cause convulsions in high doses.

Betula pendula
Birch

The diuretic and cleansing properties for which birch is used in homeopathic medicine are equally beneficial for your plants. Its ability to regulate the flow of unwanted moisture internally while cleaning things up externally is useful for apples affected by apple scab disease, and for grapes suffering from rot and mildew.

Method and applications

• **To treat fruit trees**, simmer 4oz (100g) of birch bark, flowers, and leaves in 1¾ pints (1 liter) of water for 20–30 minutes. Strain, then dilute 1 part birch to 10 parts water and spray all over the tree, on the trunk, and on the ground around the base of the tree as a preventive measure.

• **Spray diluted birch tea** in areas of the garden at risk from fungal pathogens after harvesting any affected plants. Use 1 part birch to 10 parts water. This helps to prevent the problem recurring with the next crop.

Calendula officinalis
Calendula

A popular ornamental plant, calendula—or marigold—not only looks good, but attracts a myriad of beneficial insects, too. In the wild calendula manages to come back year after year at just the right moment, lying low if the weather gets too hot or too cold in summer or winter. Perhaps this is why calendula tea works so well as a pick-me-up for humans after a period of infection or illness. Mercurial plants like calendula—and chamomile—that come and go in the field are extremely adept at accumulating and using nutrients from the soil. It is these nutrients that benefit greedy garden feeders like tomatoes, sweet corn, eggplant, peppers, potatoes, and members of the beet and brassica families.

Method and application

• **To extract the nutrients from calendula**, soak 8oz (200g) of shoots, leaves, and ideally the flowers in 7 pints (4 liters) of water and leave outside for 7–10 days. Filter off the concentrate, then dilute 1 part calendula in 6 parts of water and spray on the leaves of your crops.

Matricaria recutita

Chamomile

Chamomile tea has a calming and soothing effect on humans, and it has the same effect on stressed out plants, too. It is both a preventive and a curative treatment. When sprayed directly on the crops—or on the furrows into which they are going to be sown or transplanted—the sulfur content acts against fungal diseases, while its calcium content stimulates healing processes, promoting healthy growth in leafy crops, flowers, and vegetables that are susceptible to fungal organisms. Chamomile is also high in potassium, which benefits all fruiting and flowering crops: for maximum benefit, spray them both before and after they flower. Chamomile also plays an important role in the biodynamic garden (*see pp.92–97*).

Method and application

• **To make chamomile tea**, infuse 4oz (100g) of fresh or dried flowers in 1¾ pints (1 liter) of hot water for 5–10 minutes. Strain, then dilute 1 part concentrate in 10–20 parts of water. Chamomile tea is best made fresh and should be applied very early in the morning, just after sunrise, as a fine mist over the top of the plants.

Mentha species

Mint

Mint is an interesting plant because we use it when we want to get up close and personal with each other on romantic occasions—but in the garden it is planted strategically as a companion plant to repel unwanted insects. In concentrated form, mint tea and liquid manure will also deter and confuse flying insects, such as aphids and whiteflies—in effect you gain all the benefits of companion planting mint without the worry of it trying to take over the garden.

Methods and applications

• **To make mint tea** add 4oz (100g) of roughly torn or chopped mint to 1¾ pints (1 liter) of water. Either bring the water slowly and gently to a boil and then turn off the heat, or pour just-boiled water over the mint to avoid scalding the leaves. Let it cool overnight. Filter, and then spray without diluting.

• **For liquid manure** Soak 4oz (100g) of roughly torn or chopped mint leaves in 1¾ pints (1 liter) of tepid water. Leave outside for 3–4 days. Dilute 1 part mint in 4 parts water.

• **Use mint to enhance other plant teas** —its antioxidant properties mean the beneficial effects the teas have will linger for longer. Prepare and dilute the plant tea, then simply drop a few pieces of torn mint leaf into the tea and leave it to infuse for an hour or two before use.

 *Picea species*

Pine nut slug repellent

You can use the seeds from any pine growing in your local area to make a diluted extract that helps to protect your crops against slug damage. Applied as a spray to the target plants, the seed extract makes the leaves unpalatable for slugs. Like many plant cures, the list of ingredients is incredibly simple: all you need is $\frac{1}{8}$oz (3g) of pine seeds and $1\frac{3}{4}$ pints (1 liter) of rainwater.

1. Shake the pine seeds out of the cone and crack open the shell to extract the kernels (nuts).

2. Discard the shells, then weigh out $\frac{1}{8}$oz (3g) of nuts. Crush the seeds to a fine powder with a mortar and pestle.

3. To make a paste, gradually add a small amount of lukewarm rainwater to the crushed nuts, stirring constantly.

4. Gradually add more **water** and pour the pine nut mixture into a large bottle.

5. Pour the remaining **water** into the bottle, and seal the top.

6. Shake vigorously for about 5 minutes to mix the contents thoroughly.

7. Leave the solution to ferment in a sunny spot for about 2 weeks, stirring occasionally. To help the fermentation process, pour the mixture into a wide-mouthed jar to increase its exposure to air, and cover with muslin.

2 weeks later

8. Strain the mixture and put the residue on the compost heap.

9. Dilute the mixture, allowing 1 part concentrate to 10 parts rainwater. For best results dynamize for 20 minutes (*see pp.60–61*).

10. Apply the spray to any crops at risk from slug attacks.

The pine nut treatment may make the leaves of your crops taste slightly "resiny" for a few days, so in the days leading up to harvest you may want to try alternative slug deterrents—such as protective rings of crushed eggshells or coffee grounds.

Quercus alba, Q. robur
Oak bark

A few days of rain coupled with warm temperatures and high humidity can quickly cause an outbreak of downy mildew on tomatoes and plants in the brassica family—including cabbage, cauliflower, kohlrabi, broccoli, Brussels sprouts, kale, turnips, and radishes. Keep an eye on the weather forecast and spray an oak bark decoction as a preventive measure; it will also help to keep other pests and plant diseases, such as gray mold (*Botrytis*) and powdery mildew, at bay. The tannin content in oak bark is particularly effective at tightening and sterilizing plants against attack from chewing insects, so use the decoction to treat young seedlings, too. Oak bark also has a special place in biodynamic gardens (*see pp.102–107*).

Method and application

• **To make the oak bark decoction**, break a handful of oak bark into small pieces, and add to a saucepan of water. Bring to a boil and simmer for 20 minutes. Strain, then dilute 1 part oak with 9 parts water before spraying.

Sambucus nigra
Elder

Grow elder as a companion plant in the garden, and you will not only be able to use the flowers and berries to make wonderful homemade wine, but it will also deter unwanted pests—just rubbing a leaf or two on our skin is said to deter flies. The flowers, shoots, and leaves can also be used to make two sprays with insect-repelling capabilities.

Method and applications

• **To make elder decoction** simmer 4oz (100g) of leaves, shoots, and even the bark in 1¾ pints (1 liter) of water for 20 minutes. This helps extract the tannin, which deters aphids and thrips. Strain and spray without diluting the concentrate.

• **To make elder liquid manure** soak 4oz (100g) of leaves and other green parts of the plant in 1¾ pints (1 liter) water for up to a week. Strain and dilute 1 part elder manure to 4 parts water. Spray on crops and the soil to slow down attacks of powdery mildew, or to deter flying insects such as aphids, thrips, and cabbage butterflies.

• **Fresh elder leaves or liquid manure** can also help to control mice, rodents, and other burrowing animals—apply to areas where they live or congregate.

Symphytum species
Comfrey

Comfrey vies with stinging nettle as the most useful, versatile, and cost-effective medicinal plant for the garden, and in fact you can alternate the two to benefit from the full range of nutrients. Comfrey leaves improve compost if added to the pile, and also make a nutrient-rich, leaf-moldlike mulch for potatoes and tomatoes. Collect the leaves at the beginning of flowering—when they contain their highest nutrient levels—and soak them in water to produce a potent liquid manure for fruit and fruiting crops, such as cucumbers, melons, and tomatoes. It is rich in potassium and all the trace elements, such as boron, that all these crops need to flower and set fruit.

Method and applications

• **To make comfrey liquid manure** soak 2¼lb (1kg) of comfrey leaves in 2¼ gallons (10 liters) of rainwater and leave to ferment for 4–10 days, stirring occasionally. Strain and dilute before use.

• **To use as a foliar feed to reduce plant stress**, particularly after hail storms, dilute 1 part comfrey in 19 parts of water, and apply to plant leaves.

• **To make comfrey liquid fertilizer**, dilute 1–2 parts comfrey in 8–9 parts water and spray directly on the soil. For best results apply to moist soil after rain, in the afternoon.

Tanacetum vulgare
Tansy

Tansy can be a useful addition to the garden: it repels pests and attracts beneficial insects. A strategically placed clump of fresh tansy leaves, stems, and flowers can help to keep ticks and fleas away from the dog basket, and mites away from bedsheets. Its flowers have a similar effect when they are used as a fresh tea, decoction, cold extract, or liquid manure. Cultivate with care.

Methods and applications

• **Tansy cold extract** is an effective insecticide for whiteflies on cabbage, Brussels sprouts, and other brassicas. It also acts as a fungicide against rust and downy mildew. Soak a couple of heaped handfuls of chopped leaves in 1¾ pints (1 liter) of cold water for 2 days, then strain and spray without diluting.

• **Use tansy decoction** to combat codling moths, whose caterpillars tunnel into ripening apples and pears, and to deter flea beetles from attacking the tender young leaves of cabbage, turnips, radishes, and even flowers during dry spells. Make a cold extract but after 24 hours bring it to a boil and simmer briefly. Cool, strain, and then spray it directly on crops.

• **Tansy liquid manure** has a fungicidal effect, particularly against downy mildew on tomatoes and brassicas. Make the cold extract but leave it to soak for 7 days. Strain and then dilute 1 part concentrate in 10–20 parts of water before spraying your crops.

Taraxacum officinale
Dandelion

Dandelion flowers are packed with nutrients—calcium, copper, iron, magnesium, potassium, and silica—and biodynamic gardeners use them to make a special compost preparation (*see pp.108–113*). The flowers can also be used as a tea to stimulate growth, especially early in the growing cycle when the first two or three leaves appear—whether broccoli, cabbage, bok choy, potatoes, or plums. The spray acts as a wake-up call for the plants to concentrate and improve their flavor, primarily by using their leaves efficiently when trapping solar heat and light. This also makes the leaves stronger, tighter, and more resistant to disease, which is especially important in rainy years.

Method and applications

• **To make dandelion tea**, infuse a handful of flowers—picked early in the morning before they are fully open—in 1¾ pints (1 liter) of hot water for 5–10 minutes. Filter off the concentrate and dilute, using 1 part dandelion concentrate to 4 parts of rainwater.

• **Spray the crop and the surrounding soil.** For best results, apply the spray early in the morning, ideally under an ascending moon (*see p.52*).

Urtica dioica
Stinging nettle

The nettle is arguably the most versatile of all the plants used to treat other plants because it is super rich in life-giving nutrients—iron, magnesium, calcium, and potassium. It is an important plant to biodynamic gardeners (*see pp.98–101*). Collect the leaves and stems when the nettle begins to flower—this is when the nutrient levels are at their highest.

Methods and applications

• **Teas and decoctions** help regulate growth so plants do not attract pests and diseases; use 1 part nettle concentrate in 5–20 parts water. To make tea, soak 4oz (100g) leaves in 1¾ pints (1 liter) of hot water and allow to infuse for up to 10 minutes. For the decoction, pour 1¾ pints (1 liter) cold water over 4oz (100g) leaves, bring to the boil, and simmer for 3–10 minutes.

• **A cold extract**, made by soaking 4oz (100g) of nettle leaves in 1¾ pints (1 liter) of cold water for 24–36 hours, helps discourage mild attacks of aphids on tree fruit and vegetable crops.

• **For liquid manure**, soak nettle leaves in water for 4–10 days in the sun. Allow 4oz (100g) leaves per 1¾ pints (1 liter). Strain and dilute 1 part nettle in 10 parts water. Spray both crops and soil to stimulate root growth. To prevent stress in hot or cold weather, and to stop green leaves turning yellow with chlorosis, dilute 1:25 and water the crops directly to get sap moving again.

Kelp liquid manure

Using kelp, or seaweed, in your garden is a clever way to reclaim the nutrients washed out by rain and get them back into your soil. It is rich in potassium, which makes this fertilizer especially useful for fruit and fruiting vegetables like tomatoes, cucumbers, and peppers. A kelp feed helps plants through potentially stressful moments in their cycles: at transplanting; before flowering and after fertilization; during fruit development and ripening; and after harvest, when the soil may also need a boost.

1. Pour dried kelp or seaweed into a large noncorrosive container of rainwater. For 2¼ gallons (10 liters) of water you should expect to use around 16oz (500g) of dried material.

2. Stir well. Thanks to their watery origins, kelp and seaweed take a while to decompose in water to produce a liquid manure. Keep the mixture outside in a warm place to help speed the process.

3. Cover with cloth, or a loose lid, and leave for 6–8 weeks. The liquid manure will be brownish in color, with a pleasant, sweet, briny smell. Dilute 1 part kelp to 10 parts fresh water and spray on the soil around your crops.

Natural remedies
Compost tea

Your compost heap is full of beneficial microorganisms that are spread around the garden whenever you dig compost into the soil. A compost tea or liquid manure is a very efficient method of delivering both nutrients and beneficial organisms to the garden throughout the growing season—and it is very simple to make.

1. Stuff a net bag with nettles to make your compost tea rich in life-giving nutrients, such as iron, magnesium, calcium, and potassium.

2. Fill a second bag with comfrey to enhance the compost tea with nitrogen.

3. Fill a net bag or old pantyhose with 2lb 4oz (1kg) of your best, most vibrant, fully fermented compost and attach it to a stick along with the comfrey and nettles.

4. Suspend the ingredients in 2¼ gallons (10 liters) rainwater to ensure maximum contact between the water, compost, nettles, and comfrey.

5. Cover with burlap. Give it a good stir 3 times a day to keep the tea aerated.

4–10 days later

6. Remove the compost and dilute for use. Aerated compost teas are even more effective—use an aquarium air pump to add oxygen for 24 hours nonstop.

Foliar spray

Spraying all parts of your plants in a layer of protective microbial life will stimulate the immune system, displace disease organisms, and increase their uptake of minerals.

Strain the compost tea to prevent blockages when spraying.

Dilute 1 part tea in 10 parts of rainwater, stir, then transfer to a hand or garden sprayer.

Apply every 2 weeks to all parts of the plant to boost the immune system: these regular coatings of protective microbial life will outcompete the organisms that cause disease.

Ground drench

Compost teas are also a quick and efficient method of improving overall soil health and fertility: simply add a small quantity to the watering can and water it onto the soil.

Strain the compost tea to prevent any residue from blocking the watering can. Dilute 1 part tea in 20 parts of rainwater.

Stir well to aerate the mixture before application—beneficial microorganisms thrive on oxygen.

Water generously over the soil in large droplets whenever your crops are in need of a boost—if plant leaves are floppy and yellowing slightly, it is a good time to spray.

Natural remedies
Weed tea

In a battle for survival between weeds and cultivated plants, weeds would win every time. Their roots mine minerals and trace elements held deep in the soil, their leaves extract nitrogen from the air. They can also regenerate from a single piece of root or just a few seeds. Weeds contain the exact combination of nutrients that the garden lacks: to reclaim the nutrients without fear of spreading weeds in your compost, make a simple plant tea.

1. Gather the weeds and stuff them in a porous bag. You can use the roots, stems, and leaves of many types: the more you include, the more nutritious the tea will be. Each weed contains different amounts of minerals—nettles and dandelions are high in calcium, iron, and magnesium, and thistles are rich in phosphorus as well as trace elements like zinc and manganese.

2. Place the weeds in a container—ideally, it should be between a third and half full. Cover with rainwater until the container is nearly full.

Biodynamic gardeners also add six special preparations to help the weeds break down faster and increase the nutrient content (*see pp.86–119 and 138–139*).

3. To keep the weeds submerged, weigh them down with a brick or rock.

4. Cover with burlap and leave to ferment, stirring gently once a week or so.

2–4 weeks later

5. Remove the weeds and compost the mushy remains. The roots and seeds will not be viable after their time under water, which means there is no longer any danger of spreading weeds around the garden in the compost.

6. Strain the liquid, then dilute 1 part weed concentrate in 10–40 parts of rainwater, depending on the needs of your garden.

7. Stir vigorously for several minutes to aerate the mixture. This will stimulate beneficial microbes and make the spray more effective when it lands on the soil.

8. Water generously or spray over the soil in large droplets, ideally on a dull, cloudy afternoon in fall. Target weedy ground and areas recently converted from weeds to cultivated plants. Apply once a week for three successive weeks. The nutrients returned to the soil are easily available to crops, discouraging weed regrowth.

The
biodynamic
approach

Daily rhythms

When you get hungry or thirsty, you can always turn on the kitchen tap or open the refrigerator, and when the light fades, you can flick on a light switch. Plants don't have the freedom to pick and choose what and when they eat, or how much light they get. Being firmly rooted in the ground, they are utterly dependent on what nature provides—be it light and heat from sunshine, water from spring or fall rain, or the cold and dark of winter. The plants we eat should still be intimately tuned in to seasonal cycles, unlike our own 24/7 existence.

Growing crops using hydroponics and artificial light, and shipping food by air, using computer-controlled refrigeration, provides us with the choice of almost any fruit or vegetable we want, 365 days a year. But the flipside of this relentless choice is that cultivated plants have been tuned out of seasonal rhythms, and as a consequence, so have we. Growing at least some of our own food is the best way of tuning back in to natural, seasonal cycles.

Imitating the sun

As the sun rises higher in spring and summer, Earth receives more heat and light. This encourages seeds and plants to grow upward and outward, producing shoots, leaves, and flowers so they can reproduce. It is as if the living potential in the earth is being exhaled. Then, as the sun sinks lower in fall and winter, Earth gets less heat and light. Plants contract back into the soil, either dying off completely or dropping their leaves during dormancy. Now it is as if the earth has inhaled back everything it produced, while preparing itself for the next cycle to begin.

Periods when the earth breathes in—either seasonally during fall and winter, or daily each evening—are usually the best times to dig the soil, readying it for planting, or for planting itself, to sow seeds, and to spread compost. Sprays intended for the soil, like liquid manures or biodynamic soil sprays, such as horn manure

Seasonal rhythms

As well as daily rhythms, Earth experiences the four seasonal rhythms of spring, summer, fall, and winter. The seasons occur because Earth orbits the sun at a slight angle (23.5°). The start of each new season is marked by four days; spring equinox; summer solstice; fall equinox; and winter solstice. Equinox days have roughly equal amounts of darkness and light. The solstices mark when the sun stops getting either higher (in summer) or lower (in winter) in the sky each day.

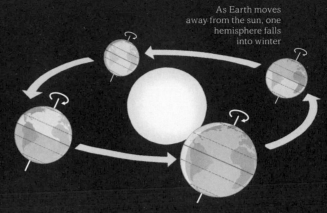

As Earth moves away from the sun, one hemisphere falls into winter

Due to Earth's elliptical orbit, the hemisphere nearest the sun enjoys summer

	Spring Equinox	Summer solstice	Fall equinox	Winter solstice
Northern hemisphere	March 20	June 20–21	September 22–23	December 21–22
Southern hemisphere	September 22–23	December 21–22	March 20	June 20–21

500 or BC are also best applied when the earth is breathing in, during the fall or evening. The periods when the earth breathes out—either seasonally during spring and summer, or daily each morning—are the best times to apply most plant teas, as well as atmospheric sprays, like horn silica 501. The aim is to help the crops grow, upward or outward, in the right way. Connecting the natural cycles of the sky above with those beneath your feet costs nothing, and makes for better gardening.

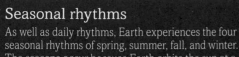

Night & day—spring & fall

Earth is lit by the sun, our nearest star, but due to its round shape, only half of our planet is lit by sunlight at any one time. However, as Earth spins on its axis, the whole planet experiences a 24-hour day-night rhythm. Biodynamic gardeners see Earth as a living organism that breathes in and out, both daily and seasonally. In the evening and during fall, the Earth breathes in, or inhales; in the morning and in spring the Earth then breathes out, or exhales.

Plants follow the natural daily cycle, with some that flower only at certain times, such as morning glory (left) and evening primrose (right).

Tuning in to nature
The moon

Weather permitting, the sun is visible every day, but our closest celestial neighbor, the moon, comes and goes, and changes shape. Recently, a new generation of gardeners has begun to rediscover the value of timing key tasks, like sowing, planting, and harvesting, to lunar cycles; best of all, working to lunar cycles is free.

Full moon—new moon cycle

An obvious celestial cycle to work to is the full moon cycle, because we can see the moon phases change with our own eyes and there i no need to consult a lunar calendar, although may make planning easier. The word *month* i derived from *moon*, and a full moon occur once a month, or every 29.5 days, to be exact.

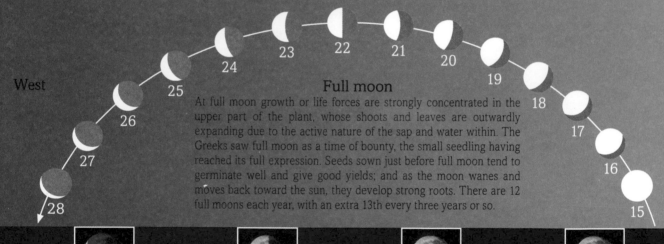

West

28 27 26 25 24 23 22 21 20 19 18 17 16 15

Full moon

At full moon growth or life forces are strongly concentrated in the upper part of the plant, whose shoots and leaves are outwardly expanding due to the active nature of the sap and water within. The Greeks saw full moon as a time of bounty, the small seedling having reached its full expression. Seeds sown just before full moon tend to germinate well and give good yields; and as the moon wanes and moves back toward the sun, they develop strong roots. There are 12 full moons each year, with an extra 13th every three years or so.

DAYS 23–28
WANING CRESCENT

DAY 22
THIRD QUARTER

DAYS 16–21
WANING GIBBOUS

DAY 14–15
FULL MOON

Pruning
The flow of sap and water from the roots up into the upper part of the plant is weaker in the run up to new moon, which makes it a good time to prune trees and shrubs.

Apply weed pepper
Full moon is a good time to make and apply weed peppers (*see p.138*). Think carefully before you use them: you may find it harder to grow a desirable related plant in the same spot at a later date.

Tracking the full moon

The cycle occurs because of how the moon, the sun, and the Earth all move relative to each other. The moon orbits the Earth, while the Earth is also spinning around the sun. When the sun is on one side of the Earth and the moon is on the opposite side—in opposition (*see p.56*)—it is full moon, and the moon appears completely round and bright in the night sky, even though it has no light of its own. The light we see is sunlight reflected off the moon's gray-white surface. Around 14 days after full moon it is new moon. The moon is much harder to see because it has moved around the Earth to lie directly between Earth and the sun. The side of the moon lit by the sun at new moon is facing the sun and so is the side we cannot see.

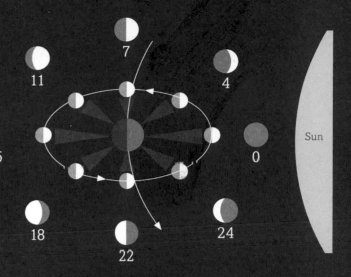

New moon

The Greeks believed new moon was a time of fertility and rebirth because this was when the moon and sun joined each other in the same part of the sky. In biodynamics, new moon is a period of inward contraction, when plant growth or life force is concentrated down toward its root system. As the moon waxes and moves away from the sun, it appears larger, and the flow of sap becomes more vigorous in the upper part of the plant. The Greeks thought the curved sliver, visible just after new moon, resembled a newly sprouting seed.

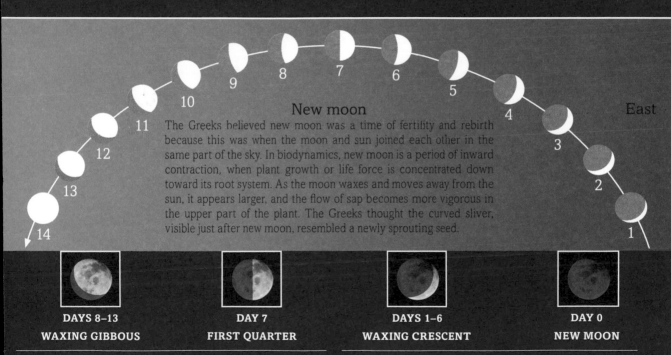

| **DAYS 8–13** | **DAY 7** | **DAYS 1–6** | **DAY 0** |
| **WAXING GIBBOUS** | **FIRST QUARTER** | **WAXING CRESCENT** | **NEW MOON** |

Sow seeds
Seeds sown during the two or three days just before full moon tend to germinate well and give good yields. This is especially true of annual crops like cucumbers, lettuce, leeks, cabbage, and spinach which form their edible, water-filled parts above ground.

Spray horn manure 500
The days leading up to a full moon are good times to apply horn manure—two days before is ideal. The forces of reproduction and growth are particularly powerful at this time, and allow all the life contained in the horn manure 500 prep to work strongly.

Apogee and perigee

Understanding how close or far the moon and Earth are from each other is useful when timing key garden tasks, such as sowing, planting, harvesting, and pruning.

The moon's boomerang orbit

It takes around 27.55 days for the moon to complete its elliptical orbit around Earth. Its closest point to Earth is called perigee; its farthest point is known as apogee. Note that biodynamic sowing calendars show how the moon spends less time in front of a star constellation at perigee than it does in front of the same constellation at apogee. This is because the moon's elliptical orbit means that its "speed," as seen from Earth, varies as it passes through the twelve constellations along its ecliptic path.

Axis tilt of the moon—6.7°

Axis tilt of the Earth—23.5°

Apogee
251,655 miles (405,500 km)

Perigee
225,744 miles (363,300 km)

Apogee

When the moon is at its farthest point from Earth, or apogee, a summer mood reigns. The moon's influence on tides is at its weakest at apogee, and so are its watery influences. For this reason, apogee is the best time to sow potatoes for a good yield that stores well. Other root or leaf crops, like carrots or spinach, sown at apogee, risk growing too quickly and running to seed because the watery influences are at their weakest.

Don't be tempted to sow something at apogee deliberately to encourage it to bolt and set seed to save for the following year (*see pp.26–27*). There is a risk that these seeds will produce a generation of plants with such a short growing cycle that they will be incapable of actually providing much food. In contrast the apogee moon's summer influences make it a good time to harvest fruit crops, such as tomatoes, eggplant, or apples for more concentrated, less watery, flavors, or to cut mature pumpkins ready for drying and curing outside.

Perigee

When the moon is closest to Earth at perigee, two things can happen. Tides are especially strong, and there is a greater likelihood of a lunar landing. In 1969, Neil Armstrong and his Apollo 11 mission team saved 26,000 miles (42,000 km) of extra flying by going to the moon at perigee. The perigee moon invokes a winter mood because the moon's watery element inhibits the sun's relationship with Earth. Seeds sown into beds prepared at perigee may germinate poorly, or the crop itself may be affected because the watery element will be too strongly manifested in the upper part of the plant. For leafy crops that need to be watery, like spinach or lettuce, the perigee moon can be positive. However, if fruit crops, such as strawberries or apples, are watery, it causes a loss of sweetness, ripeness, and flavor, and they may also store poorly.

The potentially negative effects of a perigee moon can be made worse if it coincides with a full moon. This happens once every 14–15 months, and can give rise to supermoons, when the moon is physically close and appears magnified. The days leading up to lunar perigee are a good time to balance the greater moisture the moon brings to soil by spraying *Equisetum arvense* 508 on the soil. This prevents excess growth of either weeds or fungal disease spores.

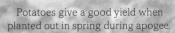

Avoid sowing seeds of crops that are prone to bolting.

Potatoes give a good yield when planted out in spring during apogee.

Keep crops prone to bolting well watered when a "summer" mood reigns.

✓ If perigee and full moon coincide, spray horn silica 501 to dry out the atmosphere.

✗ Avoid digging beds during perigee.

Lift roots like carrots at risk of rotting in wet soil.

Leaf crops, like lettuce and spinach, taste better when sown at perigee.

✗ Strawberries planted during perigee will have watery, tasteless fruit.

Ascending and descending moon

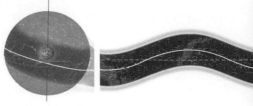

The yellow line denotes the path the moon takes in front of the constellations (*see p.54*).

The ascending and descending moon cycle is one of the easier lunar cycles to work to, because it allows you two periods of almost two weeks in which to do certain tasks. Thinking of the ascending moon as the spring–summer moon and the descending moon as a fall–winter moon makes the cycle easy to grasp.

Following the moon

Just as the sun lies lowest in the sky at midwinter (winter solstice) and highest in the sky at midsummer (summer solstice), so the moon sits lowest in the sky at the end of its descending period, and rises to its highest point at the end of its ascending period. The difference is that there are six months between the sun's winter low and summer high points (the winter and summer solstices), but the time between the moon's summer high and winter low points is just 13.65 days, or 27.3 days between the start of each ascending or descending moon period. This means that the ascending–descending moon cycle runs independently of the 29.5 day full moon–new moon cycle; the 27.55 day apogee–perigee cycle; and also the four-season, 365.25 day cycle.

This means that full moon, new moon, apogee, and perigee can all occur at any point in the moon's ascending or descending cycle. Also, the moon ascends and descends—in its "spring–summer" and "fall–winter" phases—independently of the actual season at any time of year.

Understanding nodes

Nodes occur twice a month when the moon crosses the "ecliptic", an imaginary line in the sky where eclipses occur. They can happen at full moon, causing a lunar eclipse when Earth's shadow blots out the moon, or at new moon, causing a solar eclipse when the moon hides the sun. Plants risk being inhibited if sown, hoed, or transplanted at nodes. To avoid problems view moon nodes as rest days.

Differing views

The angle at which the moon rotates the earth is 5.5 degrees, and it appears to move up and down in the sky as everything rotates. The cycle varies according to which hemisphere you are in. When the moon passes from Sagittarius to Capricornus, then Aquarius, Pisces, Aries, Taurus, and finally Gemini, it is an ascending spring–summer moon in the northern hemisphere—but in the southern hemisphere it will be a fall–winter descending moon.

Conversely, if it is a descending fall–winter moon in the northern hemisphere, it will be a spring–summer ascending moon in the southern hemisphere; but no matter where you live, the moon will still be moving from Gemini to Cancer, Leo, Virgo, Libra, Scorpius, and back to Sagittarius.

Northern hemisphere
Descending moon—fall–winter mood

node   node

Sagittarius   Gemini   Sagittarius

Southern hemisphere
Ascending moon—spring–summer mood

Sagittarius   Gemini   Sagittarius

node   node

The moon's path passes in front of Gemini to Cancer, Leo, Virgo, Libra, Scorpius, and back to Sagittarius.

The descending moon

During the descending fall–winter moon period, sap is especially vital in the lower parts of plants. This is the time to plant out seedlings from pots and seedbeds, because the roots will find it easier to get going in their new environment. Also, since plant sap contains nutrient-rich goodness, pruning is best done now. This is because any growth that needs removing contains sap whose force is less vital than it is at ascending moon. The earth-centered nature of a descending moon also means this is a good time to stimulate root activity by adding compost to the soil.

Plant out seedlings.

Dig compost into the soil.

Prune fruit trees and bushes.

Apply horn manure 500.

The ascending moon

During the ascending spring–summer moon period, sap in the upper plant parts is especially enlivened. Flowers cut now last longer before wilting, and picked fruit keeps well. The ascending moon is also a good time to take cuttings of trees or vines that you intend to graft before planting. As well as the sun and moon, all planets in our solar system follow this ascending and descending cycle as they pass in front of the 12 constellations—first ascending, then descending—as they continue their orbits.

Cut flowers stay fresh longer.

Mist crops with horn silica 501.

Take cuttings at this time.

Harvested fruit keeps longer.

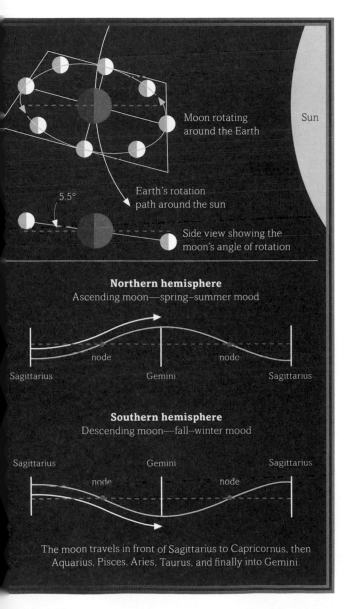

Moon rotating around the Earth

Sun

5.5°

Earth's rotation path around the sun

Side view showing the moon's angle of rotation

Northern hemisphere
Ascending moon—spring–summer mood

Sagittarius | node | Gemini | node | Sagittarius

Southern hemisphere
Descending moon—fall–winter mood

Sagittarius | node | Gemini | node | Sagittarius

The moon travels in front of Sagittarius to Capricornus, then Aquarius, Pisces, Aries, Taurus, and finally into Gemini.

The moon and the stars

In its orbit around Earth the moon passes in front of all the zodiac constellations, from Pisces to Aquarius. It takes 27.3 days to complete this cycle, and each time the moon passes a given constellation, the element associated with it—earth, water, air, or fire—is stimulated on Earth in one of four main plant organs—root, leaf, flower, or fruit/seed—which are also used in biodynamics to classify the edible parts of plants. This sidereal cycle has been seen to affect the way that particular parts of plants grow.

Aquarius
In the northern hemisphere this is a good time to spray horn silica 501 on fruit or flower crops. Plant flower bulbs in southern hemisphere garden plots.

Capricornus
Hoe weeds in the northern hemisphere. In the southern hemisphere this is the best time to work compost into the soil or apply soil sprays.

Sagittarius
Harvest fruit crops in the northern hemisphere. Prune, transplant, and feed fruit crops in the southern hemisphere.

Scorpius
The most versatile sign under which to work leaf crops in either hemisphere—and especially for sowing them in the run up to a full moon.

Libra
Sow, prune, or fertilize flowers and flowering herbs in northern hemisphere locations; but in the southern hemisphere it is a good time to pick them.

Virgo
Work compost into the soil or apply soil sprays like BC in the northern hemisphere. Remove weeds in the southern hemisphere.

Leo

Sow seeds in either hemisphere of crops that you intend to grow for their seed. Apply soil sprays or compost preps to fruit crops in the northern hemisphere.

Cancer

Prepare the soil for, sow, or spray leaf crops in the northern hemisphere. Plant or transplant perennials, hedges, or herbs in southern hemisphere garden plots.

Gemini

Fresh-cut flowers for vases, flowering herbs for drying, and salad leaf crops last longer when collected under Gemini in either hemisphere.

Taurus

Moon in Taurus is a good time to harvest potatoes—but avoid harvesting them for long-term storage if it is also near full or perigee moon.

Aries

Prune and apply tree paste to dormant fruit trees in the northern hemisphere. Apply 501 to fruit crops—and harvest—in the southern hemisphere.

Pisces

In the northern hemisphere, plant or transplant perennials like hedges and herbs. Prepare the soil, sow, or spray leaf crops in the southern hemisphere.

GEMINI

CANCER

LEO

ARIES

TAURUS

PISCES

Plant organs and the elements

The link between the plant organs and the four elements is easier to comprehend by considering how plants grow. First, they put roots in the earth. The roots create shoots and leaves, which are full of water. Flowers emerge, and transmit their scent through the air to encourage bees to fertilize them. The fertilized flowers contract due to the warmth (fire) of the sun and form seeds or fruit. When the seeds fall to the earth, they sprout new roots and a new cycle of growth begins.

In biodynamics all celestial cycles streaming in to the Earth are seen to influence plant growth. The moon, planets, and the sun all pass the 12 zodiac constellations that relate to one of the four elements: Taurus, Virgo, and Capricorn relate to the earth, and to root formation; Cancer, Scorpio, and Pisces relate to water and to leaf formation; Gemini, Libra, and Aquarius relate to air (or light) and flower formation; and Aries, Leo, and Sagittarius relate to the element of warmth (or fire) and to fruiting and seed formation.

Root, leaf, flower, and fruit days

Plant growth can be favorably enhanced by linking the part of the plant intended for harvest—such as carrot roots, lettuce leaves, edible flowers, and fruit like apples—with the position of the moon, planets, and sun in relation to the zodiac constellations. By cultivating carrots on root days—when the moon is in an earth constellation—the crop develops to its full potential, providing healthy, nutritious, and tasty carrots with the right form or shape, which will store well, if needed; and the celestial influences mean they also provide the right sustenance for body and mind. The carrots will be more tuned in to celestial rhythms if the biodynamic preparations are used.

Remember that working to the moon and stars is just one aspect of gardening successfully, and no substitute for common sense: grow crops in the soil and conditions that suit them best. And be pragmatic: it is not a crime to sow lettuce or any other crop on the "wrong" day. But it is a crime to sow nothing at all.

Moon–Saturn opposition

Oppositions occur when planets, the moon, or stars stand at an angle of 180 degrees from each other in the sky. The most familiar example of an opposition occurs every 29.5 days at full moon: the moon is directly opposite our nearest star—the sun—and Earth is in between. The different forces at work can impact the garden: the full moon on one side of Earth stimulates watery or calcium forces, enhancing growth and reproduction, which is why seeds sown at full moon tend to germinate quickly. On the other side of Earth, the sun stimulates warmth or silica forces, which aid ripeness and flavor.

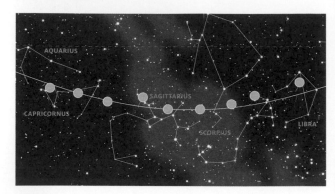

Saturn takes nearly 30 years to orbit the sun. It passes in front of all 12 zodiac constellations in its route along the ecliptic.

Nature's balancing act

For gardeners, days when the moon and Saturn are in opposition are useful times of balance and harmony in the natural world. This occurs every 27.5 days and means that Earth has the moon on one side and Saturn is directly opposite (but farther away) on the other. The moon's watery influence on fertility, germination, and yield is balanced by Saturn's warmth power that gives plants the right form, structure, ripeness, flavor, and capacity to age.

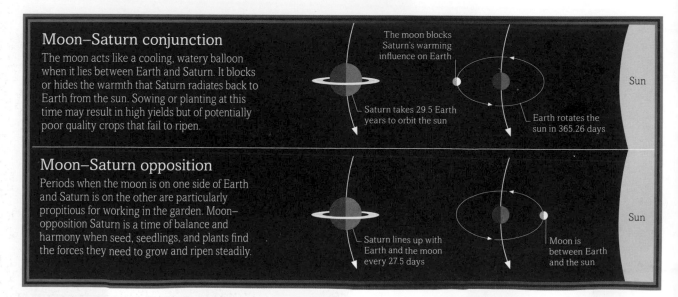

Moon–Saturn conjunction

The moon acts like a cooling, watery balloon when it lies between Earth and Saturn. It blocks or hides the warmth that Saturn radiates back to Earth from the sun. Sowing or planting at this time may result in high yields but of potentially poor quality crops that fail to ripen.

The moon blocks Saturn's warming influence on Earth

Saturn takes 29.5 Earth years to orbit the sun

Earth rotates the sun in 365.26 days

Sun

Moon–Saturn opposition

Periods when the moon is on one side of Earth and Saturn is on the other are particularly propitious for working in the garden. Moon–opposition Saturn is a time of balance and harmony when seed, seedlings, and plants find the forces they need to grow and ripen steadily.

Saturn lines up with Earth and the moon every 27.5 days

Moon is between Earth and the sun

Sun

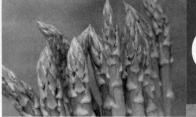

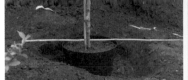
Plant perennial vegetables like asparagus.

Plant trees and shrubs.

Renew barren areas.

Saturn's warming influence arises because it acts like a mirror reflecting heat from the sun back to Earth. However the warmth Saturn sends to Earth is minimized when the moon passes in front of Saturn, completely hiding it. Fortunately, unlike moon–Saturn oppositions, these so-called moon–Saturn occultations happen only irregularly. Several may occur in the space of several months, followed by a two- to five-year gap before the next series occurs.

Things to do at opposition

The two days leading up to moon–opposition Saturn are times to prioritize key garden tasks, particularly those that will have a lasting effect. These are good times to dig compost into the soil, to plant flower bulbs, to prepare planting holes for fruit trees, shrubs, rose bushes, and hedges—and then plant them—and to move herbs and other plants that need to go into pots.

Seeds sown in the two days before moon–opposition Saturn, and those that start to germinate at that time generally produce robust plants. It makes sense to time sowing or planting high-yielding crops—such as potatoes, tomatoes, beans, and strawberries—as well as potentially fussy ones like spinach and Asian greens to the moon–opposition Saturn rhythm.

Moon–opposition Saturn periods are also highly favorable times to spray the three biodynamic spray preparations (see pp.66–85). Horn manure 500 will have an especially strong stimulating effect on soil microorganisms at moon–opposition Saturn, while horn silica 501 and *Equisetum arvense* 508 sprays respectively bring additional flavor-enhancing and strengthening effects to plants.

The enlivening, nourishing effects of teas, liquid manures, and spreading biodynamic compost are also enhanced at moon–opposition Saturn.

Create raised beds and prepare them for planting.

Apply horn manure 500 in the afternoon just before opposition.

Spray horn silica 501 early in the morning just after opposition.

Plant ornamental flower bulbs like tulips.

Plant perennial herbs in pots.

How the biodynamic movement began

Biodynamics is the oldest green farming movement. It emerged during the early 1920s, just after the end of the First World War. The organic farming movement came later, developing directly after the Second World War. Over the previous 150 years Europe had transformed itself from an agricultural to an industrial economy. Although the organic and biodynamic movements agreed that industrialization had brought some useful technological benefits, they were also concerned about its damaging and possibly irreversible side effects, such as the loss of biodiversity and habitats for birds and bees.

Industrial impact

The industrialization of agriculture really took off after the First World War. The war and the influenza pandemic that followed wiped out two generations of largely self-sufficient farmers. Millions of farm animals also died in the fighting, or from neglect and starvation. These farmers and the animals they used to plow were replaced with modern agricultural machinery developed from the newly invented military battle tanks. First World War bomb-making technology was modified to create soluble chemical fertilizers to boost yields, and nerve gas technology was used to develop weedkillers and pesticides. The use of these pesticides and fertilizers led to a loss of biodiversity and wild habitats for birds and bees, increased pollution of the soil and waterways, and crops whose high yields were offset by reduced nutritional value and rising levels of chemical residues. And as heritage seed varieties were replaced by hybrid seeds that produced more predictable yields, it meant farmers could no longer save their own seed, and became less self-sufficient.

These scientific breakthroughs served to make farming more predictable, more efficient, and safer—but also more profitable for those controlling the new technologies, and less profitable for those doing the farming. Not all farmers were happy. They

sensed that modern methods were making their soil, crops, seeds, and animals weaker and less fertile. As working animals were replaced by machines, there was less manure to compost to keep soils fertile. Modern mineral fertilizers and hybrid seeds produced bigger yields but weaker, more disease-prone crops—and much bigger weeds. Some farmers felt their long-term economic survival was becoming impossible.

A fresh approach

In 1924 a group of leading central European farmers asked Rudolf Steiner (1861–1925) to give them an alternative vision of farming. Steiner had already developed an alternative form

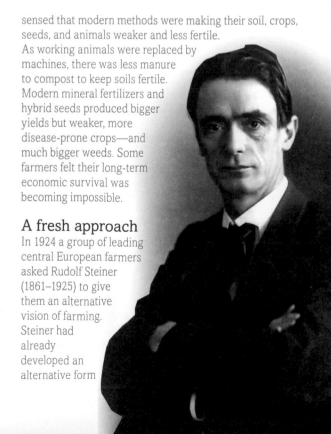

of schooling—Steiner or Waldorf education—but agriculture was his defining passion. He had grown up in a community in Austria (now part of Slovenia) where the farming methods and traditions that he witnessed as a boy had remained unchanged for centuries—and still worked just as well.

In spring 1924 Steiner outlined his alternative to modern farming in a series of lectures called *Agriculture*—and it is these ideas that have become known as biodynamics. He warned the farmers who had invited him that some of his suggestions would seem rather odd—even slightly backward—but stressed that accepting modern farming at face value would pay off in the short term only at the risk of terrible long-term consequences for human, plant, and animal health. Steiner even correctly predicted that the world's bees, who pollinate our crops, would face population collapse around the year 2000, thanks to modern pesticides.

How biodynamics works

Steiner said that healthy humans need healthy food from healthy farms. By *healthy* Steiner was clear that food must feed the physical body but must also have the power to nourish our will. Things won't change for the better unless we want them to, and we do something about it. And because we are what we eat, to help the planet we live on not just to survive but thrive, we need to grow better food. To do that, said Steiner, farmers would have to make some radical changes and accept some ideas that seem odd to our 24/7, high-tech generation but were not quite so out of the ordinary then. Steiner said each farm or garden should be as self-sufficient as possible. Animals—and their manure—make this much easier, and when Steiner was speaking, many homeowners still kept some of their own animals for meat, milk, and eggs: a cow, some pigs perhaps, and some hens. Steiner then added a new element to the self-sufficiency idea by suggesting the best way of healing damaged soil was via normal compost prepared in a special way, using six preparations. These were made from six medicinal herbs commonly used to treat ailments in humans, animals, or both: yarrow, chamomile, dandelion, and valerian flowers; stinging nettles; and crushed oak bark. Steiner said while plant roots often make the best remedies for humans, it would be best to use the flowers when healing the earth.

A handful of each of the plants would be added to the compost pile after being prepared in a special way. By this, Steiner meant exposing the plants to the sun or burying them in the soil. Steiner also suggested four of these compost preparations be sheathed in the sense organs of either a cow or a male deer (stag). This seems odd now, but in the 1920s home butchering of farm animals like cows, or game like deer, was much more common than it is today. Cow intestines were often used to make pork sausages for the table. What Steiner was suggesting was to make

sausages from chamomile flowers and feed them to the garden via the compost pile instead. He also suggested three sprays be applied to the soil, made in similar ways to the compost preparations but including cow manure, the mineral quartz (silica), and another medicinal plant *Equisetum arvense*.

Steiner said that biodynamics was a low-tech way of farming that everyone could practice. His nine preparations were made and used in very small quantities but would quickly help farms and gardens achieve a healthy, dynamic, and sustainable balance. Treating each garden or farm as an organism in its own right would eventually help us see the earth as a living organism, as part of a much wider cycle of life involving the other planets and stars in our solar system, too. Steiner didn't coin the term "think global, act local," but his biodynamic way of farming was the first to fit it, and it is as valid now as it was in 1924.

The ingredients used in the nine biodynamic preps.
From top left: Equisetum arvense (common horsetail), chamomile, dandelion, nettle, oak bark, yarrow, cow manure, valerian, and quartz.

How to dynamize biodynamic sprays

Several biodynamic preps are diluted and stirred before application to ensure the beneficial forces in the prep are transferred into the water and onto the land. The process is known as dynamizing because there is a dynamic interaction between the prep and the water in which it is stirred.

Stirring and the vortex

Stirring by hand for long periods of up to 1 hour seems like a lot of hard work, but once you get the hang of the process, it takes on a rhythm of its own. Recruit a few helpers and it can be an enjoyable social event; if it becomes a chore, it is better to stop, pour what you have been stirring onto the compost heap, and start again another time when you feel fresher and your inner will is stronger.

The aim of stirring is to create a whirlpool effect; this produces a vertical crater in the center, known as the vortex. The vortex is created because water around the edge of the stirring tank moves more quickly than the water in the middle. Once or twice a minute, reverse the direction of stirring, so the vortex crashes and a new one is created. This ensures the forces carried by the preparation being stirred are transferred to every drop of water.

As you stir, you will notice that the texture of the water changes and becomes more slippery and viscous. This is partly due to the aeration it has received, but also because the water has been opened up to celestial forces from above through the dynamizing process. Looking down into the vortex created by hand-stirring water in a bucket resembles the view of our universe from space. Planet earth spins around a star—the sun—which itself is spinning around on the edge of our spiral-shaped, vortexlike galaxy—the Milky Way—which is also spinning around in the wider universe. Life on earth depends on the ability of everything to keep on spinning, so spinning the preparations around in water, the source of life, reinforces the living processes plants need to stay vital and healthy.

How long to stir

Horn manure 500 and horn silica 501 should be stirred for 1 hour. The barrel compost (BC) is stirred for 20 minutes. Stir valerian 507 for 10–20 minutes, whether it is being added to the compost or sprayed onto crops.

Stir vigorously in one direction for about a minute, remove the stick and allow the water to spin undisturbed.

Dynamized liquids are usually applied in one of two ways. For ground sprays, shake large droplets onto the soil with a brush. Plant teas and horn silica 501 are usually applied as a fine mist on or over the crops.

Plant teas and liquid manures also benefit from a 10–20 minute stir. The aeration helps them to stick better, and makes it easier for plants and the soil to absorb the nutrients in the liquid. Aerated compost teas (*see p.40*) require longer—up to 24 hours.

Applying the spray

Dynamized liquids should be sprayed as soon as stirring ends, or not long after. Adding an unstirred liquid to one that has been stirred will nullify the effect of the stirring. Spray the unstirred liquid first, then the dynamized one; better still, stir them both.

Flowforms

Stirring by hand creates a single central vertical vortex or whirl in the water. Horizontal vortices are also effective and can be created with flowforms. These attractive water features use a solar-powered pump to encourage water to flow across a series of sculpted bowls, usually made of clay. The bowls allow the water to move in the same direction at differing speeds and form shapes as if it were eddying and flowing over pebbles in a stream. The bowls can also produce figure-eight shapes that resemble the way blood flows in living organisms. The rhythmical, oxygenating effects of flowforms enhance the water's vitality, and the sight and sound of water in a flowform is known to have therapeutic effects.

Just before the vortex collapses, break it with the stick and stir in the opposite direction. Repeat the process for the required time.

Nine biodynamic preparations—made from 7 plants, a mineral, and animal manure—

Horn silica
preparation 501

Chamomile
preparation 503

Horn manure
preparation 500

Yarrow
preparation 502

are designed to *enliven* the earth and all that grows in it.

Valerian
preparation 507

Oak bark
preparation 505

Nettle
preparation 504

Dandelion
preparation 506

Equisetum arvense
preparation 508

The 9 preps explained

Biodynamics entails the regular use of nine preparations, which deliberately expose both garden and gardener to the three realms of nature: animal, mineral, and vegetable. Biodynamics sees uniting these three realms as the best way of regenerating land that has lost its life force—and in repairing the earth, we also reconnect ourselves with natural seasonal and celestial cycles.

Horn manure 500

Sprayed on the earth, horn manure gives the garden solid foundations and charges the soil with all the life force it needs. Good soil needs the right amount of air and moisture to support worms, fungi, bacteria, and microbes, and to produce crops that are wholesome to eat. Horn manure keeps the earth's stomach well stocked. It keeps our stomachs well stocked and our senses stimulated with the food it helps produce. **Making 500** pp.66–71. **Using 500** pp.72–73.

Horn silica 501

Horn silica helps to produce nutritious food that tastes good and stores well. Sprayed over crops to maximize the forces of heat and light sent by the sun, it pulls plants upward to their limits using heat and light as bait, keeping them lean, taut, and ready to withstand pests and diseases. They stay healthy and able to produce ripe, flavorful, and wholesome crops. **Making 501** pp.74–79. **Using 501** pp.80–81.

Yarrow 502

The yarrow prep develops a sense of awareness in the compost that is transmitted to the crops when it is spread on the soil. Plants need this to survive and prosper, just as animals do in the wild. Crops able to sense changes locally—such as weather patterns—and movements of the sun, moon, planets, and stars are completely connected to their environment. This kind of total awareness helps keep plants strong. **Making 502** pp.86–91. **Using 502** pp.122–129; 136–137.

Chamomile 503

The chamomile prep ensures the garden's waste and recycling system works safely and efficiently. Garden waste is either recycled naturally where it falls on the ground, or in the compost pile before it is put back on the soil. Effectively, the land is feeding off refuse, eating leaves and other compostable items. Chamomile makes sure this earthy digestive system works as effortlessly as a cow's intestine without ever getting blocked. **Making 503** pp.92–97. **Using 503** pp.122–129 136–137.

Dandelion 506

The dandelion prep has a similar role to the yarrow prep. Yarrow makes plants aware of their surroundings; dandelion has the same effect but also helps plants tune in to what is happening underground. The dandelion flower is like a tiny sun, plunging its powerful, elastic roots deep into the underground. Dandelions give compost the power to brighten soil from within, and connect it with what is above. **Making 506** pp.108–113. **Using 506** pp.122–129; 136–137.

Stinging nettle 504

The nettle prep plays a special role, making compost more compostlike overall. Good compost is dark and earthy, neither too dry nor too moist. It contains the right worms and microbes as well as all the important minerals in exactly the right amounts. Compost infused with nettle 504 helps crop plants grow well no matter the conditions, and leave the soil in a better state than it was before—just like the nettles do in the wild. **Making 504** pp98–101. **Using 504** pp.122–129; 136–137.

Valerian 507

The valerian prep is the icing on a compost cake, sealing in the goodness contained in a well-built compost pile. Its job is to make sure the raw ingredients bake at the right temperature. Good compost needs enough tiny microbes to heat up and kill off troublemakers like weed seeds and disease organisms. When the cleaned-up material cools, worms make the compost ready to be digested safely and efficiently by the land and its crops. **Making 507** pp.114–118 **Using 507** pp.119, 122–129; 136–137.

Oak bark 505

The oak bark prep helps to create compost that gives the soil the right balance. If soil lacks balance, anything that grows there will also be unbalanced—and crops that grow too fast are likely to attract disease. Whether radishes or fruit trees, crop plants should follow the oak's example of slow, steady, reliable growth. A radish may never seem as wise or mighty as an oak, but it can grow just as strong as one. **Making 505** pp.102–107. **Using 505** pp.122–129; 136–137.

Equisetum arvense 508

This spray preparation has the job of crowd control, specifically against pests like weeds and fungal diseases attracted to gardens whose soil and plants are out of balance. *Equisetum arvense* helps prevent potential imbalances. It can be applied to the land or to crops as fresh tea or as a liquid manure, providing a gritty, silica-filled barrier that fungal diseases and opportunistic weeds cannot stand. **Making and using 508** pp.82–85.

Horn manure 500

Horn manure is the key to the biodynamic world. It is made from cow manure stuffed in a cow horn and buried for six months over winter. The dark, crumbly substance that results has populations of beneficial microorganisms far higher than those in normal compost or good soil.

Biodynamic cows are never dehorned. The horns are the cow's sense antennae —which is why cows lower their heads and point their horns at you in greeting.

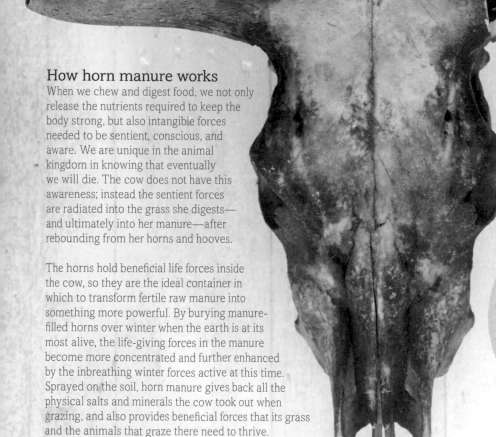

Cow horns are connected to the nasal cavity, which means that digestive gases and sentient life forces are circulated right to the horn tips before rebounding back into the cow's stomach.

How horn manure works

When we chew and digest food, we not only release the nutrients required to keep the body strong, but also intangible forces needed to be sentient, conscious, and aware. We are unique in the animal kingdom in knowing that eventually we will die. The cow does not have this awareness; instead the sentient forces are radiated into the grass she digests— and ultimately into her manure—after rebounding from her horns and hooves.

The horns hold beneficial life forces inside the cow, so they are the ideal container in which to transform fertile raw manure into something more powerful. By burying manure-filled horns over winter when the earth is at its most alive, the life-giving forces in the manure become more concentrated and further enhanced by the inbreathing winter forces active at this time. Sprayed on the soil, horn manure gives back all the physical salts and minerals the cow took out when grazing, and also provides beneficial forces that its grass and the animals that graze there need to thrive. Substitute *pasture* with *backyard*, and *grass* with *homegrown vegetables*, and we can rekindle not just life within the earth, but life within ourselves when we eat plants grown in soil sprayed with horn manure 500.

Cow horns are made of keratin with a bone core that stops just short of the tip. Gently tap out the core from the dried horn, so that the hollow cavity can be stuffed with manure.

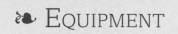

Equipment

Fresh cow manure

Cow horns—ideally from local pasture-grazed cows that have had several calves—are available from biodynamic associations. Calving rings form at the base of the horn for each calf born, making a spiral pattern similar to the vortex formed when dynamizing (see pp.60–61).

A rock or stone anvil helps to send the manure clear down to the horn tips and remove air spaces

BIODYNAMIC SPRAYS HORN MANURE 500

67

Making horn manure 500

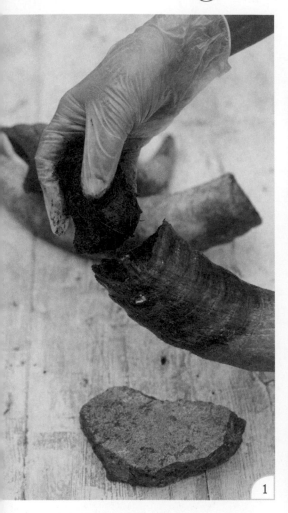

1. Stuff the horns with fresh cow manure around the fall equinox. The best manure is from female cows in milk for their calves, ideally from the pasture in which the animals are grazing. Remove any pieces of green grass or clover. Tap each horn on a rock as you fill it to help ease the manure right into the horn tip and displace any air.

2. Check each horn is tightly packed to ensure that the manure will decompose in the correct way. Pockets of trapped air will result in an incomplete transformation so it is important to displace as much air as possible.

3. Dig a hole about 30in (75cm) deep in good soil, and sprinkle in some fresh compost. Make sure the site is away from power lines.

4. Plant the horns mouth down. If necessary, arrange them in two or three layers. There is no limit to the size of the pit, or the number of horns buried in it, provided the soil is good and the correct horns are filled in the proper way.

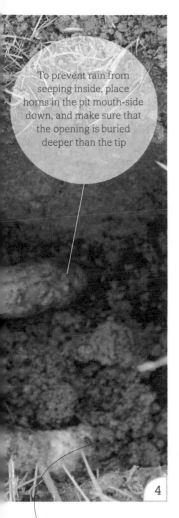

To prevent rain from seeping inside, place horns in the pit mouth-side down, and make sure that the opening is buried deeper than the tip

Carefully pack soil around each horn, ensuring that there are no air gaps

5. Backfill the hole, until the horns are covered by 12–18in (30–45cm) of soil. Mark the corners of the pit with wooden stakes.

6. In warm climates it is advisable to provide shade and shelter from direct sun and heavy rain. Spread a straw mulch over the top of the pit to prevent moisture from evaporating from the soil.

7. Lay a board at an angle over the corner stakes to provide shade and protection from very heavy rain, without compromising the airflow underneath.

8. Cover with more straw to help regulate the temperature.

10

11

6 months later, in spring

10. Lift the horns around the spring equinox, after they have spent 6 months underground absorbing the inbreathing winter forces at work when the earth is its most alive. Earthworms are partial to cow manure, so it is best to excavate the prep before they become too active.

11. Scrape off any soil that sticks to the exterior of the horns before you empty out the contents to avoid contaminating the concentrated horn manure.

12

13

Storing horn manure 500

Horn manure 500 is best made fresh each year, but you can keep it for up to 3 years, provided it is stored well and does not dry out. Place the crumbled horn manure in a glazed pottery or glass jar with a loose-fitting lid that allows the prep to breathe. Keep the jar in a dark, cool, frost-free place, surrounded by an insulating layer of peat, either in a wooden box, or in a clay container sunk into the ground.

Stone slab keeps out the weather

Drip saucer filled with peat makes a loose-fitting lid

Horn manure 500 stored in a small terra-cotta pot

Larger terra-cotta pot filled with peat

To store horn manure 500 in the garden, choose a shady spot with fairly constant conditions—avoid sites at risk of waterlogging, frost pockets, or baking sun, and any areas close to sources of radiation, such as power lines and cell phone towers. Horn manure 500 may also be stored with the compost preps (*see pp.120–121*).

12. Gently tap the horn to remove the contents. If necessary, use a piece of wire to get to anything right at the inside tip of the horn.

13. Crumble the horn manure, and store in a jar. The contents should be dark black-brown, and smell strongly and pleasantly of humus, the "earth within the earth."

Using horn manure 500

Bring your soil to life

Although horn manure is not a fertilizer, it adds a concentrated fertilizing force to the soil that benefits living organisms like beneficial bacteria, worms, and the plants that grow there. It works in tandem with horn silica 501; horn manure works on the earthy underground part of the garden from which crops grow and develop their substance and form; 501 works on the parts above ground, where crops ripen and develop flavor.

Apply ground sprays like horn manure over a large area, using a brush or conifer sprig to splash it onto the ground in large drops.

How to dilute horn manure 500

1. Fill a large container with clean, slightly lukewarm water, and add a small handful of horn manure, about the size of a golf ball.

Choose a slightly overcast day when the soil is warm and just moist. The best time is late afternoon or evening as the earth is breathing in, especially under a descending moon. The days before full moon, when reproductive and growth forces are at their height, are also good, ensuring all the life that prep 500 contains will work strongly.

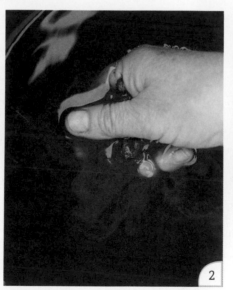

2. To dissolve the horn manure gently rub the preparation into the water using your fingers to remove any lumps.

3. Dynamize the solution for one hour by stirring clockwise and then in an counterclockwise direction to break the vortex at regular intervals (see pp.60–61). Spray horn manure soon after dynamizing it—within an hour or two at the very most.

Apply horn manure 500 to the garden and to bare soil in large, rainlike droplets. Treat the whole garden by loading the brush with the dynamized liquid and drawing it in front of your body in a spiral shape.

Apply 500 to freshly dug, hoed, or weeded soil, just before sowing seeds or transplanting.

Spring applications of horn manure 500 help to revive soil life after freezing winter conditions and heavy frost.

Applying horn manure 500 between fall and spring keeps the soil inwardly alive.

73

Biodynamic sprays

Horn silica 501

Made by filling a cow horn with silica-rich quartz, horn silica works in tandem with horn manure 500. While horn manure influences plant roots, horn silica influences the parts that are visible both to us and to the light and heat of the sun—shoots, leaves, flowers, and fruit—regulating what the crop will taste like, and how ripe it will be.

Quartz rocks can be transparently clear, milky white, or even purple-pink in color; the transparent type is the best one to use

Rainwater to make paste

Cow horn

Heavy-duty mortar and pestle to break up and grind quartz

How horn silica works

Horn silica 501 organizes the heat and light forces coming both from our sun and from the outer warmth planets like Mars, Jupiter, and Saturn. It allows plants to develop a stong connection with heat and light—which is why it is sprayed at sunrise, into the atmosphere and over the tops of the plants. Horn silica continues the work of horn manure, which gets nutrients moving in the soil, by pulling those nutrients upward into the plants and keeping the sap flowing. It also helps to give crops the perfect shape—not too firm or too floppy, or too short or too tall. The prep is made in a similar way to horn manure 500—a cow horn is filled with a paste made from ground silica and buried in the ground for six months, but this time over the summer.

Quartz rocks are often washed down from the mountains into riverbeds

&❧ EQUIPMENT

Toughened glass
work surface

Protective
glasses

A heavy glass
bottle makes an
excellent rolling
pin to crush the
ground-up silica
to a fine powder

Face mask

Making horn silica 501

1

2

1. Break the quartz rock into small
pieces when you are ready to make the
prep in late spring or early summer. You
will need to use considerable force to do
this, so use a heavy duty mortar and
pestle, or even a hammer.

⚠️ **SAFETY FIRST**
Fragments of quartz can be
extremely sharp: always wear protective
eyewear when breaking up rocks, and
make sure others—including family
pets—are well out of range of flying
shards. Wear a face mask to avoid
inhaling tiny particles of silica dust.

2. Grind the quartz pieces into a fine powder
with the mortar and pestle. Turn the powder out onto
a glass cutting board, and use a glass bottle like a rolling
pin to help crush it into a flourlike consistency.

3. Transfer the silica powder to a glass bowl or pot and gradually add clean rainwater, stirring constantly to make a stiff paste. It should be just at the point of being runny.

4. Spoon the silica paste into the horn until it is full to the brim.

5. Prop the horn upright and allow the contents to settle overnight. If water rises to the top, pour it off and add more paste so that the horn is completely full. Allow the contents to dry for a few more hours if needed, and then bury the horn.

6

6. Dig a hole around 30in (75cm) deep in a sunny, open site away from cell phone towers and electrical power lines. Ideally, choose a flower day under an ascending moon to bury horn silica.

7

8

7. Place the horn in the pit, mouth-side down to prevent rain from collecting inside.

8. Refill the hole. The horn should be covered by 12in (30cm) of good soil. Use a wooden stake to mark the site of the pit.

9

6 months later, in fall

9. Excavate the horn silica. After its 6 months underground, experiencing the "summer life of the Earth" the silica inside the horn will be filled with complementary "summer" solar forces to balance the earthly "winter" forces carried by horn manure 500.

10

11

12

10. A crust on the horn surface, or pink spots on the outside of the horn, indicates that helpful microorganisms have been at work. Carefully scrape away any fungi from the mouth of the horn to avoid contaminating the prep when you empty out the contents.

11. Use a knife to ease the contents out of the horn and into a clean bowl. The horn silica prep should be similar to talcum powder in appearance.

12. Transfer the powdery silica to a clean, clear, glass jar with a tightly fitting lid for storage.

13. Horn silica 501 keeps indefinitely as long as it remains dry. Keep it in a bright, light place that catches the morning sun every day, away from electricity. Never store horn silica in the dark.

13

Make your garden glow

Horn silica 501 is the *yin* to horn manure's *yang*. Dripped on the earth, horn manure 500 pulls roots down to give plants a solid foundation, but horn silica is wafted mistily into the bright, airy atmosphere to encourage your plants to stretch upward like the rising sun, and allow their shoots, leaves, flowers, and fruit to develop a strong connection with heat and light. Crops sprayed with the combination of 500 and 501 are more disease-resistant; have enhanced aroma, color, flavor, and nutritional qualities; and also store better.

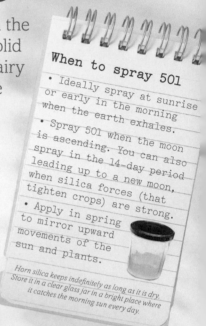

When to spray 501
- Ideally spray at sunrise or early in the morning when the earth exhales.
- Spray 501 when the moon is ascending. You can also spray in the 14-day period leading up to a new moon, when silica forces (that tighten crops) are strong.
- Apply in spring to mirror upward movements of the sun and plants.

Horn silica keeps indefinitely as long as it is dry. Store it in a clear glass jar in a bright place where it catches the morning sun every day.

How to dilute horn silica 501

1. Take a pinch of horn silica and add it to a bucket of lukewarm rainwater. The precise amount depends on the size of the area to be sprayed, but a little goes a long way: 1 level teaspoon of horn silica is all you need for around 11 gallons (50 liters) of water—enough to treat 2½ acres (1 ha).

2. Stir the solution for one hour in clockwise and counterclockwise directions to break the vortex at regular intervals (see pp.60–61).

3. Pour the dynamized liquid into a sprayer with a fine nozzle. Make sure that you spray the solution as soon as possible after stirring—it remains potent for three hours at the very most.

Practical considerations

Choose a day that is likely to be warm and at least partly sunny—do not spray silica if heavy rain is forecast. Aim to finish applying 501 by mid-morning to avoid scalding the leaves. Spray the horn silica solution as a fine mist upward over the top of your garden plants and seedlings rather than onto the soil. By treating the atmosphere the silica acts as a lens to focus the sun's heat and light and connect them with your crops.

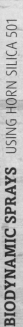

Equisetum 508

One of the easiest biodynamic preps to make, silica-rich *Equisetum arvense* 508 is used to treat both the crops and the soil in which they grow. It is essentially a tea or liquid manure that is made from common horsetail and applied as a spray to prevent plants from being outdone by weeds or damaged by noxious pests, rot, mildew, and other debilitating fungus disease organisms.

Unique qualities

Equisetum arvense comes from a family of plants that predates the dinosaurs. It thrives by shady river banks, ditches, and lakes where soil is damp and light is often poor. Most plants weaken and succumb to pests and diseases in dingy conditions, but the luminous fronds of *E. arvense* contain the highest levels of silica in the plant kingdom, and it even reproduces from fungal spores. It is the silica that makes 508 sprays so effective by tightening crops and making them less appetizing for pests.

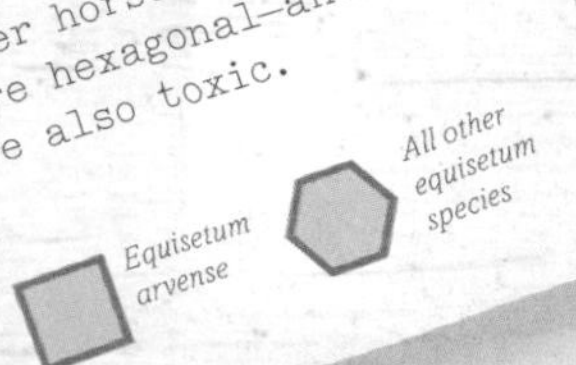

How the 508 sprays work

Equisetum arvense is not the only silica-rich biodynamic prep, but it works differently from horn silica 501. Both revolve around the idea that silica makes plants healthier, tastier, and longer lasting in storage, but horn silica 501 encourages upward movement and a connection with the celestial forces of light and heat. In *Equisetum arvense* 508 tea or liquid manure the silica works downward, using the brightening and drying effects to push disease organisms down, off, or away from the crops and back into the soil where they belong. For maximum effect apply 508 sprays a few days before a new moon because that is when plants inwardly contract anyway, naturally shielding themselves against pests and diseases.

Which horsetail?

Horsetail has a large extended family so make sure you use the right one. Cut into the stem to find out: the common horsetail looks square in cross section; all other horsetails look more hexagonal—and they are also toxic.

Equisetum arvense

All other equisetum species

Collect the fronds and stems just before or at midsummer, when the concentration of silica is highest. You can use them immediately or keep them dry in airy shade until needed. They should retain their green color and dry, firm, spiky feel.

Making equisetum tea 508

1. Extract the silica from *Equisetum arvense* by making a decoction. Use 2–4oz (50–100g) of fronds in 2–5 pints (1–3 liters) of rainwater.

2. Bring to a boil, cover, and simmer for about 30 minutes. Then remove from the heat—with the lid on the pan—and leave it to cool.

3. Strain off the pale yellow-green or brown equisetum concentrate.

4. Make the spray, diluting 1 part equisetum in 40 parts rainwater, and then dynamizing for 15 to 20 minutes (*see pp.60–61*). This helps the tea stick to the plants and makes the treatment more effective.

5. Pour the tea into a garden sprayer.

6. Use a fine setting and apply directly to the crops, misting upper and lower leaf sides. Spray at 2-week intervals unless heavy rain is forecast.

Equisetum 508 tea may be used in tandem or mixed with other sprays like oak bark decoction (*see p.36*) and tree paste (*see pp.132–135*), which both have disease-suppressing effects.

Making 508 liquid manure

2 weeks later

Mold on the surface indicates that your liquid manure concentrate is ready to use. It will smell like sulfur, especially if the equisetum fronds were left in the liquid during the fermenting process. To extend the life of your liquid manure concentrate starter, simply fill it up from time to time with fresh *Equisetum arvense* 508 tea.

1. Make the equisetum decoction (*see facing page*) and pour it into a bucket, with or without straining off the fronds.

2. Cover with a burlap bag and leave it to ferment for 3–10 days in a warm place.

3. Dilute the concentrate. Allow 1 part equisetum to 5–19 parts of water.

4. Dynamize the solution by stirring for 15–20 minutes.

5. Use equisetum manure 508 as a fine mist on plants, and also as a soil drench applied with a watering can. It is a very useful preemptive measure 2–3 days before perigee, or full moon, when watery lunar forces are strong. You can also mix 508 with stinging nettle liquid manure to produce a spray that cleanses and stimulates the soil.

BIODYNAMIC SPRAYS EQUISETUM 508

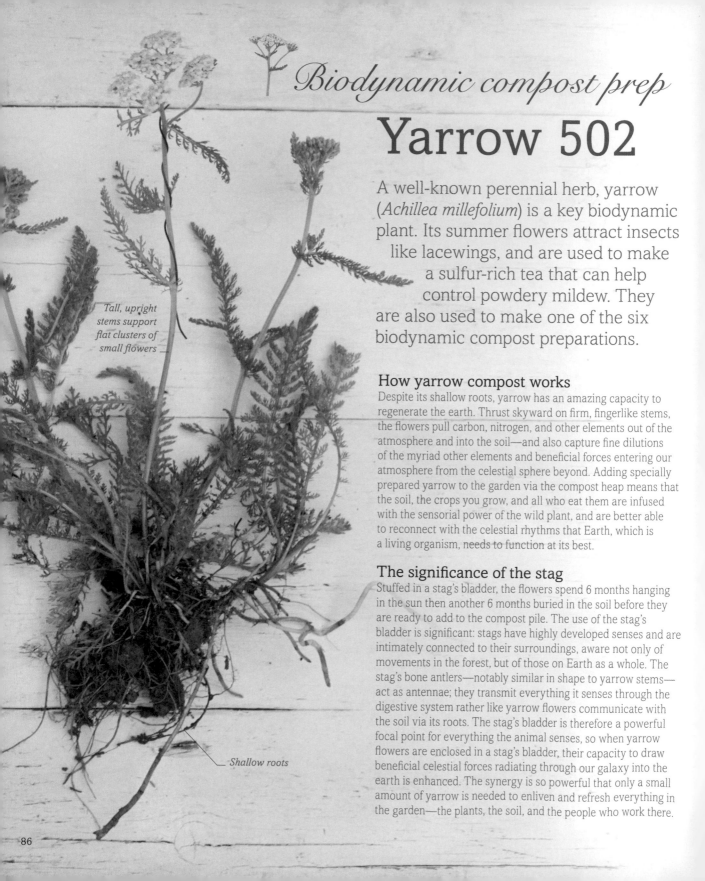

Yarrow 502

A well-known perennial herb, yarrow (*Achillea millefolium*) is a key biodynamic plant. Its summer flowers attract insects like lacewings, and are used to make a sulfur-rich tea that can help control powdery mildew. They are also used to make one of the six biodynamic compost preparations.

Tall, upright stems support flat clusters of small flowers

Shallow roots

How yarrow compost works

Despite its shallow roots, yarrow has an amazing capacity to regenerate the earth. Thrust skyward on firm, fingerlike stems, the flowers pull carbon, nitrogen, and other elements out of the atmosphere and into the soil—and also capture fine dilutions of the myriad other elements and beneficial forces entering our atmosphere from the celestial sphere beyond. Adding specially prepared yarrow to the garden via the compost heap means that the soil, the crops you grow, and all who eat them are infused with the sensorial power of the wild plant, and are better able to reconnect with the celestial rhythms that Earth, which is a living organism, needs to function at its best.

The significance of the stag

Stuffed in a stag's bladder, the flowers spend 6 months hanging in the sun then another 6 months buried in the soil before they are ready to add to the compost pile. The use of the stag's bladder is significant: stags have highly developed senses and are intimately connected to their surroundings, aware not only of movements in the forest, but of those on Earth as a whole. The stag's bone antlers—notably similar in shape to yarrow stems—act as antennae; they transmit everything it senses through the digestive system rather like yarrow flowers communicate with the soil via its roots. The stag's bladder is therefore a powerful focal point for everything the animal senses, so when yarrow flowers are enclosed in a stag's bladder, their capacity to draw beneficial celestial forces radiating through our galaxy into the earth is enhanced. The synergy is so powerful that only a small amount of yarrow is needed to enliven and refresh everything in the garden—the plants, the soil, and the people who work there.

❧ EQUIPMENT

Dried yarrow flowers

Warm water

Wire cutters

Stag bladder (available from your local biodynamic association) from a native species such as European red deer or North American white-tailed deer

Yarrow flowers

String and scissors

Garden wire to protect the prep

Making yarrow 502

GREAT FLOWER DAY TASK

Yarrow blooms in midsummer, so collect, dry, and store the flowers for use the following spring. Pick the flowers on a sunny day. Wait until all the flower heads in each cluster are open, and cut off the florets. Trim off the stems to ensure they don't harden and puncture the bladder. Dry the flowers on slatted trays then store in a jar until you are ready to make the preparation in early spring.

1. Make yarrow tea by pouring warm—not boiling—water over a handful of flowers. The tea is used to rehydrate the bladder, and to moisten the dried flowers used for stuffing so they are less likely to cause the sheath to split.

2. Prepare the sheath by making a small cut about two fingers wide at the tip of the bladder (near the urinary tract) to create a balloon-shaped bag or envelope.

3. Soak the bladder in yarrow tea until it is soft. When you remove it, you should be able to separate the two sides at the opening. Put the sheath to one side.

4. Add yarrow flowers to the bowl and allow them to absorb the remaining tea. Work the tea into the flowers with your hands, adding more if necessary, until the flowers feel slightly moist—like freshly baked bread or sponge cake. They should not be dripping wet.

5. Use your fingers to compact the stuffing slightly before you push it into the bladder.

6. Pack the yarrow mixture into the sheath. Use your thumb or a wooden dowel to push the mixture firmly into the bladder and expel as much air as possible.

7. When the sheath is full, tie off the opening with string. Remove any fat that clings to the bladder to avoid attracting birds and animals when it hangs outside.

8. Hang the bladder in a dry, sunny location high in a tree, or under the eaves of a building. It must remain intact until fall, so make sure that there is room for it to swing in the wind without banging against anything that could cause it to split— it's worth surrounding the bladder with a wire cage or netting that will also protect it from animals and birds.

Six months later, in fall

9. Put a layer of soil in a terra-cotta pot, add some fresh garden compost, place the bladder in the center, and cover with more soil and compost so that the entire bladder is in contact with the soil. Cover the pot with a tile or a piece of slate: this prevents you from damaging the bladder when you dig it up. Bury the pot in a shallow hole around 12in (30cm) deep and leave it alone over winter, when the earth is breathing in.

Six months later, in late spring or early summer

10. Dig up the yarrow compost between late spring and the summer solstice.

11. Gently lift the yarrow out of the pot. It will be extremely fragile—the bladder may have rotted away, but the flower stuffing will hold its shape.

12. Carefully separate the yarrow from any soil and what remains of the bladder membrane using a blunt knife.

13. Crumble the compost and store it in a glass or pottery jar surrounded by peat moss as soon as possible to keep it from drying out.

Using the prep

Yarrow 502 is generally used in concert with the 5 other compost preps.

- To make biodynamic compost, see p.122.
- For the barrel compost prep (BC), see p.126.
- To enhance homemade plant sprays and liquid manures, see p.136.
- For storage, see p.120.

Chamomile 503

Chamomile (*Matricaria recutita*) is the "keep calm and carry on" plant that brings a regenerating, life-giving quality to both garden and gardener. Its roots loosen compacted earth so other plants can find the food and water they need, and a tea from the flowers helps to unblock plant sap, preventing stress from excess heat or cold. The flowers are also used to make one of the six biodynamic compost preparations.

How chamomile compost works

Composted chamomile flowers encourage the natural cycle of growth, decomposition, and new growth to occur in an efficient, healthy way that ensures nothing is wasted. Their life-enhancing properties allow all the raw materials in the compost heap to break down in the correct way, ensuring the finished pile has a stable nitrogen content. The chamomile compost preparation is also rich in balanced proportions of both sulfur and calcium; these allow the pile to inwardly direct life-giving forces released during decomposition, so they stay in the heap and are not lost to the atmosphere.

Chamomile sausages

The flowers are composted inside a cow's intestine, which is cut into short pieces to make sausages and then buried in the soil for six months over winter. In the cow, the intestine holds in the forces and substances that engender healthy life and growth—just like chamomile does in the compost. Placing the flowers in the intestine in the soil allows the chamomile to attract into itself the vitality that enhances its inherent power to cleanse soil, keep it vital, and regulate decomposition. Once it is added to the compost heap, the chamomile prep brings these life-enhancing qualities back to the garden: the soil finds the biodynamic compost easy to digest, which means crops can then find exactly the right amount of food and water they need to force themselves out of the soil and develop into healthy plants to enable the next cycle of growth to continue.

EQUIPMENT

Warm water for chamomile tea

Cow intestine (available from your local biodynamic association)

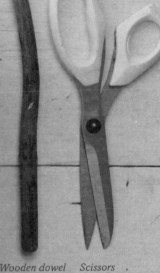

Wooden dowel *Scissors*

Funnel

String

Dried chamomile flowers

Making chamomile 503

Chamomile or mayweed?

There are several varieties of chamomile, so make sure you use the right one. Look for true or German chamomile (*Matricaria recutita*)—the strain with a strong, pure scent used in herbal tea bags. It is often confused with *Chamaemelum nobile* —Roman chamomile, also known as mayweed— which has a more bitter taste. To check the identity of your plant, cut open the yellow cone supporting its flowers: on German chamomile the cone is hollow inside, but the cone for mayweed is solid.

Chamomile   Mayweed

True chamomile flowers resemble badminton shuttlecocks, but aim to pick them before their petals are fully open

Mayweed flowers have a much flatter profile

Spread out the flowers in a tray lined with netting or blotting paper, and turn them every so often. They should retain a rich, clean smell, with no hint of dustiness or mold.

Collect chamomile flowers from early spring— ideally on sunny mornings with an ascending moon— before they are fully open, when the petals are still horizontal. Dry the flowers in a warm, airy place out of direct sunlight, and store them until you make the prep, usually in fall. Dried chamomile has a rich aroma, so keep it in a lidded glass jar to protect it from moths and their caterpillars, as well as mice.

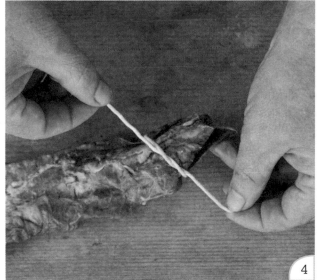

1. To prepare the casing and make the chamomile sausage a manageable size, cut a piece of cow intestine 10–16in (25–40cm) long. Trim off any excess fat.

2. Soak the casing in warm water until it becomes soft and rehydrated.

3. Roll the casing up your thumbs to separate the sides of the tube and remove any obstructions.

4. Use string to tie off one end of the tube, and set the casing aside while you prepare the stuffing.

5. To make chamomile tea, sprinkle a handful of fresh or dried flowers into warm water and leave to infuse for a few minutes.

6. Place the flowers in a bowl and rehydrate them with a small amount of chamomile tea. The flowers should be just moist—damp, but not soaking wet.

7. Roll up the casing around the spout of a wide-mouthed funnel. The top of a cut-down plastic bottle is perfect for this task.

Alternative method

If you wish, you can make the chamomile preparation in the same way as yarrow 502 (*see pp.86–91*). It will take a full year to mature, but it may be more potent for absorbing the celestial forces at work in the summer months. The process is similar, but if you can collect enough chamomile in early spring you can use the freshly picked flowers to fill the casing —there is no need to dry them first. Protect the sausage from wind damage, birds, animals, and insects with a wire cage covered in fine netting, and then hang it out in a sunny location. After 3–4 months take it down and bury the prep at the fall equinox, as described above.

6 months later, in spring

11. Dip up the chamomile prep. Lift the pot around the spring equinox, before earthworms become active and wriggle their way inside to devour the chamomile. Gently brush off soil sticking to the casing.

12. Open the sausage. Use a knife to slice lengthwise down the middle and scrape out the chamomile flowers.

13. Crumble the composted flowers to allow them to dry slightly before storing in a glass or pottery jar, insulated by peat.

8.

9.

10.

8. Fill the intestine with moist chamomile, adding a few small clumps at a time. Use a wooden dowel to press the flowers down the length of the tube.

9. Continue filling the casing until the sausage is firm to the touch, but not so tightly packed that it is in danger of splitting open.

10. Fresh chamomile sausages may attract burrowing animals, so place the sausage in the center of an unglazed terra-cotta pot packed with soil and fresh compost. Cover the pot with tiles and bury it mouth-down in the ground—aim to provide a thick blanket of fertile, humus-rich soil around 12in (30cm) deep.

12.

13.

Using the prep

Chamomile 503 is used in concert with 5 other compost preps.
• To make biodynamic compost, see p.122.
• For the barrel compost prep (BC), see P.126.
• To enhance homemade plant sprays and liquid manures, see p.136.
• For storage, see p.120.

Nettle 504

Stinging nettles do their best to grow in out-of-the-way places, but are a real asset to the garden: wherever they grow they leave behind soil that is darker, earthier, richer, and healthier than before. They are also superb companion plants, attracting ladybugs that feed on aphids. Their extraordinary soil-improving properties can be delivered to the garden in fresh teas and liquidz manures as well as in the compost as one of the biodynamic preps.

Unique qualities

There are many types of nettles, but perennial stinging nettle, *Urtica dioica*, is indispensable in biodynamic gardens. It naturally congregates on bare, compacted land, where its shallow roots reveal an extraordinary ability to drag nutrients from deep in the earth up to the topsoil and enrich the soil so that other plants can thrive. The flowers and seeds are tiny and easy to miss. They appear across the central, most shaded part of the plant, indicating that the nettle concentrates its tremendous power and all its reproductive force at its center, on its stem and leaves. This may explain why they sting so much—it is a sign of how the nettle perfectly captures and balances solar energy from above and the earth's minerals from below.

How nettle compost works

The nettle prep is made using the leaves and stems, which are buried underground for a year in a site exposed to the sun. This enhances both the plant's ability to mediate between the earth and the sun, and its natural power to help soil regenerate and enrich itself. The forces in the nettle are so powerful that no animal sheath is needed. Added to the compost heap, the nettle prep helps garden soil adapt individually to all the different plants being grown, so the soil becomes more "intelligent." The overall effect is to promote balance by keeping things flowing properly—it prevents blockages like compacted soil that starve roots of air, water, food, and light, or sap flowing so weakly it makes crops more prone to hunger, thirst, and pests.

Collect stinging nettles when their sting is most potent—in midsummer when the plants are in flower

&❧ EQUIPMENT

Let the nettles wilt and compress them slightly before burying

Making nettle 504

1. Harvest nettles in midsummer as they are flowering. Use a scythe—and wear protective gloves—to cut down the nettles near the base of the stems.

2. Leave the nettles to wilt for a few hours. Choose a shady spot and protect from rain, if necessary. Wilting exposes the nettles to the forces of the midsummer sun—and you'll be able to pack more nettles into the container.

3. Chop the leaves, stems, and flowers into an unglazed clay pot. The container will protect the nettles from earthworms eager to feast on the iron-rich contents, and also makes the prep easier to excavate.

4. Pack as many nettles into the pot as you can, pressing them down firmly.

5. Cover the pot with a piece of tile or slate, using string to hold the lid in place.

6. Choose an open, well-drained site in a sunny spot for your nettle pit. Dig a hole large enough to hold the pot, and deep enough to ensure the nettles will be covered by at least 12in (30cm) of soil.

7. Bury the pot upside down. This will reduce the amount of rainwater penetrating the pot during its time underground.

8. Add some fresh compost, and then fill in the hole. Use stakes to mark the spot where the prep is buried, and leave it alone for at least one full calendar year.

12–15 months later

9. Excavate the nettle pit. The resulting dark black, flaky compost has a distinctive smell, a bit like a leafy forest floor after light rain. Run the excavated material between your thumb and forefinger: if the skin looks like it has been dipped in black octopus ink, your nettle prep is of the highest quality. Crumble it into a glass or pottery jar and store it with the other preps.

Using the prep

Nettle 504 is generally used in concert with the 5 other compost preps.

- To make biodynamic compost, see p.122.
- For the barrel compost prep (BC), see p.126.
- To enhance homemade plant sprays and liquid manures, see p.136.
- For storage, see p.120.

Biodynamic compost preps

Oak bark 505

The oak tree is one of the strongest, mightiest, and longest-lived plants. Throughout its journey from tiny acorn to towering tree it must grow steadily and protect itself from the elements. The protection is provided by its tough, weather-resistant bark—and this is the point of interest to the biodynamic gardener.

How oak bark compost works

Oak bark compost helps to stop plants from getting harmful diseases. Plants that grow in the wild are inherently healthy, but cultivated plants can get sick if the soil in which they grow has been damaged or weakened. Plants that grow too fast or too slowly are also more likely to suffer from pests and diseases. This is nature's way of getting rid of unbalanced plants. Oak bark compost helps correct weaknesses and imbalances in the soil, allowing all garden plants to grow steadily and stay healthy like the mighty oak itself.

Encouraging balance

The prep is made by stuffing crumbled bark into the skull of a farm animal and leaving it to soak under water over winter. Like oak bark, the skull is full of calcium, and with the right amount of calcium plants produce balanced, healthy growth. The oak bark compost supplies calcium in a way that allows the garden to regulate or "think" for itself, so it is composted in the part of the skull that holds the animal's brain. The swampy burial site is also significant: the mud represents the earth, and water, the moon. Crops grow best and stay healthier when the earth and moon are in balance; by placing the skull somewhere both earthy and watery the calcium-rich bark can bring a balancing influence to the garden.

For best results use bark
from a native species such
as the white oak (Quercus
alba) in North America or
English oak (Q. robur)
in Europe

A pig skull—here,
shown after
excavation—is
often used, but
cow, horse, sheep,
or goat skulls are
also suitable for
making the prep

Finished oak bark
compost is a rich
and earthy black

Crumbled oak bark
used to fill the skull

Making oak bark 505

Wedge a box against the tree to collect the shavings

1. Collect the bark from mature living oak trees on still, dry, sunny days from late summer to early fall. Use a rasp or a coarse file to scrape off the crumbly outer layer of bark.

⚠️ Wear gloves and protective goggles to protect your hands and eyes from stray bark.

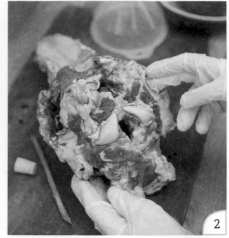

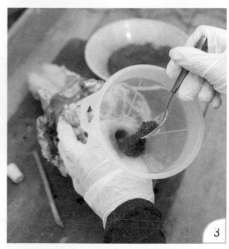

2. Ask your butcher to remove the brain through the hole at the base of the skull that connects the spinal cord (the foramen magnum). Take care to leave the membrane inside—the meninges lining—intact.

3. Pack the cavity with the powdered oak bark, using a funnel to help.

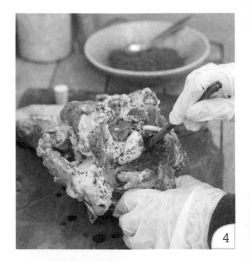

4

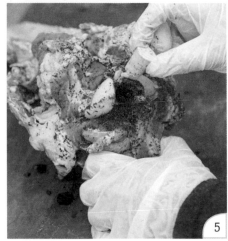

5

6

6. To create swamplike conditions, partially fill a wooden water barrel with rainwater and add a few spadefuls of soil.

7

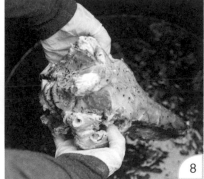

8

4. Press the bark down firmly with a wooden dowel to pack in as much bark as you can and expel as much air as possible.

5. Seal the hole with a cork, or a piece of bone held in place with clay.

7. Add some old leaves to the barrel, which will decay over winter.

8. Place the skull in the "swamp" —weigh it down with a heavy rock or brick, if necessary.

9. Add more leaf debris and soil to ensure the skull is completely covered.

10. Top off with more rainwater, and then cover with a heavy lid to prevent animals from getting trapped.

11. Connect the barrel to a downspout to ensure your mini swamp has a regular supply of fresh rainwater. If this is not possible—or if the water level drops below the outlet on the water barrel—occasionally just top off the barrel with enough rainwater to create an overflow.

12. Open the tap slightly to allow rainwater to drip slowly through the barrel—or drain a little water out every now and then—to mimic the slow-running water found in swamps.

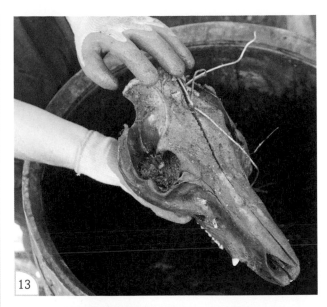

13

15

14

16

⧗ *Six months later,*
in early spring

13. **Lift the skull** out of the barrel, and gently hose it down with clean water.

14. Break open the skull with light blows from a chisel, or a hammer and a wedge. Avoid hitting too hard: the skull is flakier and less dense after its time in the swamp, and if it disintegrates, you may lose the contents.

15. The oak bark should be earthy black in color with a soft texture.

16. Ease the composted bark out of the cavity with a knife, crumble, and store in a glass or pottery jar.

Using the prep

Use oak bark 505 with 5 other compost preps.

• To make biodynamic compost, see p.122.

• For the barrel compost prep (BC), see p.126.

• To enhance homemade plant sprays and liquid manures, see p.136.

• For storage, see p.120.

Dandelion 506

Tenacious and vigorous, the dandelion (*Taraxacum officinale*) is popular with children who love to blow away the fluffy seed heads. Adults may curse when they appear in the lawn, but from a biodynamic perspective when the plant uses its strong rubbery root to punch holes in the ground, it opens up compacted soil, exposing the earth to the light of the sun and other celestial bodies, so that new plants soon thrive there.

Dandelion flowers are like little yellow suns connected to the earth via a strong, deep taproot.

How dandelion compost works

The dandelion prep provides garden soil with a fine-tuned ability to sense and draw in just the right amount of what it needs in the way of light, heat, water, or food from the rest of the garden and its neighbors. The composted flowers not only draw the light and heat of the sun, and the balancing influences of Saturn, Jupiter, and Mars into the garden, but underneath it, too. The dandelion prep gives the soil the inner brightness and sensitivity it needs to be able to provide crops with the liverlike power to filter exactly what they need from the soil, producing high-quality food that tastes as good as it looks.

Dandelion pillows

The flowers are encased in a cow's mesentery, and buried in the ground for six months over winter. The mesentery completely encloses the cow's digestive organs, holding in and concentrating the streams of influence from the sun, planets, and stars that pass through the cow and make her manure so life-enhancing. Light and heat from the sun are also captured by dandelion flowers that stream them down into the earth, where they are released for other plants to use. By enclosing the dandelion flowers in the mesentery—which concentrates these same heat and light influences—it reinforces the dandelion's special ability to help other plants connect with both their immediate local environment and the celestial sphere above.

Warm water for dandelion tea

Cow mesentery (available from your local biodynamic association)

String, needle, threader, and scissors

Dried dandelion flowers

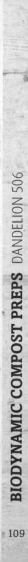

Making dandelion 506

Picking the moment for dandelions

Dandelions have a hotline to the sun: their petals unfurl as it rises and close at night or on overcast days. You'll need to start early and only pick half-open flowers to beat pollinating insects—once pollinated even decapitated flowers go to seed.

Half-open flower

The central petals on a half-open—and unpollinated—flower are closed and folded inward like a small cone.

Fully open flower

Fully open flowers are often pollinated; they may develop into fluffy seed heads that are unsuitable for use in the prep.

Collect the flowers in early spring—ideally on sunny mornings with an ascending moon— and as early in the day as possible, before the petals are fully open. Spread out the flowers on flats in a warm, airy place, and turn them occasionally to ensure they become completely dry. Store the flowers in jars or paper bags until it is time to make the prep.

Fresh dandelions ready to dry   Dried dandelion flowers   Discarded seed heads

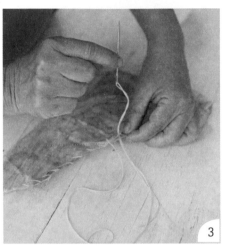

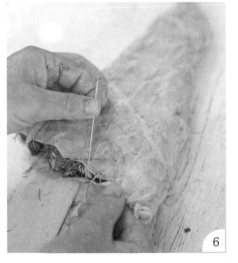

1. To make dandelion tea, add some dried flowers to warm water and allow it to stand for a few minutes.

2. To create the sheath, cut a piece of the mesentery sheet around 8–14in (20–35cm) wide, and soak it in some of the warm tea until it is rehydrated. It should become soft and easy to handle.

3. Fold the sheet in half. Thread a needle with string and stitch up the side and along the base to make a pouch.

4. Put the flowers in a bowl and pour over a small amount of dandelion tea to moisten them. The flowers should be damp, but make sure that they are not soaking wet.

5. Fill the pouch with the flower mixture. Press the flowers way down inside until you have made a small dandelion pillow.

6. Seal the opening of the dandelion package by stitching it together with more string.

7. Dig a hole about 24in (60cm) deep in a sunny site in fall. Ideally, choose a day when the moon is descending, and in an earth-root constellation. Line the sides and base of the hole with heavy tiles to protect the pillow from burying animals.

8. Backfill the lined hole with a thick layer of good soil seeded with fresh compost until you are about a third of the way up. Alternatively, you can prepare an unglazed terra-cotta pot with soil and compost as for yarrow 502 (*see p.90*).

Alternative method

If you wish, you can make the dandelion prep using the same technique as for yarrow 502 (*see pp.86–91*). It takes a year to mature, but hanging the mesentery from a tree for 6 months over the summer allows it to benefit from the exposure to sun's heat and light. Follow the process here, but prepare the mesentery in spring. Make a wire cage to protect the prep from wind damage, birds, and animals, then hang it out in a sunny location. Take down and bury the prep at the fall equinox, as described above.

9. Place the dandelion pillow in the soil, cover with a thick layer of soil and compost, then top with tiles or slate —it should be around 12in (30cm) deep. Fill in the rest of the hole.

10. Mark the spot, label it, and leave it alone for 6 months until spring.

11

13

12

14

6 months later, in spring

11. Dig up the dandelion pillow. The mesentery sheath should still be intact and will not have broken down much at this point.

12. Slice open the pillow with a knife to reveal the composted dandelions. They may smell musky and earthy, but this is perfectly normal.

13. Put the contents into a dish and prepare it for storage. Crumble it in your fingers, and look out for worms—return them to the compost heap.

14. Scrape off as many flowers as possible from the sheath. Store the excavated prep in a glazed pot or glass jar.

Using the prep

Use dandelion 506 with 5 other compost preps.

- To make biodynamic compost, see p.122.
- For the barrel compost prep (BC), see p.126.
- To enhance homemade plant sprays and liquid manures, see p.136.
- For storage, see p.120.

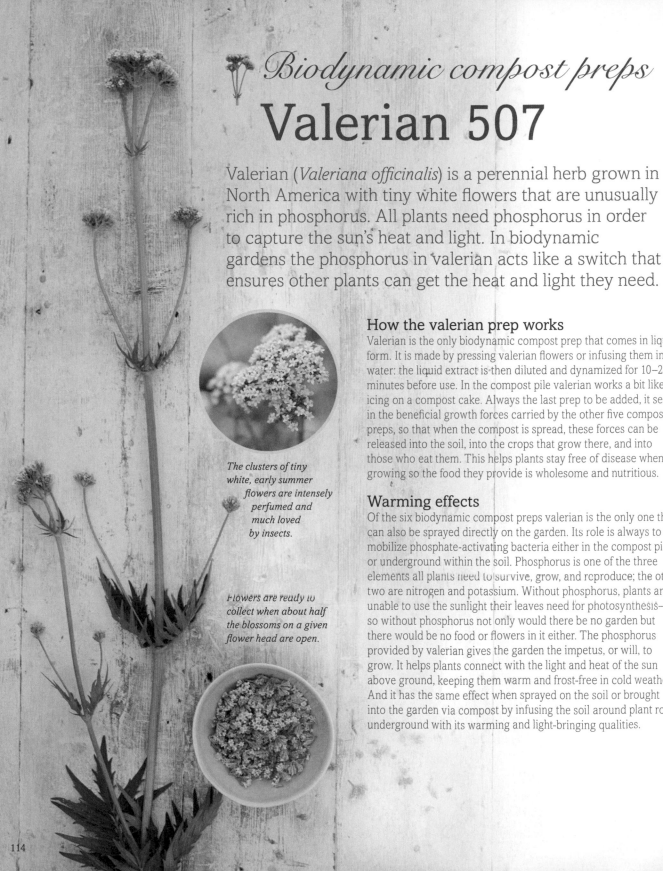

Valerian 507

Valerian (*Valeriana officinalis*) is a perennial herb grown in North America with tiny white flowers that are unusually rich in phosphorus. All plants need phosphorus in order to capture the sun's heat and light. In biodynamic gardens the phosphorus in valerian acts like a switch that ensures other plants can get the heat and light they need.

The clusters of tiny white, early summer flowers are intensely perfumed and much loved by insects.

Flowers are ready to collect when about half the blossoms on a given flower head are open.

How the valerian prep works

Valerian is the only biodynamic compost prep that comes in liquid form. It is made by pressing valerian flowers or infusing them in water: the liquid extract is then diluted and dynamized for 10–20 minutes before use. In the compost pile valerian works a bit like icing on a compost cake. Always the last prep to be added, it seals in the beneficial growth forces carried by the other five compost preps, so that when the compost is spread, these forces can be released into the soil, into the crops that grow there, and into those who eat them. This helps plants stay free of disease when growing so the food they provide is wholesome and nutritious.

Warming effects

Of the six biodynamic compost preps valerian is the only one that can also be sprayed directly on the garden. Its role is always to mobilize phosphate-activating bacteria either in the compost pile or underground within the soil. Phosphorus is one of the three elements all plants need to survive, grow, and reproduce; the other two are nitrogen and potassium. Without phosphorus, plants are unable to use the sunlight their leaves need for photosynthesis—so without phosphorus not only would there be no garden but there would be no food or flowers in it either. The phosphorus provided by valerian gives the garden the impetus, or will, to grow. It helps plants connect with the light and heat of the sun above ground, keeping them warm and frost-free in cold weather. And it has the same effect when sprayed on the soil or brought into the garden via compost by infusing the soil around plant roots underground with its warming and light-bringing qualities.

❧ EQUIPMENT

Rainwater to dilute

Wooden dowel

Funnel

Clear glass bottle
and cork for
infusing flowers

Dark glass
bottle for
storage

String

Use a strainer or
muslin to strain
the infusion

Fresh valerian
flowers

Valerian 507 Infusion recipe

- Approximately 1oz (30g) fresh valerian flowers

- 5 floz (150ml) tepid rainwater

Makes about 4 floz (100ml) valerian 507.

For a longer shelf life store in small bottles 1 floz (20ml).

Making valerian 507

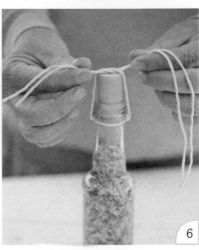

1. Pick valerian flowers with their supporting pods (calyx) in early summer, ideally on days with an ascending moon. Often the best time is around the summer solstice, but be guided by the weather. The flowers in each cluster will open individually; their petals start to fall about 2 weeks after opening, and this is the moment to start collecting. Don't forget to leave some flowers for the insects.

2. Use a funnel and a stick to fill a clear glass bottle with the flowers.

3. Pack the flowers right down inside the bottle using the stick.

4. Pour rainwater into the bottle, allowing for a ½in (1–2cm) air space at the top, below the base of the cork.

5. Use a cork to seal the bottle. Press it in firmly, but make sure you keep an air space to allow the flowers to ferment.

6. Tie the cork to the neck of the bottle to ensure it doesn't pop out during the fermentation process.

7. Attach the bottle to a tree branch in a sunny location out of the wind, and leave it to hang for 3 days.

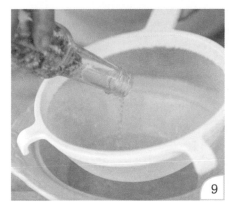

3 days later

8. Take down the bottle. If the liquid is a clear yellow-amber color, your valerian juice is of the highest quality, but a cloudy green liquid is almost as good.

9. Strain the liquid with a strainer, or pour it through a piece of muslin or an old piece of pantyhose. The solids will be discarded, but squeeze out as much liquid as you can before you throw them on the compost heap.

10. Pour the liquid concentrate into a green or brown bottle, and seal with a cork. Always leave an air gap between the cork and the liquid. Within a few weeks the liquid should be a transparent green-yellow color. It should smell like the picked flowers, but with more depth and ripeness.

11. Store valerian 507 with the other compost preps (*see p.120*). Lay the bottle on its side to keep the cork wet and prevent it from shrinking. Valerian keeps for years if stored well, and should also keep its scent.

Alternative method: Juicing

You can also make valerian 507 by pressing freshly picked flowers to extract their liquid content. The technique is simple, but it may have a shorter life than juice made using the infusion method. If mold develops during storage, the valerian juice will no longer be suitable for use with the other preps in the compost pile, or as a frost-prevention spray.

Collect the flower pulp as it emerges

Run the pulp back through the juicer to extract more liquid

Flower juice is ready to store

1. Use a manual juicer to press the flowers. This relatively gentle method reduces the risk of oxidization and ensures the valerian juice is not contaminated with bad energy from electrical currents.

2. Press the flowers through the machine. Collect the pulp and push it back through the juicer to ensure you extract the maximum amount of juice from your flowers. Work quickly to stop the juice from browning while it is in contact with the air.

3. Funnel the valerian juice into a green or brown bottle, and seal with a cork or a fermenting cap. This prevents air from getting in, but allows gases released by acid fermentation in the juice to escape. Store the bottle with the other compost preps.

Using valerian 507

Keep frost at bay

In the compost pile valerian 507 is valued for its insulating warmth, which surrounds the heap and seals in the growth forces delivered by the other compost preps. In early spring and fall, this warming quality can be deployed as an effective guard against frost: simply spray valerian 507 directly over your soil, and even onto the plants themselves.

Valerian 507 must always be diluted and dynamized before use in the garden or on the compost heap.

Dynamizing valerian 507

1

2

1. Prepare the valerian by diluting 1 part concentrate in 19 parts of warm rainwater. The pale yellow-green liquid has an intense floral smell.

2. Dynamize by stirring for 10–20 minutes, creating a vortex in clockwise and counterclockwise directions.

3

3. Gently mist fruit blossoms and other plants at risk from early or late frost on the afternoon or evening before frost is forecast, and repeat each day if necessary. The valerian surrounds the plant with a protective warmth that reduces frost damage—so you should still get a crop from early-flowering fruit trees like apples.

More uses for 507

Valerian 507 is also used with the 5 other compost preps.
- To make biodynamic compost, see p.122.
- For the barrel compost (BC), see p.126.
- To enhance homemade plant sprays and liquid manures, see p.136.
- For storage, see p.120.

The biodynamic preparations

Storing the preps

The compost preps have radiant qualities that dissipate if they are not stored correctly, so pack the preps in peat to keep them at their best. Peat is a natural insulator against radiation that not only preserves the radiant qualities of each prep but also protects them from electromagnetic radiation from power lines and cell phone towers. You can store them inside, but many biodynamic gardeners prefer to keep their preps in closer contact with the Earth.

1. Sink a wooden box into a hole in a cool, dry, shady spot with no risk of floods.

2. Line the box with peat—or use pure, fibrous coconut fiber (coir) as an alternative.

3. Label the prep jars and press them into the peat, storing them away from electrical outlets. The peat helps protect the etheric forces in the preps from radiation and electrical currents, and insulates the preps from each other.

4. To protect the top, fill a cotton bag or hemp sack with peat to create an insulating pillow that fits comfortably inside the box.

5. Place the pillow over the prep jars. They should be completely surrounded by peat.

6. Cover the box with a weatherproof lid set at an angle to encourage the rain to run off. A piece of slate is ideal—easy to lift to gain access, but weighty enough to withstand wind and accidental knocks.

Horn manure 500 should also be stored in peat, so if you are short on space you can keep it in the same box as the compost preps.

Horn silica 501 should not be stored with the compost preps. Always keep it in a light place—for example, on a bright windowsill that catches the sun each day (see p.79).

Individual storage sites

If you have the space, you can store the preparations in separate areas of the garden, but make sure the conditions are consistent for all the compost preps. Keeping the preps apart further reduces the possibility of their radiant qualities blurring in storage. You can create robust shelters using terra-cotta flowerpots filled with peat or fibrous coir, and plunging the prep jar (here, containing horn manure 500) into the center. Use a drip saucer filled with peat as the lid of the pot, and cover the hole with a stone slab.

Making a biodynamic compost heap

The most effective way to get the compost preps into the garden is to include them in the compost pile when it is built. Their beneficial forces radiate through the heap from the moment the pile starts breaking down until its transformation into dark, earthy-smelling material is complete.

1. Start the heap by spreading a thin layer of twigs and prunings over the bare soil to help airflow at the base of the pile. Keep the pile moist, but not wet, to encourage fermentation.

2. Layer the heap to ensure carbon-rich, woody material is balanced by the soft green waste rich in nitrogen.

3. Scatter crushed eggshells over the heap to increase the calcium content.

4. Shred your woody waste if you can to help it break down faster.

5. Alternating the layers of green and brown material helps you provide a balanced diet for the bacteria in the heap.

Making a prep ball

To prevent the solid compost preps—yarrow 502, chamomile 503, nettle 504, oak bark 505, and dandelion 506—from blowing away in the wind, wrap a pinch of each prep in an individual ball made of old potting mix or good quality fresh soil before adding the ball to the pile.

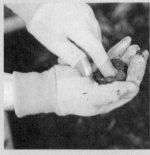   

Roll some soil or potting mix into a ball and use your finger to make a well in the center.

Take a pinch of one the preps and place it in the well.

Close the ball around the prep and squeeze to hold the prep securely in the center.

The prep ball is ready to be added to the compost heap.

6. Make a prep ball for each individual solid compost prep using fresh soil or old potting mix to encase each prep.

7. Arrange the prep balls on the surface. When the pile is complete they will be in the ideal position at the heart of the your new compost heap.

8. Continue to build the heap in layers, adding more brown and green material to create a balanced heap. Bear in mind that for the finished compost to achieve a C:N ratio close to 30, for every bucket of brown woody material, you will need around 3 buckets of soft green waste.

9. Add more eggshells and continue adding more material in layers until your bin is full.

10. Dilute the valerian 507 using 1 part valerian to 19 parts rainwater. Dynamize for 10–20 minutes using your hand or a stick to stir vigorously in clockwise and counterclockwise directions.

11. Splash the dynamized valerian over the compost heap in large droplets to provide insulating warmth and to seal in the forces activated by the other compost preps. Cover the finished heap with some old carpet, paper bags, or cardboard to prevent the pile from becoming too wet in the rain, and also to keep the temperature up.

More ways to make biodynamic compost

If you garden on a much smaller scale and cannot generate enough waste to make perfect biodynamic compost in one season, there are other techniques you can use to get the preps into your garden.

Small or existing heaps

Many gardeners constantly add waste to the compost heap as and when it appears. This "cool" composting method takes longer to make usable compost, but is more practical for many. Add the preps when you turn the heap—or if you choose not to turn it, plunge them into the center with a stick.

1. Plunge a stick into the heap until you reach the center. Wiggle it back and forth to create a chute. Make a chute and a ball for each solid compost prep.

2. Drop the prep balls down the chutes. Close the holes, sprinkle with dynamized valerian 507, and cover.

Activate your compost with BC

Barrel compost (BC) is compost made using fresh cow manure (*see pp.126–131*). Add a layer of BC to the compost pile to gain all the benefits of preps 502–507—and added cow power, too.

Use compost starter

Compost starter, or activator, is a dried version of BC, available from biodynamic associations. Each time you are ready to add kitchen or garden waste to the bin, sprinkle about a teaspoon of the starter into the bin first, and then add the new material.

Making barrel compost

Barrel compost (BC) is a great option for gardeners unable to generate or store waste in the proportions needed to build a perfect compost pile in one try. It was developed in the 1970s by Maria Thun, who aged cow manure in a barrel, then diluted the resulting compost in water and sprayed it on the land. BC has many different uses—and is known by almost as many names, including cow patty pit (CPP) and manure concentrate.

Maria Thun's barrel compost

The inspiration for BC came from the "birch pit preparation," devised by German livestock farmers to recycle cow manure from animals wintering in their barns. These farmers had attended Rudolf Steiner's 1924 Agriculture Course, so they were aware that by adding the six biodynamic compost preps 502–507, the manure would be imbued with extra powers to regenerate the soil, the crop, and those who ate it. They shoveled cow manure from the barns into long trenches lined with fresh birch branches to keep it well aired—the birch pits—and then added the compost preps. Within a few months the manure and straw bedding became dark, earthy-smelling compost that could be spread back on the cow pastures and crop fields. The empty pits would be refilled with fresh barn material, creating a continual cycle of fertility.

Maria Thun re-created the birch pit idea on a much smaller scale. Her barrel compost was intended to be made in relatively small quantities with a quick turnaround, so there was no need to line the pit with birch to increase airflow. Instead, the manure was vigorously aerated before it was tipped into the barrel, by mixing in a handful each of basalt dust—to aid healthy decomposition—and calcium-rich eggshells after scientific data suggested oat, celery, and tomato crops grown on limestone soils contained fewer radioactive residues left by nuclear bomb tests and accidental leaks. After transferring the mixture to the barrel, Thun added the compost preps and left the rest to nature.

A wooden half barrel with the base removed provides a compact hole with easy access, and ensures the manure is in contact with the soil.

A shallow brick-lined pit is a good alternative to a half barrel. It keeps the contents cool, moist, and well-ventilated throughout its time in the ground.

The benefits of BC

Traditional compost takes a year to mature, depending on the climate, but BC decomposes faster and can be ready in half the time. The simple ingredients and speedy turnaround make it an ideal biodynamic compost spray, delivering a blast of cow power, as well as the compost preps. An application of BC in fall is particularly beneficial since it helps the soil digest fallen leaves and other organic matter left over from the previous growing season. It is also interesting to note that after the nuclear accident at Chernobyl in 1986, tests by the German Ministry of Agriculture showed that plants treated with BC contained 55 percent fewer radioactive residues than their untreated counterparts.

❧ EQUIPMENT

Fresh cow manure—your local
biodynamic association may
be able to help find a supplier

Yarrow 502

Chamomile 503

Nettle 504

Oak bark 505

Dandelion 506

Valerian 507

Basalt dust—
available from
local biodynamic
associations

Crushed eggshells
—collect them
over time, and
dry them in the
oven to keep mold
from developing

Recipe for BC
- Approximately 44lb (20kg) fresh cow manure
- 3oz (75g) crushed eggshells
- 4oz (100g) basalt dust
- 2 units yarrow 502
- 2 units chamomile 503
- 2 units nettle 504
- 2 units oak bark 505
- 2 units dandelion 506
- 2 units valerian 507

127

Making barrel compost

1. Remove the base from a clean half barrel and sink it into a hole, so that the top third of the barrel remains above ground level.

2. Turn the cow manure onto a mixing board or a hard surface, and add crushed eggshells to raise calcium levels.

3. Add the basalt dust. This helps plants to decompose in a healthy, efficient way, enriching the soil for the next crop.

4. Stir for 1 hour to ensure the mixture is thoroughly aerated. Work from the outside into the center, and move around the board in a circle—effectively turning the mixture in a spiral. The process can be easier, less tiring, and more fun if 2 or 3 helpers mix from opposite sides.

5. Wet the interior of the barrel to help prevent the prep and the barrel from drying out.

6. Put the manure mixture into the barrel. After an hour of stirring, it should have a mousselike consistency.

7. Make six holes in the surface with a stick—one hole for each of the compost preps.

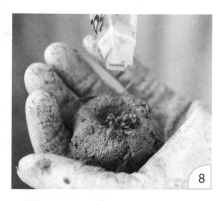

8

11

9

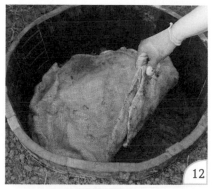

12

10

13

8 weeks later

Empty the barrel onto the mixing board, and stir again, working all the way around the board to aerate the mixture. Put it back in the barrel and add another set of the compost preps. Water with dynamized valerian, and cover the pit as before. Depending on your climate and the weather, your BC should be ready in about 5 months.

Fresh cow manure

Finished BC

8. Make a prep ball for each solid compost prep (*see p.123*). Flatten a patty of the manure mix in the palm of your hand, place a pinch of the prep in the middle of the patty, and roll it into a ball.

9. Drop each prep ball into one of the holes. Close each hole immediately.

10. Dynamize the valerian 507 (*see p.119*) and pour about half the mixture into the final hole. Close the hole.

11. Splash more valerian over the top of the mixture in the barrel.

12. Use the last of the valerian to wet a burlap bag, and place it over the manure mixture. The breathable insulation the sack provides protects the barrel from temperature extremes.

13. Cover the pit with a large board set at an angle to protect the BC from rain and the drying effects of direct sun.

Using barrel compost prep

Give your plants a kick-start

When it is ready to use, barrel compost (BC) resembles rich, dark, fine soil with a clean, intensely earthy smell. BC is precious and potent stuff packed with power from the compost preps, so it is often diluted and used as a spray. It has an enlivening effect on the soil, its structure, microbial life, and texture; use it when you transplant seedlings and young plants to ensure they have a good start.

The four-leaf stage is the perfect time to give your seedlings a biodynamic boost.

How to dilute BC

1. Pour a generous handful of BC into rainwater. As a general rule of thumb, allow 3 parts BC to 20 parts water. The amounts will vary according to the condition of the soil, and the size of the area to be covered, as well as how you intend to use it.

For ground sprays on average garden soil expect to use around 3 gallons (15 liters) of water per acre (0.4ha).

2. Stir vigorously for about 20 minutes to dynamize the BC solution. Break the vortex at regular intervals with a change of direction: stir clockwise and then counterclockwise throughout the 20-minute period.

3. The BC solution is ready to use. For best results, apply BC when the earth is breathing in—in the afternoon; during periods when the moon is descending; and in fall. As this is an earth spray, the optimal time to apply BC is on root days, when the moon is passing through Taurus, Virgo, or Capricornus.

Place your seedlings in the BC bath and allow them to soak up the goodness for about an hour.

Diluted BC is an excellent foliar spray: apply it to the undersides of leaves with a mister.

Diluted BC may also be applied as a ground spray, using a brush to flick large droplets onto the soil.

Put a pouch filled with raw BC in your watering can to boost plants as you water.

Add a handful of raw BC to the soil when transplanting.

Using the preps
Tree paste

What's the difference between a mound of bare soil and a tree trunk? Answer: there isn't one—at least not from the biodynamic gardener's perspective. In biodynamics, the tree trunk is seen to be a tall cylinder of bark filled not with wood, but with enriched soil. The leaves growing from the woody parts of the tree are considered to be little different from lettuce, arugula, spinach, or any other edible leaf crop in the vegetable garden: they're just a little bit higher up off the ground.

When you apply tree paste with a brush, make sure you coat the trunk from all angles so that every bit of bark is covered. This is the only way the cambium layer below will benefit from the paste's influence.

The benefits of tree paste
Just as vegetables taste better if the soil is fed and reinforced with biodynamic compost, or kept healthy with applications of horn manure 500, *Equisetum arvense* 508, and compost sprays such as BC, so the food that trees produce—apples, plums, pears, and so on—tastes better if the trunk or "soil cylinder" is treated with the biodynamic preparations in the same way as garden soil. In addition to using solid compost or soil sprays, you can paint or spray a runny tree paste onto the tree trunk during winter, or after your fruit trees are pruned.

How tree paste works
After emptying the vegetable plot, you put biodynamic compost back into the garden to make sure that the next set of crops grow in soil and subsoil filled with renewed vitality. Tree paste is effectively the compost used for trees. It is spread on the outer bark and works on what is called the cambium—the growing layer between the bark on the outside and the tree trunk on the inside. The cambium is really the subsoil or root system for the tree's shoots and leaves, and the paste provides a life-enhancing stimulus from the outside that makes the tree healthier within.

As well as enlivening the inner workings of the tree and providing what it needs to maintain balanced fruitfulness, tree paste also seals crevices in the bark used by overwintering pests, such as codling moth caterpillars. These pests hide over the

winter in loose bark then attack apples and pears by tunneling into their fruit—which can make for a nasty surprise when you cut open an apparently healthy fruit.

When to apply tree paste
Tree paste may sound like a treatment for plants, but in fact it is a remedy for the soil part of the tree—which is why it is best applied under a descending moon, when the earth is breathing in. The ideal time of day for tree pasting is during the afternoon, again because this is when the earth breathes in. For fruit trees target periods when the moon stands in front of the warmth-fruit constellations of Sagittarius, Aries, and Leo. On citrus trees treat only the base of the trunk.

Just like good compost, tree paste can be applied more than once between fall and spring: after leaf drop to strengthen the tree trunk and branches; a second time after pruning to seal pruning wounds from potential infection; and for a third and final time at bud burst in spring to reduce the threat from any fungal disease organisms that have become active as temperatures warm up.

❧ INGREDIENTS FOR TREE PASTE

BC puts the six
biodynamic compost
preparations into the mix

Equisetum arvense 508 tea
offers general protection
against fungal diseases

Fine sand
(silica or builder's
sand) boosts the
mineral content

Cow manure
infuses the mix
with its grass
content and
its revitalizing
digestive forces

Potting clay (or
bentonite) also
enhances the
mineral content

Tree paste recipe
• 1 part clay
• 1 part fine sand (or
diatomaceous earth)
• 1 part fresh cow
manure
• 1 unit of horn manure
500
• rainwater to dilute
• (optional) equisetum
tea 508
• (optional) a generous
handful of BC

Horn manure 500
binds the ingredients into
one dynamic whole

Making tree paste

1. To prepare the clay, place the potting clay or bentonite in a bucket with a little rainwater, and chop it with a spade to achieve a smooth texture with no lumps. If you garden on clay soil, you can use it as a base for the clay paste: just add some soil to a bucket of rainwater and stir it to remove the lumps. Be sure to remove any small rocks, wood fragments, or pieces of root.

2. Make the equisetum tea with rainwater (*see p.84*) and use it to dissolve the horn manure. Dynamize the liquid by stirring for 1 hour, changing direction at regular intervals. Alternatively, you can add the horn manure to warmed rainwater in the usual way (*see p.72*).

3. If you are using BC to enhance the paste, add it to the horn manure 500 mixture for the last 20 minutes of stirring.

4. Pour the dynamized liquid into the bucket with the clay, and then gradually stir in the fresh cow manure to infuse the mixture with the cow's digestive forces.

5. Gradually stir in the sand. Use the spade with a chopping and swirling motion to combine the sand, aerate the mixture, and break up large lumps. Add more rainwater if it becomes too thick.

6. The finished tree paste should have the consistency of pancake mixture or all-weather paint—a thinnish paste that is sloppy enough to apply to tree trunks with ease.

7. Use a whitewash brush to apply the freshly made tree paste to fruit trees or vines between late fall and late winter, after pruning but before bud burst. Make sure every crevice in the bark is covered with the paste, right down to ground level. you'll need about 3½ pints (2 liters) for one mature tree. Pour leftover paste onto an unfinished compost pile.

For large numbers of trees, make the paste with bentonite and diatomaceous earth to get a finer texture, and apply with a coarse-nozzled sprayer. Use an old piece of pantyhose to prevent the nozzle from clogging up.

Enhance your liquid manures

Add the compost preps to homemade liquid manures and fertilizers, and your garden will benefit from their goodness whenever you use them. Make the manure as usual, by pouring rainwater over the plant material. Here, marigolds are used to make a liquid manure that repels insect pests like greenflies and blackflies.

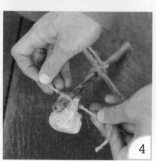

1. Make a prep ball for each of the five solid compost preps 502–506, using finished compost or good soil from your garden (*see p.123*).

2. Wrap each ball in muslin to ensure they will remain intact when they are added to the liquid manure.

3. Make a cross using two clean sticks and some twine to hold the preps in place.

4. Attach a prep ball to each end of the cross, and one—traditionally nettle 504— at the center.

5. Place the prep cross in the liquid manure.

6. Dilute the valerian. A ⅛ fl oz (5ml) capful will be sufficient for about 10 fl oz (300ml) of water. Dynamize the valerian for 10–20 minutes.

7

8

7. To dynamize valerian in a bottle, close the cap and hold it horizontally. Sweep it from side to side to create the vortex, keeping the bottle level the whole time.

8. Splash the valerian into the liquid manure.

9. Use a clean rock to keep the preps submerged.

9

10

11

10. Leave it to ferment as appropriate. This marigold manure is left undisturbed for 2 weeks, then stirred each day.

11. To use the manure, remove the preps, strain, dilute as appropriate, then dynamize for 10 minutes before spraying. For marigold manure dilute 1 part marigold concentrate in 10 parts of water, and apply as soon as insect pests are seen.

Getting the most from the compost preps

A little of every compost prep goes a long way, so whether you make liquid manure in a small bucket or a large bin, you only need a single unit of each prep—or a generous portion of BC. To make the preps go further, and gain maximum benefits throughout the growing season, it is worth making fertilizers and plant tonics in the largest quantities you can manage as early in the year as you can.

Suspend BC in the liquid manure (here, seaweed) instead of the individual preps.

With the preps added, weed tea is an even richer source of nutrients for crops.

Wrap the preps in leaves and drop them into the liquid (here, a compost tea).

Making weed pepper

The preps make plants so strong they resist most pests and diseases, but weeds can still be a problem. Ashing or peppering weeds discourages them from populating the area treated—and unlike herbicides, it leaves no residue in the soil or groundwater, and has no adverse effect on wildlife.

GREAT FRUIT DAY TASK

1. Collect the seeds of the weed that needs ashing—here, docks—from the garden you intend to treat. For best results, choose a fruit day under an ascending moon.

If you are dealing with more than one type of weed, keep their seeds separate. Do not be tempted to mix different weed seeds together before burning them: for the ash concentrate to be effective, each type of weed must be burned on its own.

2. Burn the seeds on a wood fire, ideally at full moon. Use a metal pan with holes in the lid to allow smoke to escape without the ash.

3. Cool the ash and store it in a jar until you need it. The element of fire transmits a negative force to the weed that discourages it from reproducing where the pepper is applied.

Ash and sand pepper

Add 1 dessert spoon of ash to ¼ bucket of sand for 1 acre (0.4 ha). Aerate for 10 minutes. Once a year, at spring or fall equinox or summer solstice, apply pepper to the soil on three successive days: the day before, the day of, and the day after a full moon. Repeat over four years.

Weed ash soil spray

A homeopathic potentized solution may be useful for large areas. Like the sand method, this long-term treatment can take up to four years to be effective.

1. Grind the ash for 1 hour with a mortar and pestle sealed in a plastic bag to keep any dust from escaping.

2. Dissolve 1 part weed ash in 9 parts of rainwater, and pour into a bottle.

3. Shake the bottle for 3 minutes to make a D1 solution, or potency.

4. Measure out 1 part of the D1 solution.

5. Add 9 parts water, pour into a bottle and shake for another 3 minutes to make a D2 solution.

6. Repeat the 1:9 dilution and 3-minute shake until you reach D4 potency; this may be stored in a dark bottle.

7. Dilute the solution to D8 before use, then add a capful to a spray bottle. To use it, first hoe the soil on a fruit day with a descending moon to stimulate weed germination; water lightly, if needed. On the next root day with an ascending moon, hoe again, and apply the weed ash spray early in the morning when the soil is still moist with dew.

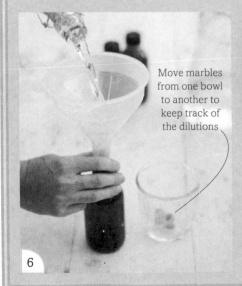

Move marbles from one bowl to another to keep track of the dilutions

Biodynamic garden planner

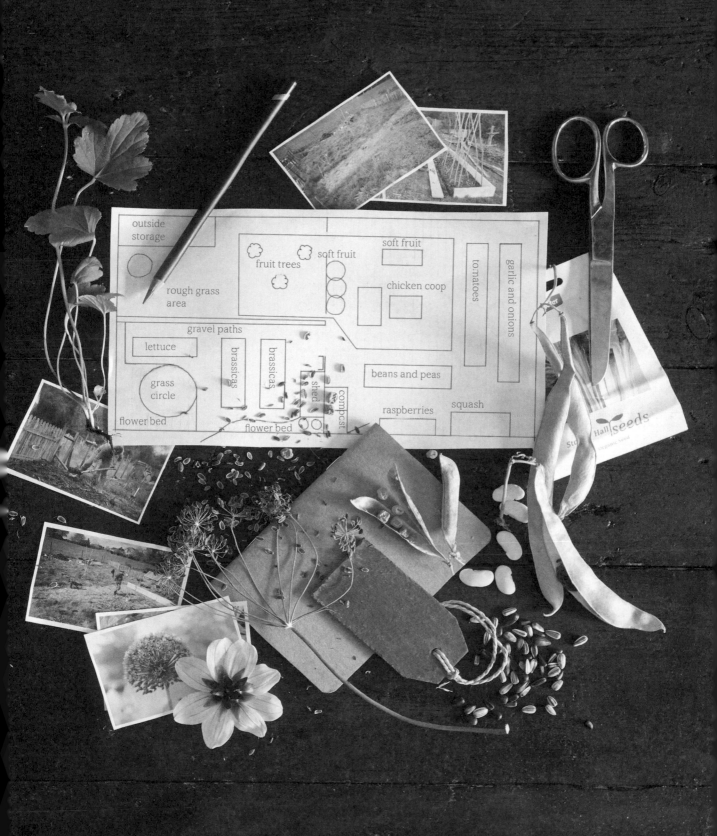

Plant trees and other perennials after the fall equinox.

Apply BC in fall after clearing beds and borders.

Prepare and bury horn manure 500 for excavation in spring.

Collect oak bark and make preparation 505.

Far from signaling the end of the growing year, fall in the biodynamic garden is a time of potential for new life.

The gardening year

A key aim of biodynamics is to transform your garden into a self-sustaining living organism, and one way to achieve this is to reconnect it with natural seasonal cycles.

Fall potential

Fall is the start of the biodynamic year, a time of fresh beginnings and new potential. Between the fall and spring equinoxes the earth is at its most vibrant and inwardly alive. For this reason, the fall equinox is the beginning of a window of opportunity to plant perennials like fruit trees, shrubs, and hedges.

Whatever remains of last year's compost can be dug into the soil while it is still workable and not rain-sodden or frozen by frost. Use this compost for planting new fruit trees, or to prepare the ground for crops like broad beans that are planted early. Then the key task for fall is to make new batches of biodynamic compost for the year ahead: prepare oak bark 505 and those preps that overwinter below ground as the earth starts to breathe in again.

Winter quiet

Winter is the quietest time in the garden as far as growing is concerned. Even so, no garden should be left bare over winter: the risk of soil and nutrients being washed away is too great. Instead, sow overwintering cover crops like beans, barley, clover, and vetches to feed the soil while protecting it. And if you have a

Save seeds from your healthiest plants to sow in years to come.

Mulch around crops to help retain moisture and keep down weeds.

Turn maturing compost piles and add compost preps 502–507.

Collect weeds and make a tea to return the nutrients to the soil.

Winter

Dig over empty beds; let frost break up clods into a fine tilth.

Protect tender herbs and shrubs from the cold with garden fabric.

Apply tree paste to protect trees from overwintering pests.

Sow seeds under cover in late winter for the earliest harvests.

means of growing under cover, you can begin to sow seeds and raise new plants, ready for transplanting in the spring. Resist the temptation to prune most fruit trees now, at least until after the winter solstice. Winter pruning can encourage disease or even death by letting frost into the plant.

Spring growth

As spring comes around, the sun's rising and ever-widening arcs encourage fresh green growth and bring warmer temperatures. Birds, insects, bees, and mammals start to become more active, and it's a busy time for the biodynamic gardener, too.

Overwintering crops need harvesting so the ground can be cleared for sowing new crops or transplanting seedlings, when temperatures and the often very changeable spring weather are just right. Now is also a good time to prune fruit trees and other perennials, as the sap pushing from within helps to keep pests out.

Summer harvest

As spring turns into summer, plants needed for teas and for biodynamic preparations can be harvested: first chamomile, dandelion, and yarrow, and then around midsummer valerian, stinging nettle, and horsetail.

Water use becomes critical during these months if crops are to survive. A single missed day of watering can cause sensitive crops like spinach, arugula, and lettuce to bolt, and summer brassicas to turn woody. Even compost piles need protection from the sun.

Late summer to fall is the peak period both for harvesting crops and composting green waste. Encourage annual crops and perennial fruit to ripen before the weather turns with sprayings of horn silica 501. Some crops can be sprayed after harvest too, to maximize the yield of carbohydrates that the fruiting shoots send down to the plant roots, feeding microorganisms in the soil.

Spring

Spring equinox marks the moment when day is longer than night, and the rising sun pulls the sap upward within plants.

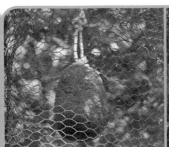
Fill and hang yarrow 502 high up in a dry, sunny place.

Mist horn silica over crops—and make more if necessary.

Flick diluted horn manure 500 on the soil to raise fertility.

Protect fruit blossoms from late frost by spraying valerian 507.

Know your plants and what they need

If the same crop is grown in the same place over and over again, without a break, the soil loses its balance. Minerals get depleted, soil pests build up, and quality and yields diminish. Rotate your crops to prevent this from happening.

Growing in raised beds makes it easier to plan crop rotation.

Crops fall into three main types: hungry crops that leave the soil poorer than it was before; soil-building crops that leave the soil enriched; and other crops that can fit in anywhere as long as the soil is freshly prepared for each new season. Start by feeding the soil with either biodynamic compost, well-matured manure, or by sowing green manures. The next step is to grow whichever crop is best suited to how the soil was prepared. Fruit trees are not rotated, for obvious reasons, and other perennial crops, such as asparagus, horseradish, rhubarb, raspberries, and black currants, can remain in the same spot for years.

KEY

L	Light feeders
H	Heavy feeders
M	Medium feeders
+	Add nutrients
−	Take away nutrients
n	Neutral

Managing soil fertility

Biodynamic growers classify vegetables according to which organ is intended for eating, but using this as the basis for rotation can be unhelpful. For example, a succession of root, leaf, flower, and fruit/seed crops could be achieved if turnips, Brussels sprouts, cauliflower, and mustard were grown in the same spot. Since they are all brassicas, however, this would encourage disease. Instead, it is better to categorize and rotate crops according to their feeding needs.

Nutrient givers L +

Crops in the legume family can provide a net nutrient benefit to the soil they are grown in by fixing nitrogen from the air, which is then released into the soil. Follow with nitrogen-hungry crops in the brassica family.

• peas and beans, including green, broad, and runner beans, as well as snow peas.
• green manures, such as vetches and clovers, can be sown in empty ground over winter to replenish nitrogen levels and prevent erosion.

Nutrient takers H −

Cucurbits like freshly composted soils, as do the nightshades (except potatoes, which prefer a soil composted the previous fall). Other heavy feeders include brassicas and leafy beets.

• brassicas, such as cabbage, Brussels sprouts, broccoli, and cauliflower—add lime if needed.
• leafy greens like chard, spinach and endive, plus celery and celeriac.
• cucurbits, such as zucchini, squash, and cucumbers.
• nightshades, such as peppers, tomatoes, and sweet corn.

Moderate requirements M n

Crops with moderate nutrient needs will usually be able to live off any residual fertility from general crop rotation, but you can also apply BC to help activate soil microorganisms.

• onions
• garlic
• chives
• shallots
• smaller leaf crops, like lettuce
• carrots
• beets
• parsnips

Crop family groups

Individual garden crops belong to larger crop families whose members often share similar care requirements in order to thrive. Understanding the characteristics of each crop family will help you to provide for their needs and achieve higher yields.

Allium family

Includes onions, garlic, shallots, chives, and leeks

Crops in the allium family prefer rich soil that is neither too acidic nor too fertile, and as such they can follow members of the brassica family in crop rotations. Give alliums a site with good air flow, and for firm, tasty bulbs, avoid overwatering Use the horn manure 500 spray to keep the soil friable and free draining. Use the horn silica 501 spray to encourage allium crops to develop pungent but not overpowering flavors.

Cucurbit family

Includes zucchini, squash, pumpkins, cucumbers, marrows, gourds, and melons

Crops in the cucurbit family are among the hungriest plants in the garden and will thrive in soil that has been generously composted. They are also some of the thirstiest, needing regular watering, as well as being heat lovers who prefer to grow in full sun in a sheltered spot. Cucurbits are trailing plants; pinch off their growing tips and sideshoots to control yields and improve flavor. Growing cucurbits vertically up a trellis saves space, but make sure the trellis is strong enough to support potentially large quantities of often weighty fruit.

Brassica family

Includes cabbages, kale, broccoli, Brussels sprouts, cauliflowers, Asian greens, rutabaga, turnips, radishes, and arugula

Hardy brassicas like kale, sprouts, and rutabagas will thrive in most winter climates but can be prone to the root disease clubroot (see p.147). Brassicas like a nitrogen-rich soil so can follow legumes in crop rotation. They also dislike acidic soils, which should be dressed with a sprinkling of lime. Leafy brassicas need frequent watering to get going and liquid feeds from comfrey, nettle, and kelp to stay strong.

Nightshade family

Includes tomatoes, potatoes, sweet corn, peppers, eggplant, and okra

Members of the nightshade family and sweet corn are high maintenance, hungry plants but worth it for their high yields. As fruiting vegetables from hot climates, they need warm, richly fertile soils. In cooler climates, start seeds off under cover so they germinate well before the last frost, giving them time to ripen before temperatures drop in fall. Horn silica 501 sprayed at flowering promotes ripening. Regular watering and liquid manure feeds promote good yields.

Legume family

Includes peas, beans, and many green manures

Legumes could almost be called the something-for-nothing family, because their roots leave the soil enriched with nitrogen (see p.146). Legumes are easy to grow, but need support from bean poles or pea sticks for their tendrils to cling to. Horn silica 501 sprays help guide these plants upward, toward the ripening light and heat of the sun. Most edible legumes grow in summer, but broad beans can grow over winter, too. Vetches and clovers are overwintering legumes, sown as cover crops. They protect fallow land from erosive winter rains, leaving it fertile for garden crops due to be sown the following spring.

Beet family

Includes beets, Swiss chard, spinach beet, spinach, New Zealand spinach, and red orach

Members of the beet family can be grown for their leaves or, in the case of beets, for both the root and leaves. Beet crops grow best when allowed to grow quickly, meaning in freshly composted, fertile soil. Almost constant watering in dry weather is needed to prevent a check in their growth. Keep the leaves disease free by spraying Equisetum arvense 508, and well fed with nutrient-rich sprays like nettle, comfrey, and kelp.

Crop finder

Rotate annuals to keep everything in balance. Although biodynamics groups plants by their edible part—roots, stems and leaves, flowers, and fruit—this is not a basis for crop rotation.

KEY
 Root days
 Flower days
 Leaf days
 Fruit days

Rotation group 1

This group of plants leaves the soil well fed. The bean family are legumes, which means they pull nitrogen out of the air and push it down into their roots. When their roots are dug in, the nitrogen is released into the earth. The soil is then ready for the next set of crops, usually medium or heavy feeders, or leafy crops that need a good supply of nitrogen.

Soybeans

Glycine max

p.214

Runner beans

Phaseolus coccineus

p.211

Lima beans

Phaseolus lunatus

p.214

Green beans

Phaseolus vulgaris

p.212

Peas

Pisum sativum

p.210

Broad beans

Vicia faba

p.213

Swiss chard & spinach beet

Beta vulgaris subsp. *cicla* var. *flavescens*

p.186

Chinese broccoli

Brassica oleracea Alboglabra Group

p.189

Broccoli sprouts

Brassica oleracea Italica Group

p.178

Rotation group 3

This is a fairly versatile group of onions, root, and stem crops that can be squeezed in anywhere as long as the soil has been well worked, and has a friable or loose texture for good drainage. They require only moderate levels of fertility, meaning soils into which compost or other organic matter has been added, but not too recently.

Onions

Allium cepa

p.154

Green onions

Allium cepa

p.158

Shallots

Allium cepa Aggregatum Group

p.155

Celeriac

Apium graveolens var. *rapaceum*

p.165

Horseradish

Armoracia rusticana

p.170

Red orach

Atriplex hortensis var. *rubra*

p.201

Beets

Beta vulgaris subsp. *vulgaris*

p.162

Endive

Cichorium endivia

p.199

Mustard greens

Brassica juncea

p.191

Rutabagas

Brassica napus Napobrassica Group

p.163

Kale

Brassica oleracea Acephala Group

p.193

Rotation group 2

Members of the brassica family, especially leafier ones, need plenty of food and water, and benefit from following soil-boosting legumes or well-manured crops like potatoes. To prevent clubroot disease, try to leave soil free of brassicas for three years, or add lime to keep the soil neutral (pH 7). It pays to keep careful notes of which brassica was planted where.

Cauliflower

Brassica oleracea Botrytis Group

p.176

Cabbage

Brassica oleracea Capitata Group

p.184

Brussels sprouts

Brassica oleracea Gemmifera Group

p.185

Kohlrabi

Brassica oleracea Gongylodes Group

p.190

Broccoli

Brassica oleracea Italica Group

p.177

Bok choy

Brassica rapa Chinensis Group

p.188

Napa cabbage

Brassica rapa Pekinensis Group

p.187

Turnips

Brassica rapa Rapifera Group

p.168

Arugula

Eruca vesicaria subsp. *sativa*

p.196

Radishes

Raphanus sativus

p.164

Japanese bunching onions

Allium fistulosum

p.159

Welsh onions

Allium fistulosum

p.159

Leeks

Allium porrum

p.157

Garlic

Allium sativum

p.156

Celery

Apium graveolens var. *dulce*

p.194

Chicory

Cichorium intybus

p.200

Radicchio

Cichorium intybus

p.202

Carrots

Daucus carota

p.167

Florence fennel

Foeniculum vulgare var. *azoricum*

p.195

Rotation group 3

Continues on next page

BIODYNAMIC GARDEN PLANNER CROP FINDER

147

Rotation group 3

continued

Jerusalem artichokes

Helianthus tuberosus

p.171

Rotation group 4

These are another flexible group of crops that can be grown almost anywhere. They need to be part of an annual rotation, but do not have to follow the same patterns as other crops as long as they are grown in a different spot each year; tomatoes are an exception. They need moderate to high levels of fertility added at planting (or transplanting in the case of strawberries) and benefit from regular doses of liquid manures.

Sweet potatoes

Ipomoea batatas

p.161

Lettuce

Lactuca sativa

p.197

Okra

Abelmoschus esculentus

p.223

Sweet peppers & chili peppers

Capsicum annuum

p.220

Melons

Cucumis melo

p.233

Parsnips

Pastinaca sativa

p.166

Scorzonera

Scorzonera hispanica

p.169

Cucumbers & gherkins

Cucumis sativus

p.216

Pumpkins & winter squash

Cucurbita maxima, C. moschata, C. pepo

p.218

Zucchini & summer squash

Cucurbita pepo

p.215

Potatoes

Solanum tuberosum

p.160

Spinach

Spinacia oleracea

p.192

Marrows

Cucurbita pepo

p.217

Strawberries

Fragaria x ananassa

p.225

Tomatillos

Physalis ixocarpa

p.224

Salsify

Tragopogon porrifolius

p.169

Corn salad

Valerianella locusta

p.198

Tomatoes

Solanum lycopersicum

p.219

Eggplant

Solanum melongena

p.221

Sweet corn

Zea mays

p.222

Perennial crops that are not rotated annually

These crops stay in the same place for years, or even decades, so good site and soil preparation is critical. Remove all perennial weeds, and provide planting holes filled with the right mix of soil, compost, sand, or rocks needed for drainage.

Asparagus
Asparagus officinalis
p.203

Citrus fruits
Citrus species
p.242

Sea kale
Crambe maritima
p.205

Globe artichokes
Cynara scolymus
p.179

Figs
Ficus carica
p.241

Apples
Malus domestica
p.234

Apricots
Prunus armeniaca
p.240

Sweet cherries
Prunus avium
p.236

Tart cherries
Prunus cerasus
p.237

Plums, gages & damsons
Prunus domestica, P. insititia
p.238

Peaches
Prunus persica
p.239

Nectarines
Prunus persica
p.239

Pears
Pyrus communis
p.235

Rhubarb
Rheum × hybridum
p.204

Black currants
Ribes nigrum
p.229

Red currants
Ribes rubrum
p.230

White currants
Ribes rubrum
p.230

Gooseberries
Ribes uva-crispa
p.228

Blackberries & hybrid berries
Rubus fruticosus
p.227

Raspberries
Rubus idaeus
p.226

Blueberries
Vaccinium corymbosum
p.231

Cranberries
Vaccinium macrocarpon
p.232

Grapevines
Vitis species
p.243

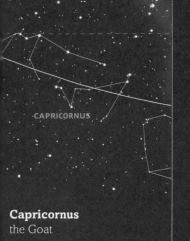

Capricornus
the Goat

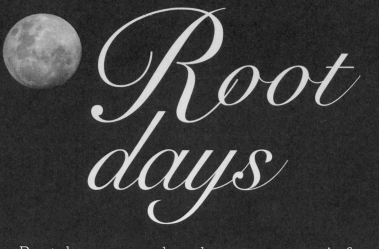

Root days

Root days occur when the moon passes in front of the star constellations of Capricornus, Taurus, and Virgo, which relate to the element of earth. Almost every plant puts its roots in the soil, but for biodynamic gardeners after a high-quality, consistent harvest with good storage potential, these are the days to cultivate roots, tubers, and bulbs like carrots, potatoes, and onions. Most root day crops have the edible part below ground, but the bulbous stems of leeks also develop best when tended on root days. Ideally, aim to prepare the soil for these crops on root days too; for maximum benefit plan your weeding, digging, or hoeing—and the application of soil sprays like horn manure 500 or barrel compost—for afternoons, especially during descending moon cycles, when the earth is breathing in.

Taurus
the Bull

Root days and lunar cycles

❧ The moon visits an earth-root constellation every 9 days and spends between 2 and 3 days in each.

❧ In the northern hemisphere the moon is ascending when it travels through Capricornus and Taurus.

❧ The moon is descending when it passes in front of Virgo, the largest of the zodiac constellations.

Virgo
the Virgin

Things to do on...

Root days

A special connection to the earth means that root days are ideal for any task that benefits the soil, be it digging, spreading compost, or applying ground sprays. If you are planting or transplanting trees, shrubs, or perennials, these are good days to choose since they encourage plants to establish strong foundations under ground.

• **Under a descending moon** the earth breathes in, making this the best time for planting root crops—especially perennials that stay in the same place for years like horseradish—or transplanting root crop seedlings. This is also the best time to apply soil sprays.

• **Under an ascending moon** the earth breathes out, which means this is the best time to spray the tops or leaves of root crops with teas and liquid manure feeds.

• **In the 2–3 days before full moon** sow root crops to encourage stronger germination—this is especially useful for sensitive, hard-to-germinate root crops like parsnips.

• **The watery influences of the full and perigee moon** make these times to avoid harvesting root crops for winter storage. They are more liable to rot.

• **Moon–opposition Saturn** is a good time to prepare the ground for potentially abundant yet tricky crops like potatoes.

Beets

Onions

Descending moon periods are the best times to work compost into the soil.

Lift and prepare roots like parsnips for wi storage before the ground gets too much f

Hill up potatoes on root days—roughly every 9 days rather than every week.

Sow scorzonera and other root crops just before full moon for optimal germination.

Root days are a good time to make biodynamic compost, using the compost preps.

Tackle weeds around root crops whenever you see them.

For best results thin or transplant root crop seedlings like beets on root days—even when grown under cover.

Apply soil sprays like horn manure 500 and BC in the afternoons when the earth breathes in.

Harvest root vegetables when the moon is descending to maximize storage potential.

Make the barrel compost prep with compost preps 502–507 to give your soil a boost.

Collect oak bark for compost preparation 505.

Onions
Allium cepa

Onions are slow growers, but good keepers. Mature onions may stay in the ground until needed if the weather stays dry, but once pulled they store well indoors. They come in various sizes and may have yellow, white, or red skins. You can grow onions from seed or plant sets—immature bulbs grown from seed the previous year. Growing onions from seed takes a little more work, but allows you to plant a wider range of beautifully shaped and flavored heritage varieties.

SITE AND SOIL PREPARATION

Onions like sun or light shade with good airflow in fertile, well-drained, non-acidic soil. Add biodynamic compost or well-rotted manure to make the soil friable, well before planting.

SOWING AND PLANTING

For best results, sow or plant onions on root days under a descending moon. Sow seed ¾in (2cm) deep in rows 12in (30cm) apart. Firm the soil well to obtain compact onions.

ROUTINE CARE

Onions need a little water to get started, but are liable to rot in wet soil. Cut off any flower buds and hand weed or hoe, but avoid bruising or dislodging the bulbs. Excessive hoeing makes soil powdery and prone to drying out; spraying 500 on the soil, in the afternoon under a descending moon in spring and fall, helps it to retain moisture. As the bulbs swell, gently scrape soil away from them to help them to form; spray 501 above them to help the plants stay firm and tasty.

HARVESTING AND STORING

Start pulling onions as soon as their tops start dying back and falling over—lightly loosen the roots and lay them on their sides to dry in the sun. Store in cool, dry, airy place away from potatoes and in single layers, or in plaits or nets.

TROUBLESHOOTING

If the weather is usually wet or humid, spray *Equisteum* 508 as a fresh tea over all parts of the plants under an ascending moon, or as a liquid manure, on both onions and soil, under a descending moon, to deter fungal disease.

Collecting seeds

• Onions are biennials, so they flower and set seed in the second year. Sow seed after midsummer to form sets. If the winters are too wet to leave them in the soil, lift them in early winter and replant in spring.

• Support the flower stems with stakes. When a flower turns brown, cut it with a bit of stem on a sunny day. Place in a paper bag to dry, then shake to release the seeds.

• Allow only one variety of onion to flower to avoid cross-pollination. For the same reason, cage plants if any other members of the onion family are flowering close by.

Onions repel carrot rust flies—and carrots return the favor, repelling onion flies.

The aromatic leaves of mint confuse pests and deter attacks by onion flies.

Marigolds attract hoverflies, which dine with gusto on aphids and onion flies.

	SPRING	SUMMER	FALL	WINTER
Sow				
Harvest				

Time to harvest: **26–48 WEEKS** • Sow, plant, or thin 2–4in (5–10cm) apart, depending on variety

Rotation information: **ROTATION GROUP 3 • LIGHT FEEDERS**

Shallots
Allium cepa
Aggregatum Group

Shallots take up little space, are even easier to grow than onions, especially if you plant bulbs or sets, and you can grow them each year from the previous season's crop. Just remember to save the healthiest shallots—ideally around ¾in (2cm) in diameter—for planting out as the next crop.

SITE AND SOIL PREPARATION

Shallots love an airy site on well-drained, moisture-retentive soil that is not too acidic. Prepare the soil well before planting with enough mature compost to make it friable but not powdery. If the soil is already well composted, spray it with horn manure 500, rather than BC, in the afternoon under a descending moon.

SOWING AND PLANTING

Plant sets as soon as the soil is workable: in winter in mild areas, in early and mid-spring, or in late fall to overwinter. Space rows 10–12in (25–30cm) apart. To reduce the risk of bolting, plant and sow on a root day under a descending moon, but avoid lunar apogee.

ROUTINE CARE

In dry years, water the sets in to make sure that the roots settle firmly into the soil. Water only in dry weather if they start wilting. To improve flavor and storage life, mist horn silica 501 over the shoot tops, in the afternoon under an ascending moon, once the shoots start to wilt.

HARVESTING AND STORING

Shallots will be ready to harvest, ideally under an ascending moon, once their tops wither, 4–5 months after planting. You could also pull smaller offsets much earlier for vegetable sautées and salads. Ripe shallots should be firm and dense in the hand, with no soft areas. Shallots store for several weeks, or even months, in a dark, cool, frost-free, airy place if dry and cleaned of mud or soil. Divide them into small lots in slotted flats, net bags, or old pantyhose, or plait and hang them if you have space. They do not keep well or as long in humid settings, such as a refrigerator. Compost sprouted bulbs or chop the sprouts into salads, like chives.

TROUBLESHOOTING

Shallots resist most pests and diseases and, like other members of the onion family, make good companion plants, discouraging pests with their scent (*see facing page*). If the new shallots around the original set are only tiny, it means that the soil lacked enough compost. A soft shallot is a sign that too much or immature compost was used.

Collecting seeds

• Shallots may be left to flower like onions, and the seed harvested from their spent flower heads (*see facing page*).

• To create new sets, sow seed under cover from late winter for transplanting in mid-spring, or outdoors in mid- to late spring. Thin the seedlings to 1in (2.5cm) apart and transplant them to 2in (5cm) apart. Make sure that the seeds are kept well watered.

PLANTING SETS

New shallots, or sets, form in clusters around a single newly planted shallot, so they are commonly grown from sets.

Plant sets pointed side up: push each into the soil, leaving the tip showing.

The new shallots grow in clusters around each previously planted set.

WEEDING SHALLOTS

Shallots may be smothered by weeds, so keep the bed clear. If the weeds develop deep roots around shallots, pulling them out can disturb the crop—the shallots may stop growing if their own roots dry out.

	SPRING	SUMMER	FALL	WINTER
Sow				
Harvest				

Time to harvest: **16–20 WEEKS** • Sow, plant, or thin 6–8in (15–20cm) apart

Rotation information: **ROTATION GROUP 3 • LIGHT FEEDERS**

Garlic
Allium sativum

Garlic is easy to grow and stores exceptionally well so it can be eaten all year round. It is possible to become self-sufficient in garlic, beginning with just a single, good quality clove, but be sure to start off with garlic that is certified disease-free, and from a horticultural supplier rather than from a supermarket.

SITE AND SOIL PREPARATION

Garlic needs a warm site in full sun with well-drained soil that is reasonably fertile. Boost free-draining, rocky, or really sandy soils with well-matured compost; this helps the soil retain moisture without becoming waterlogged, which would cause the garlic to rot. Work the soil to a fine tilth. Add lime to acidic soil (below pH 6.5).

SOWING AND PLANTING

Choose good-sized, solid bulbs, peel off the papery outer skin, and break them into cloves. During a descending moon, spray the soil with horn manure 500 the evening before planting. Save some 500 and soak the cloves overnight to encourage better rooting. The following afternoon push the cloves into the soil, flat part first: this is where the rootlet forms. For year-round garlic, plant in late fall and again in late winter. Garlic needs to experience cold winter weather.

ROUTINE CARE

The soil should be slightly moist but never wet, so water only in very hot dry spells, adding a spray of chamomile tea. Hoe to remove weeds, taking care not to damage the bulbs.

HARVESTING AND STORING

Harvest from late spring through summer on root days when the moon is descending and the garlic leaves are turning slightly yellow. Using a fork, lift the plant carefully to avoid bruising. Cut off the roots and stems for garlic that is to be eaten immediately; leave the stems on and weave them together into plaits to store bulbs. Hang in a dry, airy place for a week or two to dry them out.

TROUBLESHOOTING

Avoid planting where other members of the onion family have been grown in the previous two years. Spray *Equisetum arvense* 508 as a fresh tea in humid weather to prevent mildew.

Collecting cloves

• Only hardneck types of garlic produce flowers, and even these rarely bear viable seeds. Although you could try collecting your own garlic seeds, they are likely to prove disappointing.

• To raise your own plants, save some of the healthiest, plumpest bulbs harvested during the summer, and store them in a cool, dry place. In fall, carefully break them open, taking care not to damage their skins, and plant the cloves as described above.

PLANTING CLOVES

Garlic is planted as individual cloves, with up to 20 cloves contained in each bulb. Discard any cloves that are damaged or show signs of mold because they can quickly decay in the soil.

Push the cloves into the soil by hand, with the pointed tips facing up and resting just below ground level.

Harvest when garlic leaves begin to yellow, loosening the soil gently with a fork to avoid damaging the bulbs.

Retaining the leaves makes it easier to hang up the bulbs to dry for storage.

	SPRING	SUMMER	FALL	WINTER
Sow				
Harvest				

Time to harvest: **24–28 WEEKS** • Plant 2in (5cm) deep, spaced 6in (15cm) apart in rows 12in (30cm) apart

Rotation information: **ROTATION GROUP 3 • LIGHT FEEDER**

Leeks
Allium porrum

Leeks can be ever present in the garden——as young seedlings early in the year, baby vegetables in summer, and a mature crop in the depths of winter. They are treated as roots because their edible part is a thick stem that stays white and sweet by being blanched, kept from sunlight by being buried in the earth.

SITE AND SOIL PREPARATION

Leeks like a bright, airy site on deep, fairly rich, loamy clay that does not get waterlogged. Dig in some mature compost just before planting, grow them where compost was spread for a previous crop, or spray horn manure 500 under a descending moon before or during planting.

SOWING AND PLANTING

For early leeks, sow under cover from midwinter, harden off and transplant during mid-spring, and harvest in early fall. For a winter harvest sow maincrop leeks outside in mid- to late spring for transplanting by midsummer at the latest. Leeks are always sown first, then transplanted as 6in (15cm) seedlings to allow the process of heeling up soil gradually around the stems to blanch them. Transplant under a descending moon on a root day, dropping the leeks into holes made with a dibber in furrows 6in (15cm) deep. Cover the roots with soil by watering them in, ideally with barrel compost.

ROUTINE CARE

Hoe to aerate the soil and keep weeds down, and gradually heel the earth up around the stems as they grow taller and wider. Water in dry spells, using a sprinkler head to avoid washing soil away. Add a dose of 1 part kelp or stinging nettle liquid manure to 9 parts water.

HARVESTING AND STORING

Pull leeks on root days under an ascending moon in dry weather and store them unwashed as they come out of the ground in a dark, airy place. They will keep for 1–3 months. Frost-hardy varieties that were sown in spring can be left in the ground until late winter.

TROUBLESHOOTING

Avoid heeling the leeks up high too early: this gets soil into the stems and make them gritty, or even causes them to rot. Leeks resist most diseases and help nearby plants repel pests.

Collecting seeds

• Leave one or two leek plants in the ground for the winter and insert stakes for support. They will flower in midsummer, producing seed.

• When the stems turn yellow, cut them 12in (30cm) below the seed head. Just one leek will provide more than enough seed for two seasons.

• Take the stems inside and hang them upside down in a dry, well-ventilated place. Strip the seeds off once they are fully dry. Store them in a labeled paper packet in an airtight container.

PLANTING LEEKS

Whether sown under cover or directly outside, leek seedlings are always transplanted into their final locations because they need to be planted deeply to blanch their stems.

Lift the seedlings and trim the roots lightly to make them easier to plant.

Make a hole for each seedling. Drop it in gently, but do not backfill the soil.

Water the seedlings in, allowing the water to carry soil into the hole.

	SPRING	SUMMER	FALL	WINTER
Sow				
Harvest				

Time to harvest: **4–5 MONTHS** • Plant seedlings 5in (13cm) apart in rows 12in (30cm) apart

Rotation information: **ROTATION GROUP 3 • MEDIUM FEEDER**

Green onions
Allium cepa

Green onions form small edible white or red bulbs, and green shoots, which pack a punch in salads and in Asian cooking. They thrive in similar conditions to other family members—onions, chives, and shallots—but because they take little space, are a useful catch crop between slower-growing vegetables.

SITE AND SOIL PREPARATION

Green onions grow best in a sunny site with light, well-drained, finely tilthed soil which is not too acidic. Work biodynamic compost or well-rotted manure into the soil before sowing. If your garden soil is unsuitable—heavy clay or very sandy, for example—grow them in pots instead.

SOWING AND PLANTING

Sow indoors or under cover between late winter and early spring for late spring and summer eating. Sow winter-hardy varieties in early to mid-fall for harvest the following spring, and cover winter-grown onions with cloches if the weather is harsh. Time soil preparation and direct sowing to a descending moon period, first making furrows in soil that is well weeded and raked, and watering them the day before sowing, ideally with horn manure 500. Sow thinly and shallowly, then cover with soil and firm in. If you are transplanting seedlings, tease out the roots and dig wide, deep holes to avoid cramping them when backfilling. Sow every two weeks for a regular supply.

ROUTINE CARE

In the three weeks the seeds take to germinate, water the bed lightly, especially in dry weather. Stop watering once the plants have established unless there are drought conditions. Any plants that are inadvertently bumped or lifted during thinning or weeding can be watered back into place, rather than firmed back in. Once the plants are established but not fully grown, spray the bed with horn silica 501 early one morning to keep the shoots firm and maximize flavor. Moon–opposition Saturn is an especially good time for this.

HARVESTING AND STORING

Start pulling the onions when they are about 6in (15cm) tall, on root days under a descending moon. Target areas where plants are cramped and pry them from underneath with a small fork. The green shoots can be pinched off or cut with scissors as a garnish for salads.

TROUBLESHOOTING

Avoid mulching or overwatering—the onions will be soft at best, rotten at worst. Onion thinnings left lying around attract onion flies.

Collecting seeds

• Allow plants to overwinter, protecting them with mulch.

• In spring one bulb will form on the top of a green shoot and produce a flower with black seeds.

• Cut the stalk and take it indoors to harvest the seeds.

• To avoid cross-pollination, allow only one variety of onion to flower at a time.

COMPANION PLANTS
Pungent green onions are a useful companion to carrots because onions help to mask their scent, which entices carrot rust flies. They can also be sown directly between time-consuming crops such as sweet corn.

PICK PURPLE
Although green onions typically have white stems and green leaves, there are several more colorful types available that produce purple-flushed bulbs or stems. They are grown in much the same way as traditional types and taste similar but add a splash of color to salads and stir-fries.

	SPRING	SUMMER	FALL	WINTER
Sow				
Harvest				

Time to harvest: **8 WEEKS** • Plant out ¾in (2cm) apart

Rotation information: **ROTATION GROUP 3 • MEDIUM FEEDERS**

Welsh onions
and Japanese bunching onions
Allium fistulosum

Unlike most onions, Welsh and Japanese bunching onions form no bulb to speak of but are prized for their flavorful green or white stems, which are used in Asian dishes, or eaten raw in salads. Hardy, multistemmed bunching onions produce tender green shoots, while single-stemmed Welsh onions are planted as annuals and look like small leeks—their white stem is cut at soil level.

SITE AND SOIL PREPARATION

Welsh and Japanese bunching onions prefer a fertile soil, dressed with fully matured, earthy biodynamic compost. They need an airy, sunny site with fine-textured, free-draining soil, which is not acidic. Before sowing hoe twice: first to stimulate weeds, and then to knock them down. Spray the soil with horn manure in fall and spring, and stinging nettle liquid manure in early summer.

SOWING AND PLANTING

Sow on root days under a descending moon in spring for annual Welsh onions or in fall, for winter-hardy varieties—their shoots need to be at above ankle height before the first frost. Plants sown in fall can be transplanted out in spring for a summer harvest. Sow seeds shallowly and barely cover them with soil, patted down with the back of a rake. Water them in with barrel compost to give them a good start.

ROUTINE CARE

With bunching varieties, space gets tight in onion plots, and inevitably weeding has to be done by hand. Stand or kneel on a plank while weeding to avoid compacting the soil and encouraging even more aggressive weeds.

For firm stems with good flavor, spray horn silica 501 during an ascending moon in the early morning when the stems are one third of their maximum height, and again when they are nearly fully grown. Lightly hoe soil up around the stems of Japanese onions to blanch them.

HARVESTING AND STORING

Harvest single stems on root days when the moon is descending. The plants will keep growing as long as not too many are taken.

TROUBLESHOOTING

Once the plants are established do not overwater. Onions are good companions for most crops, except beans, peas, and asparagus.

Collecting seeds

- Allow the plants to grow through the winter, protecting them with mulch, if required.
- In spring a bulb will form on the top of one green shoot per plant, from which the flowers will develop. Cut the stalk carefully and take it indoors to harvest them.
- Prevent cross-pollination by only allowing one type of onion to flower at once, or cage plants if other onions are flowering nearby.

JAPANESE ONIONS

This variety of Welsh onions, is grown for its strongly flavored stems. The plants are hardier, so don't need winter protection, and tolerate poorer soils than most other onions. The stems are at their best in their second year.

Onion flowers are edible as well as beautiful, and can be added to salads and soups for flavor and color.

EGYPTIAN ONIONS

Also known as tree onions, perennial bulbs of *Allium cepa* Proliferum Group are planted in spring and harvested as small bulbs produced at the top of a tall flowering stem in summer. Their yield is small, but they can be used as a hot flavoring, or pickled.

	SPRING	SUMMER	FALL	WINTER
Sow				
Harvest				

Time to harvest: **12–14 WEEKS** • Sow seeds 1in (2.5cm) apart and thin to 9in (23cm) apart.

Rotation information: **ROTATION GROUP 3 • MEDIUM FEEDERS**

Potatoes
Solanum tuberosum

One of the world's most important crops, potatoes are rich in vitamin C and fiber, and can be cooked in many ways. Although they take time to grow, the taste and texture of freshly dug, homegrown potatoes cannot be matched by any bought at the supermarket.

SITE AND SOIL PREPARATION

Potatoes like full sun, and slightly acidic clay-loam soil that is well drained and easily worked. Add plenty of mature compost the fall before planting during a descending moon. Spray the soil with horn manure under a descending moon, just before or when planting.

SOWING AND PLANTING

Seed potatoes can be planted under a descending moon. Plant early potatoes in early spring, main potatoes in mid-spring, and storage types in late spring. Early types are chitted before planting—set them in flats inside in a light, frost-free place until the eyes sprout. When planting, line the trenches with chopped comfrey, and plant around lunar apogee for a better crop.

ROUTINE CARE

A week after the foliage emerges, earth up and spray the soil with *Equisetum arvense* 508 tea to remove disease spores. Earth up again a few weeks later, before the foliage blocks easy access. Spray horn silica 501 over the beds two or three times, especially when the weather is warm and humid. Avoid hoeing or earthing up on leaf days or a perigee moon before midsummer to prevent pests and fungal diseases.

HARVESTING AND STORING

Potatoes are harvested when the moon is descending. Lift early and main crops in summer when their flower buds start to form. Dig up storage types during fall as the foliage dies back, before the first frost. Harvest on root days. Store the tubers in a heap (*see right*) or in the dark in a cool, airy place under cover. Small amounts can be stored in large paper bags.

TROUBLESHOOTING

If a late frost is forecast during spring, protect the foliage by spraying the soil with valerian 507 the night before. Potatoes do not need watering when planted unless the soil is very dry. In dry summers, water the plants thoroughly but infrequently. Make sure the soil in the planting trenches and that used for earthing up is evenly textured. This will make harvesting easier, and encourage the crop to be more evenly sized and healthier overall.

Collecting your own tubers

• Potatoes can be raised from seed but the resulting plants are not consistent, and require two years to produce a worthwhile harvest.

• Growing plants from tubers you have collected is more reliable than seed. Harvest them in summer or fall, and choose smaller tubers that are healthy and undamaged. Store these in a cool, dark, well-ventilated place until spring.

MAKING A HEAP

Smaller harvests of potatoes can be easily stored under cover in large paper bags. To store larger quantities, however, making a heap outside is the best option, and it will last until spring.

Choose a sheltered, well-drained site and stack the tubers in a pyramid on a 8in (20cm) thick layer of dry straw.

Cover the pile with a thick layer of straw, weighing it down with soil. Cover the straw completely with soil.

Lightly firm the soil without crushing the tubers. Collect the potatoes as needed.

	SPRING	SUMMER	FALL	WINTER
Plant	■			
Harvest		■	■	

Time to harvest: **20–24 WEEKS** • Plant early potatoes 14in (35cm) apart; main and storage 15in (38cm) apart

Rotation information: **ROTATION GROUP 3 • MEDIUM FEEDERS**

Sweet potatoes
Ipomoea batatas

Originating in tropical South America, sweet potatoes are not really potatoes at all, but part of the morning glory (bindweed) family. Their sweet-tasting flesh is delicious baked, mashed, or fried, and is packed with vitamins A and C, plus calcium and potassium. Their pretty trumpetlike flowers are welcome in the garden, too.

SITE AND SOIL PREPARATION

Sweet potatoes need a sheltered spot in full sun with plenty of space for their trailing stems. They require well-drained, sandy-loam soil into which plenty of dark, earthy-smelling compost, based on cow or horse manure, has been worked. Avoid adding chicken-manure compost, which encourages leaves not roots.

SOWING AND PLANTING

Sweet potatoes are grown from cuttings called slips that can be bought ready to plant, or grown from tubers stored from the previous year (*see right*). Plant them under a descending moon after the last frost or just after the spring equinox—whichever comes first. Cover the soil if necessary to warm it to at least 52°F (12°C). For better drainage and a bigger crop, plant slips in earthed-up ridges, adding some aged but warm horse-manure to act as a storage heater. Plant the slips 3–6in (8–15cm) deep into the ridges, leaving the top two leaves poking out.

ROUTINE CARE

Water freshly planted slips regularly until they establish, and spray them under a descending moon, at least once, with stinging nettle, comfrey, or kelp liquid manure to stimulate healthy growth. Weed around them carefully to avoid damaging the tubers forming underground. Once established, plants need little watering, even in dry spells.

HARVESTING AND STORING

Dig up sweet potatoes in early fall, before the leaves get hit by the first frost, or they will rot in storage. Choose a day when the moon is descending.

Loosen the soil with a garden fork, then use your hands to collect them. Tubers taste best if cured before storage (*see right*).

TROUBLESHOOTING

Avoid overwatering, especially on heavy clay soils, or the tubers produced will be thin and tasteless. If the roots are of poor quality despite being watered moderately, the soil drainage needs improving for next time. To do this, dig mature biodynamic compost into the soil with 15 percent sand to a depth of about 8in (20cm).

CURING AND STORING

To improve the flavor of the tubers, sweet potatoes should be cured after harvesting. Place them under cover, keeping them humid and at a temperature of 86°F (30°C) for three weeks. Turn them every few days, then store them in a cool, dry place indoors. There is no need to exclude light—they won't turn green like potatoes. Handle as little as possible.

Growing slips

• Take a healthy tuber, stored from last year, and suspend it in a jar of water, which you should change every few days, and stand it on a bright windowsill. Shoots will develop after a few weeks, which you should twist off at the base once they reach 12in (30cm) tall.

• The leafy shoots are then placed in jars of water until they produce roots, which can then be potted, ready to plant out.

• Slips can also be taken from whole tubers overwintered in dry sand, which is watered and warmed up in spring. Five or six leafy sprouts will form on each tuber, which can then be rooted in water, as above.

	SPRING	SUMMER	FALL	WINTER
Plant				
Harvest				

Time to harvest: **20–24 WEEKS** • Plant 30in (75cm) apart

Rotation information: **ROTATION GROUP 3 • MEDIUM FEEDERS**

Beets
Beta vulgaris subsp. *vulgaris*

Very space efficient, beets grow as well in small city center gardens as in larger neighborhood plots. Beets are nourishingly rich in Vitamin B and iron, and are easy to cook and store. The fresh, young leaves can also be cooked as greens.

SITE AND SOIL PREPARATION

Beets need an open site with rich but light soil, with high nitrogen levels. Soil that was well composted for a previous crop, such as brassicas, over the previous winter is suitable.

SOWING AND PLANTING

In spring sow beets outside where they are to grow. Ideally, do this under a descending moon, on a root or leaf day. Sow maincrop beets thinly 1in (2.5cm) deep and in rows 12in (30cm) apart. Sprinkle mature, finely sifted compost into the furrows and keep the seed bed moist after sowing. For earlier crops, sow beets outside under cover in early spring or in flats indoors in late winter and then transplant outside. Sow the seeds shallowly ½in (1cm) deep in rows 6in (15cm) apart.

ROUTINE CARE

Keep the soil lightly hoed to stop weeds and prevent the soil from crusting after watering, at least until leaves are big enough to shade out weeds. The bigger the leaves get and the more the crop swells, the less—if any—watering is needed, just enough to stop the beets from going woody.

HARVESTING AND STORING

Start pulling beets from 8 weeks, when their tender, half-sized tops emerge out of the ground. Continue pulling full-sized beets until light frost comes. After heavy frost they become woody. Twist rather than cut the leaves off to seal the juices in. Maincrop beets can be stored over the winter in a cool room in boxes of sand. For optimal storage avoid harvesting beets on leaf days or at other unfavorable celestial periods, such as nodes or lunar perigee of a full moon.

TROUBLESHOOTING

Avoid sowing beets too early when the soil is still cold—they are liable to bolt. When hoeing or digging up ripe beets, be careful not to damage the skins, which causes bleeding.

Collecting seeds

- Grow 20 beets of the same variety, without allowing them to flower.
- Dig up the roots in fall and cool store inside during winter.
- In spring trim the tops, replant them outside, and let them flower during summer. Stake the tall flowering stems to keep them from falling over.
- Collect seeds when the flower heads have browned. For pure seeds, do not allow beets to flower at the same time as any other members of the beet family, or Swiss chard.

GROWING BEET TOPS

Beets are closely related to chard, and have edible leaves that can be lightly picked as the roots develop. They can also be grown as microgreens to harvest as tender-leaved seedlings. Sow the seeds into small pots and pull the seedlings whole, once they are large enough to use.

HERITAGE BEETS

In addition to the traditional beets with their dark red roots, there are also yellow and striped types. These are raised and used in the same way, but cause less staining when cooked.

Red on the outside, when sliced, striped beets reveal their attractive flesh.

	SPRING	SUMMER	FALL	WINTER
Sow				
Harvest				

Time to harvest: **8 WEEKS** · Thin or transplant to leave 3in (8cm) between plants

Rotation information: **ROTATION GROUP 3 · MEDIUM FEEDERS**

Rutabagas

Brassica napus
Napobrassica Group

Also called swedes or Swedish turnips, rutabagas are larger and more globe shaped than their fellow brassica, the turnip, and their orange-yellow root flesh is sweeter and creamier. They can be eaten baked, roasted, boiled, or mashed, and are also delicious when added to soups or stews.

SITE AND SOIL PREPARATION

Rutabagas like light, fertile but not freshly composted soil. It should be well drained but not so thin it is ever allowed to get too dry. Dig mature compost into the soil in mid-fall before planting, or sow rutabagas in a plot recently vacated by nitrogen-fixing legumes and spray barrel compost on the soil.

SOWING AND PLANTING

Sow rutabagas outside when the soil has warmed up, from early spring—under cover to protect from frost—or in late spring in the open. Continue sowing until midsummer. Thin in stages, starting when seedlings are 1in (2.5cm).

ROUTINE CARE

Rutabagas taste best when they do not experience a lack of food or water, or too much weed competition. Spray horn manure 500 while hoeing the soil to keep weeds down between plants. When the rutabagas start to swell, spray horn silica 501 in the morning, preferably the day after 500 was sprayed. Do not let the soil dry out since rutabagas become woody or split as soon as the next watering occurs.

HARVESTING AND STORING

Early sown rutabagas are ready in mid-fall, with others to follow. Rutabagas are hardy and, except in very cold climates, may be left in the ground until early spring. A thick layer of straw provides enough protection from the cold until lifting. If the ground will freeze solid, lift the rutabagas by prying them out without bruising them and store in boxes of sand in a cool, dry place. For optimal storage, harvest rutabagas on root days; avoid harvesting on leaf days.

TROUBLESHOOTING

If the season starts out rainy, spray oak bark decoction or *Equisetum arvense* 508 as a liquid manure to keep downy and powdery mildew away. If the soil dries out, rutabagas attract flea beetles, which eat holes in the leaves. Hang sticky traps above the plants to trap them: shake the plants if necessary. Add lime to the soil to lift the pH if clubroot is a problem.

Collecting seeds

• Allow several rutabaga plants to overwinter in the ground and leave them to flower in spring.

• Collect the seed in early summer, once the seed heads are mature.

• Rutabagas are a member of the *Brassica napus* family, which includes rapeseed (rapeseed oil). Cross-pollination will occur if they flower near each other at the same time. Prevent this by caging your plants to ensure pure seeds.

SOWING
SEED IN FURROWS

Sow the seeds finely to reduce the amount of thinning that will be required as the seedlings develop. Keep plants moist, especially after thinning, to avoid checking their growth, which affects their flavor.

RED-SKINNED RUTABAGAS

Traditional rutabagas produce roots that are purple-flushed on top and white below. However, some varieties have completely red skins, which adds color to cooking.

	SPRING	SUMMER	FALL	WINTER
Sow				
Harvest				

Time to harvest: **UP TO 26 WEEKS** • Thin to leave 6–9in (15–23cm) between plants

Rotation information: **ROTATION GROUP 2 • MEDIUM FEEDERS**

Radishes
Summer and Winter
Raphanus sativus

Summer radishes, with their crisp, peppery flesh and thin skins are the most widely grown. However, winter radishes and Asian daikon are also well worth considering for their versatility.

Anyone thinking of buying their first pet is told to start with a houseplant, and if it is still alive after a year, then any future pet should be in good hands. A similar rule could apply to vegetables, with radishes in the role of trial plant. While summer radishes are the quickest crop to grow from sowed seeds, the longer, larger, and spicier-tasting winter version takes somewhat longer. Growing sweet and tender roots without problems requires real planning and attentiveness.

SITE AND SOIL PREPARATION
Radishes like fine, fertile soil that retains moisture. Dry soils can be improved quickly by adding biodynamic compost or finely chopped leaf mold. Or, add compost, then grow other crops there for 1–2 years. To avoid bolting, sow later batches of summer radishes in partial shade.

SOWING AND PLANTING
Spray the soil with stinging nettle liquid manure before planting to improve its texture. Sow seeds in two weekly batches at the start and end of each descending moon period, ½in (1cm) deep in spring, 1in (2cm) in summer. Winter types are sown from midsummer as temperatures cool.

ROUTINE CARE
For the best roots, sow thinly in the ideal soil type, thin regularly, and keep plants moist. To avoid plant stress, water in the evening, and spray the bed with chamomile tea or yarrow early the following morning. Weed carefully, using a hoe.

HARVESTING AND STORING
Pull summer radishes young and tender, 4–6 weeks after they were sown. Winter radishes mature in 6–10 weeks from late fall onward, and can be eaten raw or cooked. Lift them, removing the leafy tops, and store in boxes of sand, or leave them in the ground until needed. Mulch plants with straw during really cold spells.

TROUBLESHOOTING
Flea beetles create small holes in the leaves, and can be a problem when the soil is too dry, or plants have not been watered. Spray the soil with horn manure 500 and BC to keep it earthy and spongy, improving moisture retention.

Collecting seeds
• To prevent cross-pollination, only allow one type of summer or winter radishes to flower at the same time. Also ensure that summer and winter types do not flower together. Seed quality is improved if at least 20 plants are left to flower.

• For summer radishes, select the strongest bulbs and replant them 10in (25cm) apart to give the seed heads space to develop. Stake if needed and collect the seeds in early fall.

• Winter types can stay in the soil in winter or can be lifted. Replant the roots in spring and harvest the seeds in summer.

Summer radishes form colorful red roots, often with white bases, and are usually eaten uncooked in salads.

Winter radishes have thick skins and tough flesh. They can be eaten grated into salads or cooked in stir-fries.

Daikon forms roots up to 14in (35cm) long. Use them like other winter types.

	SPRING	SUMMER	FALL	WINTER
Sow				
Harvest				

Time to harvest: **20–24 WEEKS** • Sow, plant, or thin 2–4in (5–10cm) apart

Rotation information: **ROTATION GROUP 2 • MEDIUM FEEDERS**

Celeriac

Apium graveolens
var. *rapaceum*

Mother Nature forgot about celeriac when handing out beauty genes, but she filled its knobbly white bulbs with the vitamins, minerals, and fiber we need to keep the mind and body healthy over winter. Grate raw celeriac into salads, or use it cooked to add a nuttiness like parsnip and a pepperiness like celery to stews, casseroles, and soups.

SITE AND SOIL PREPARATION

Celeriac needs moist, well-drained soil, rich in potassium, and recently dressed with well-rotted manure. Choose a site in full sun.

SOWING AND PLANTING

Sow seeds indoors, covering lightly with sandy compost—they need light to germinate. When planting out, dig the holes large enough for the crown to rest on the soil: it should not be buried. Time sowing, pricking out, and planting to root days with a descending moon. Spray horn manure 500 just before or when planting out.

ROUTINE CARE

Water well to prevent bolting, and apply *Equisetum arvense* 508 as a fresh tea in damp weather, or before lunar perigee, to deter fungal diseases. In midsummer, mulch with leaf mold or comfrey to retain moisture and deter weeds. With good mulching and watering, additional liquid manures are not necessary. When the bulbs start to swell, apply horn silica 501 once between summer solstice and fall equinox; spray in the afternoon to improve winter storage.

HARVESTING AND STORING

Cut under the bulb with a knife, leaving rootlets in the soil to attract beneficial worms. Use BC once the bed is clear to promote healthy decomposition of the rootlets, leaves, and residual mulch over winter. Store the bulbs in boxes of sand or a cool room for winter.

TROUBLESHOOTING

Ensure the compost used to prepare soil is fully fermented to reduce slug attacks, and grow onions nearby to deter carrot rust flies. In hot weather, celeriac may suffer water stress—the bulbs may crack and taste woody. If no compost is available, sow vetch as a cover crop before celeriac to add nitrogen and improve soil drainage and nutrient availability.

Collecting seeds

• Save seed from a plot of 12 celeriac plants, which must be of the same variety. Grow them in the normal way without allowing them to flower.

• Leave them in the ground over winter, or in colder regions, dig up the roots in fall, cool store them inside, and replant them in spring.

• Let the plants flower in summer. Collect seed as each flower head ripens, usually the central one first, and sideshoots later.

• Celeriac will intercross with celery if both are allowed to flower at the same time.

FROST PROTECTION

Celeriac is ready to harvest from fall onward, and keeps best if it is left in the ground until needed. Although it is hardy, celeriac can be damaged by winter weather, so mulch around the roots with a thick layer of straw, or cover the plants with fabric.

If using straw, work it in well between the plants so it is less likely to blow away. Top it off, if required, in winter.

COMPANION PLANTING

Cabbage white butterflies dislike the scent of celeriac and celery, making them a good crop to grow alongside all brassicas, including kale and cabbage. Growing celeriac near lettuce, spinach, and peas is also thought to improve their yield.

	SPRING	SUMMER	FALL	WINTER
Sow				
Harvest				

Time to harvest: **20–24 WEEKS** • Sow, plant, or thin 2–4in (5–10cm) apart

Rotation information: **ROTATION GROUP 3 • MEDIUM FEEDERS**

Parsnips

Pastinaca sativa

Like marathon runners, parsnips start slowly, keep going for ages, and finish strongly in winter after the competition fades. Their long taproots are loaded with fiber, vitamins, and sweet, nutty flavors, and before sugar was available they were used to sweeten cakes and jams.

SITE AND SOIL PREPARATION

Choose a sunny site. Parsnips often follow brassicas in a rotation since they like well-worked, rock-free, slightly acidic soil that was well composted for a previous crop. Compost made in part from comfrey leaves is rich in the potassium parsnips need. Fresh compost causes parsnips to fork. At a descending moon, dig the bed roughly in winter to let the frost break up large clods; in late winter, work the soil to 8–12in (20–30cm) deep to remove any compaction and allow the roots to swell. Rake to a fine tilth. Ten days before sowing, cover the soil with fabric or cloches to warm it.

SOWING AND PLANTING

Sow direct as soon as conditions allow, under a descending moon, with three seeds per group in rows 12–14in (30–35cm) apart and 1in (2.5cm) deep. Space 4–6in (10–15cm) apart for short or intermediate roots, 8in (20cm) apart for large ones. Cover seeds lightly and firm gently. Sow radishes (*see p.164*) to mark the rows and make weeding easier until the parsnips sprout. To boost the seed, spray the bed soon after sowing with stinging nettle liquid manure, or with comfrey liquid manure if a comfrey-enriched compost was not used for the previous crop on the plot.

ROUTINE CARE

Weed carefully to avoid disturbing the roots. When the tops begin to swell,

mist horn silica 501 over them, in the morning at an ascending moon, to improve sweetness and taste. Spray 501 again, especially if storing the crop indoors over winter, a month before harvest.

HARVESTING AND STORING

Parsnips are ready when their leaf tops wilt in late fall. The hardy roots taste better if pulled after a frost and can stay in the ground over winter until required. Mark the rows with stakes if snow is forecast, to locate them easily. Parsnips may rot in very wet, cold soil; store instead in boxes of sand (*see right, bottom*).

TROUBLESHOOTING

Parsnips germinate poorly, so it is best to buy fresh seed each year. Do not start them in cell packs indoors because they transplant badly.

Collecting seeds

• For the best quality seed, collect from at least 20 plants of the same type, grown in the usual way.

• Leave the plants over winter and allow them to flower the next summer. If you have to lift the roots for winter because of poor conditions, replant them in spring.

• Stake the tall flower stems to prevent them from falling over. Collect seeds when the flower heads turn brown, and dry them before storing.

KEYS TO SUCCESS

Parsnip seed is sensitive to poor growing conditions and can be difficult to germinate. However, once the seedlings appear, they are easy plants to grow.

Gently thin seedlings sown in groups to leave the strongest ones. Water the remaining seedlings to settle the soil.

Parsnip roots may split and spoil if the soil becomes dry in warm weather, so keep them well watered in summer.

To store roots in a cool place indoors, lift them, remove the tops, and pack with separation in boxes of sand.

	SPRING	SUMMER	FALL	WINTER
Sow				
Harvest				

Time to harvest: **17–42 WEEKS** • Thin to 4-8in (10-20cm) apart, depending on variety

Rotation information: **ROTATION GROUP 3 • MEDIUM FEEDERS**

Carrots
Daucus carota

People first grew carrots as medicine, not food, and for good reason—carrots are rich in vitamins A, B, and C, fiber, and minerals such as calcium. They are sweet, easy to grow, take up little space, and they are delicious raw or cooked.

SITE AND SOIL PREPARATION

Carrots need fertile soil, but the tips fork in soil enriched with fresh compost. Under a descending moon, spread a fine layer of aged compost or, even better, grow them on a plot after heavy feeders such as brassicas. On heavy, rocky soils, work in fully mature compost mixed with sand, then build raised beds and fill with 4:1 parts fine-textured soil to aged compost.

SOWING AND PLANTING

Sow under a descending moon, and spray horn manure 500 in the afternoon before sowing for stronger rooting. Direct sow early, quick-growing carrots from late winter under cloches or cold frames; sow maincrops in mid-spring, and then every 14 days for a constant harvest. Sow thinly, ½in (1cm) deep in furrows 6–12in (15–30cm) apart. Cover with soil, firm, water lightly, and keep moist until germination in 7–21 days. To mark the rows, sow radishes, spinach, or lettuce with the carrots to harvest while the carrots fill out. On very sandy soil, intersow dill or cornflowers to provide phosphorus, which helps carrots to have a sweeter flavor.

ROUTINE CARE

Thin and eat the seedlings after the lacy leaves start to develop. Keep the soil moist for the first month or so and then water only if very dry. To obtain the sweetest flavor, spray horn silica 501 in the morning over the bed when the green tops are starting to form.

HARVESTING AND STORING

In the 30 days before lifting, spray 501 on a root day afternoon with a descending moon to concentrate the sugars and improve storage life.

TROUBLESHOOTING

To prevent carrot rust flies, thin on cool evenings, firm the soil, and put thinnings straight in a bucket to take away—do not place them on the ground. Grow aromatic plants like chives upwind to confuse flies, and use 2ft (60cm) tall natural barriers such as lavender, rather than garden fabric, to block out the flies.

Collecting seeds

• To obtain the best quality seeds, lift at least 20 of the best plants in fall, grown in the usual way, and store until spring.

• Replant the roots in spring and allow them to flower. Support tall flower stems with stakes, if needed.

• To prevent cross-pollination, make sure that no other carrot varieties or wild carrots (Queen Anne's lace) flower nearby at the same time.

• Cut the tops when the flowers are dry and brown; clean the seed by swirling it in a strainer to remove any chaff.

ROOTS AND SOILS

There are many heritage carrot varieties available, from white to purple. Long, slim carrots prefer deep, easily worked, sandy loam. Stubbier carrots can handle a firmer, clay-rich soil, if it is aerated.

STORING CARROTS

You can leave maincrop carrots in well-drained soil over winter until needed. On heavier soils, where they may rot, lift and store them in a cool, dry place, for up to five months in boxes.

Stack layers of undamaged carrots and soil mix in cardboard boxes.

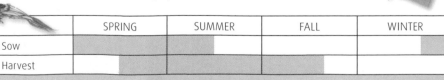

	SPRING	SUMMER	FALL	WINTER
Sow				
Harvest				

Time to harvest: **7–18 WEEKS** • Thin to 1in (2.5cm), then to 1½–3in (4–8cm), or farther for large-rooted varieties

Rotation information: **ROTATION GROUP 3 • MEDIUM FEEDERS**

Turnips
Brassica rapa Rapifera Group

These often unappreciated roots are like rutabagas, but smaller, faster growing, and more white than yellow; there are also red-skinned varieties. They may be sweet enough to be eaten raw or as turnip greens. Turnips are winter hardy and easy to raise from seed; if you sow early and in batches you can harvest them nearly all year round.

SITE AND SOIL PREPARATION
Turnips prefer loamy, clay soils that drain well without drying out, perhaps in part shade. Do not sow where brassicas have grown in the last three years or on thin soil, which causes turnips to grow unevenly and become brittle. Spray horn manure 500 on the soil at or just before sowing, under a descending moon in the afternoon; in warm conditions, do this just after rain.

SOWING AND PLANTING
Make the earliest sowings under cover from late winter onward, under a descending moon if possible, for mid- to late spring crops. Sow in mid-spring just before the last frost, on soil manured for an earlier crop, for early to midsummer turnips. Then sow every 2–3 weeks until late summer to harvest from mid-fall into spring. Sow turnips for winter harvest on soil cleared of an early crop such as potatoes or peas.

ROUTINE CARE
Sprinkle the plant with weak chamomile tea in dry weather in early morning. Spray oak bark decoction on foliage during a break in wet weather to ward off fungal disease. Spray horn silica 501 in the morning as the turnips swell to obtain smooth, shiny, firm roots. Apply stinging nettle tea to the leaves two weeks before pulling turnips to intensify the flavor.

HARVESTING AND STORING
Early spring sowings are tender enough after two months to be grated raw. Cut turnip greens from these and late summer sowings in spring. Pull late spring and early summer sowings from mid-fall to early winter—they are less frost-tolerant than rutabagas. Remove the tops and store for a month or two in a clamp or box of sand.

TROUBLESHOOTING
Turnips lose their creamy sweetness and firm texture if they get too big, so pull them early: they taste best and are easier to peel and chop.

Collecting seeds
- Turnips will cross-pollinate with other members of the *Brassica rapa* family, like napa cabbage (*see p.187*), if they flower at the same time.
- For seed, grow turnips in the normal way, but leave them unharvested outdoors in winter. In cold climates, lift the roots and bring them under cover to replant deeply in spring.
- The plants will flower in spring—support the long stalks with stakes and twine.
- Pick the seed pods as soon as they brown.

GROWING TURNIPS
Sow seeds directly into the soil in rows 9–12in (20–30cm) apart and ¾in (2cm) deep. In wet areas, sow in low but firm ridges to aid drainage. Thin seedlings when the first leaves appear, if needed.

Thin to spacings recommended for each type, from 2in (5cm) apart for long roots to 6in (15cm) apart for globular turnips.

Lack of watering in dry spells causes roots to crack and attracts leaf-nibbling flea beetles; damage is mostly cosmetic.

Pull turnips once they reach a usable size, typically the size of a golf ball.

	SPRING	SUMMER	FALL	WINTER
Sow				
Harvest				

Time to harvest: **9–42 WEEKS**, depending on season and variety • Sow or plant 2–6in (5–15cm) apart

Rotation information: **ROTATION GROUP 2 • MEDIUM FEEDERS**

Salsify
and scorzonera
Tragopogon porrifolius, Scorzonera hispanica

Something of a delicacy, the roots of these closely related crops are highly nutritious, with a bitter, oysterlike flavor; they are also called oyster plant or vegetable oyster. Salsify has white, thick roots and black salsify, or scorzonera, is longer, more slender, and darker-skinned.

SITE AND SOIL PREPARATION

Salsify and scorzonera are easy, if slow, to grow, but produce the best roots in finely textured, sandy but rock-free soil that is well dug to at least 12in (30cm). Work this type of soil at planting. To avoid clays or loams becoming lumpy, dig in mature biodynamic compost in late fall or dig and spray BC on the soil in the evening. Another option is to spray the soil with horn manure 500 in fall to stimulate soil life and healthy soil decomposition, then spray BC on an afternoon just before sowing to transform decomposition processes into soil-building processes. A site in full sun is best. All this soil preparation is done under a descending moon.

SOWING AND PLANTING

The seeds are best sown on an early spring afternoon under a descending moon. Sow several seeds to each station, 1½in (3–4cm) deep. Thin the seedlings to the strongest ones, once they have their first pairs of leaves.

ROUTINE CARE

The seeds germinate slowly, so keep the furrows well watered and as weed-free as possible through the growing season, and particularly during germination. Spray horn silica 501 at fall equinox over the plants in the afternoon to concentrate their flavors.

HARVESTING AND STORING

Lift roots from mid-fall onward, once at least 12in (30cm) long, under an ascending moon. Salsify and scorzonera in particular are hardy enough to stay in the ground over winter, especially if protected with a straw mulch. However, salsify loses its flavor if left too long. Keep both roots in a root cellar until spring; salsify stores best with its top removed.

TROUBLESHOOTING

To discourage carrot rust flies, grow scorzonera among rows of carrots.

Collecting seeds

• For the best quality seeds, save them from a plot of about 20 plants of one variety of either salsify or scorzonera.

• Grow the plants in the normal way, leaving them outdoors over winter, and allow them to flower in summer. Salsify's flowers are purple, scorzonera's are yellow.

• Collect the seeds when the flower heads become brown.

HARVESTING

Dig out scorzonera (shown here) or salsify with a fork or trowel to avoid bruising or snapping the long, thin roots. Otherwise, they can quickly lose their freshness.

BONUS CROP

You can harvest the summer flower buds of both salsify and scorzonera. Let the plants grow over winter and pick the buds just before they open, with 4in (10cm) of stem. Cook them like asparagus or add to stuffing.

Harvest the flowers on the day of use, because they soon deteriorate.

	SPRING	SUMMER	FALL	WINTER
Sow				
Harvest				

Time to harvest: **30-46 WEEKS** • Thin salsify to 6in (15cm) apart, and scorzonera to 12in (30cm) apart

Rotation information: **ROTATION GROUP 3 • MEDIUM FEEDERS**

Horseradish

Armoracia rusticana

Horseradish is easy to grow, and can be planted to make good use of forgotten corners of the garden. The roots have a pungent and peppery taste and smell, and should be scrubbed, grated, and peeled under water to avoid irritation. The root adds spice to hot and cold condiments, like traditional horseradish sauce, for use with a variety of meat and fish dishes. It can also be used in the preparation of an effective fungicide to use on fruit trees.

SITE AND SOIL PREPARATION

Horseradish grows in full sun but prefers partial shade. Soils must be deep, rich, and moist, rather than waterlogged or too dry. Although it can be grown as an annual from seed, it easily grows from roots left in the soil after harvesting.

SOWING AND PLANTING

Horseradish can be sown annually late winter to early spring under a descending moon. However, plants are usually raised from last year's roots. When the moon is descending, and ideally in the afternoon, cut off the top third of the root and plant the lower piece 2in (5cm) deep, at a slight angle. Backfill with soil and compost.

ROUTINE CARE

Horseradish needs little care, apart from watering it during really dry weather.

HARVESTING AND STORING

The roots are mature after nine months, and are largest and tastiest when lifted under a descending moon after the first winter frost. Roots can be lifted throughout winter. Store them cool, in sand or a pile if there are a lot of them, or singly in the refrigerator in a plastic bag.

TROUBLESHOOTING

Horseradish is a brassica, so avoid problems by growing it where other brassicas have been grown in the preceding couple of years at least. If sown and harvested annually, horseradish should not produce any of its small, white flowers. If flowers appear in the second year, pinch them out. Weed the plot by hand, rather than by digging, to avoid damaging the roots. Do not allow discarded root pieces to regrow where they are not wanted.

Raising plants

- Although horseradish flowers, it doesn't produce seed.
- Horseradish is propagated by digging up the roots in fall and slicing off small sideshoots.
- Store the sideshoots under cover during winter in a box of sand, or in pots of dry compost.
- Replant the sideshoots in pots during spring. Plant out in late spring when the fresh green tops begin sprouting.

HORSERADISH TEA

Horseradish tea can be used to protect pit-forming fruit trees, such as nectarines, peaches, and plums, from brown rot, a fungal disease. Apply as a spray three times during spring and summer.

Roughly chop up 1oz (30g) of root or leaves. You may prefer to dice the root under water to avoid eye irritation.

Bring the roots or leaves to the boil in a covered saucepan, then allow to cool for 24 hours without removing the lid.

Filter the cooled tea. It is applied in April, May, and at the end of August.

	SPRING	SUMMER	FALL	WINTER
Plant				
Harvest				

Time to harvest: **20–24 WEEKS** • Sow, plant or thin 8–12in (20–30cm) apart

Rotation information: **ROTATION GROUP 2 • MEDIUM FEEDERS**

Jerusalem artichokes

Helianthus tuberosus

Jerusalem artichokes have no link to Jerusalem and are not members of the artichoke family. They are like a smaller, subtly nuttier version of the potato, but unlike potatoes produce much taller stems, and can be grown in a dedicated bed for several years before needing to be moved.

SITE AND SOIL PREPARATION

Jerusalem artichokes like soil that is rich in humus, moisture-retentive, drains well, and is not too acidic (below pH5). It thrives in an open location. Dig in plenty of biodynamic compost during a descending moon before planting.

SOWING AND PLANTING

Buy tubers the size of an egg and plant them during a descending moon in early spring, once the soil is workable, 4–6in (10–15cm) deep.

ROUTINE CARE

Spray horn manure 500 over the bed in fall and spring at descending moon time. As the stems emerge, remove any weeds, and earth up soil around them. Keep plants well watered, and stake to provide extra support. During descending moons, spray plants with any leftover teas from other gardening tasks, especially yarrow, dandelion, chamomile, and yarrow and comfrey. Spray the soil with stinging nettle liquid manure if you have any spare, just after rain to keep the soil airy. Pinch off the tops and any flowers in late summer to focus the plant's energy on root formation. Spray horn silica 501 a week or two before you do this, early one morning during an ascending moon.

HARVESTING AND STORING

The tubers can be lifted early winter to spring under a descending moon. Lift every piece of root to prevent regrowth. Store tubers in a dry, frost-free place in moist earth.

TROUBLESHOOTING

Use straw mulch or cloches to stop the ground from freezing during harvest, and mark the rows, if necessary. Dress permanent beds with fresh biodynamic compost each year, and create a new bed every four or five years. Deter slug attacks using pine nut extract.

Collecting tubers

• Jerusalem artichokes are raised from tubers, not seed, which are planted in spring.

• Grow the plant in the normal way throughout summer and lift the tubers in fall.

• Retain a number of healthy tubers, each no larger than an egg, and store them under cover in a box of sand or in pots of compost.

• Pot them and let them grow under cover in spring, ready to plant out once the risk of frost has passed.

SAVING ENERGY

Jerusalem artichokes are unusual because some of the plants flower every summer, but others never do. Either way, the blooms are best removed to conserve energy, although they do make nice cut flowers.

BARRIER PLANTING

With its tall stems and dense form, Jerusalem artichokes can be planted as a windbreak to other crops in exposed gardens. Plant them at the edge of a bed or garden, and provide support.

	SPRING	SUMMER	FALL	WINTER
Plant	▮			
Harvest				▮

Time to harvest: **30–36 WEEKS** • Plant 12–18in (30–45cm) apart in a grid pattern

Rotation information: **ROTATION GROUP 3** • **MEDIUM FEEDERS**

Aquarius
the Water Carrier

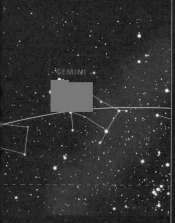

Gemini
the Twins

Libra
the Scales

Flower days

Flower days are the periods when the moon is passing in front of the constellations of Aquarius, Gemini, and Libra. They relate to air or light—the element in which plants flower. Edible flower crops, such as globe artichokes, broccoli, and cauliflower, cultivated on flower days produce high-quality, consistent yields, and store well. Ornamental flowers and shrubs also benefit from the rhythm of the air-flower constellations—as do the bees and beneficial insects feeding on their pollen! Flowers picked on these days are more intensely scented; cutting them on flower days helps the plants produce stronger sideshoots, and more top-quality blooms. Flowers for drying will also retain their shape and color longer.

Flower days and lunar cycles

The moon passes an air-flower constellation roughly every 9 days, and spends 2–3 days in each.

In the northern hemisphere the moon ascends as it travels through Aquarius and into part of Gemini.

The moon's descending cycle then begins in Gemini and it continues to descend as it passes Libra.

Things to do on...

Flower days

The garden feels at its most alive on flower days: the scents from plants in flower become heightened, and insects navigating by smell appear especially active. These are the days to cultivate ornamental beds and borders as well as edible flower crops.

- **Under an ascending moon** the earth breathes out and the upper parts of plants are at their most vital, so this is the best time to pick flowers for drying.

- **Under a descending moon** the earth breathes in, which means it is a good time to plant bulbs and divide flowering herbs ready for replanting.

- **Moon–opposition Saturn** is a good time to plant or transplant perennial herbs: the strong calcium–silica influences that result promote strong roots and enhanced aromas and flavors.

- **In the 2–3 days before full moon** sow seeds of annual flowers for stronger germination. Full moon is also a good time to collect flowers for the biodynamic preparations.

- **The perigee moon** induces an inward contraction in plants, so it is the perfect time to deadhead flowers with fading blossoms as their sap returns underground.

- **When the moon is at apogee** companion flowers like tansy are at their most aromatic: grow them in pots and move them close to the crops they protect.

Nasturtium

Broccoli

Bury horn silica 501 on a flower day around spring equinox.

Harvest baby artichoke hearts for preserving in olive oil.

Cut down stinging nettles to use in teas, liquid manures, and the compost prep 504.

Plant ornamental flowers that attract beneficial insects.

Choose flower days to dig up, divide, replant, or store ornamental bulbs and tubers like dahlias.

Harvest winter cabbage and other leaf day crops for long-term storage.

Collect flowers for drying on flower days: they retain their shape and color longer.

Prune flowering shrubs like roses on flower days with a descending moon.

ick dandelion heads before they are fully pen and dry them for compost prep 506.

Harvest chamomile flowers for teas and the chamomile compost prep 503.

Collect flowers for the valerian compost prep 507, and juice or infuse them on the same day.

Cauliflower

Brassica oleracea
Botrytis Group

Cauliflower heads, or curds, can be picked almost all year round but they need year-round space and attention too—especially, good soil preparation and watering. In smaller gardens cauliflower sown in spring and harvested late summer are a better choice than overwintering types, which may need protection from cold.

SITE AND SOIL PREPARATION

Choose an open, sunny site where no other members of the cabbage (brassica) family have been grown in the previous three years. On an overexposed site, the stems of these large plants will rock, and the roots will fail to support them. The soil should be neutral or only very slightly acidic (pH6.8 is ideal). Dig in plenty of mature biodynamic compost, ideally made partly from cow manure, and spray horn manure 500 once or twice under a descending moon.

SOWING AND PLANTING

Seeds can be started off indoors from midwinter, or sown in furrows outside from mid-spring for harvest in late summer and early fall. Ensure the soil is well worked and friable, and tread it flat before you sow, ideally on flower days, under a descending moon. Harden off transplants and water the night before planting. While the moon is descending, plant them up to their first leaves for good rooting, and water in.

ROUTINE CARE

Cauliflower must be kept well watered, well fed, and on firm ground. When the moon is descending, spray stinging nettle liquid manure on the soil and on the plants (as a feed). Early in the morning on flower days, spray horn silica 501 when direct-sown plants have 4–5 leaves, and transplants have at least 5–6 leaves;

spray again as the plant reaches full height, before the curds start to form. Yarrow tea can be applied as a pick-me-up in unsettled weather.

HARVESTING AND STORING

Fall-harvested cauliflower ripens in cool weather. Cut the main stem below the curds as they start to swell, ideally on a cool morning on flower days under an ascending moon. The florets should be firm and tight. If too many ripen together, pull a whole plant and hang it upside down in a dry, cool place; it will last two weeks.

TROUBLESHOOTING

Cauliflower can be tricky if the soil is poor, too acidic or dry, or if transplanted badly. Planting celery nearby will deter cabbage white butterflies from laying their eggs.

Collecting seeds

- Cauliflower flowers and sets seed in its second summer. Avoid collecting seed from plants that bolt in their first year.

- Save seed from at least 20 plants to prevent inbreeding. Dry the flower heads indoors, then pull off the seeds.

- Cauliflower will interbreed with other brassicas, so prevent others from flowering at the same time, or cover their blooms with paper bags.

VARIETIES TO TRY

Traditional cauliflower are grown for their dense white heads but there are also purple-flowered varieties to try. These need the same growing conditions, and offer color and subtly different flavors to your cooking.

Purple cauliflower is unique and rich in antioxidants, and has a sweet, mild, and nutty flavor, with no bitterness.

SUN SCREEN

White-flowered cauliflower heads should be shaded from the sun to keep their color and prevent scorching. As soon as the heads form, cover them with plant leaves, tied at the top. Do this on a dry day to avoid trapping moisture that could cause decay.

Release the leaves temporarily after heavy rain to allow the curds to dry.

	SPRING	SUMMER	FALL	WINTER
Sow				
Harvest				

Time to harvest: **20–26 WEEKS** • Sow seed ¾in (2cm) deep, plant at least 10in (24cm) apart in rows 10in (24cm) apart.

Rotation information: **ROTATION GROUP 2 • MEDIUM FEEDERS**

Broccoli

Brassica oleracea Italica Group

Broccoli is tasty and fairly easy to grow, with a single flower head that is harvested before winter, followed by a small crop of tender side spears. The bluish-tinged florets resemble small cauliflower heads, although they are fluffier and less compact. More exotic varieties include 'Romanesco', which has tasty, pointy-peaked florets, the color of pistachio ice cream.

SITE AND SOIL PREPARATION

The ideal site for broccoli is sunny with good wind protection and has fertile soil that is friable but contains humus, and drains well. Dig in plenty of biodynamic compost the fall before sowing, then spray the bed with horn manure 500 under the descending moon in the weeks before sowing.

SOWING AND PLANTING

Transplanted broccoli performs poorly so grow it from seed, sown directly or started off indoors in biodegradable pots. Start sowing outside under cover in early spring and continue succession sowing during flower days, preferably with a descending moon, until midsummer. Water the furrows first with stinging nettle liquid manure. Sow two or three seeds per station and carefully thin out the weaker ones later.

ROUTINE CARE

Broccoli needs regular watering to prevent uneven growth. Hoe to keep weeds down and mound the soil up a little around the base of the plants, but avoid damaging the roots. When the seedlings have four or five leaves, spray comfrey liquid manure over the bed and on the main stems, and both sides of the leaves. Later, spray horn silica 501 early in the morning after the flower heads have started to develop. Protect the florets from the sun using a large leaf (cabbage is ideal) and the flowering shoots from cool fall nights with fabric.

HARVESTING AND STORING

Pick broccoli sown in spring from late summer, and summer-sown types in mid-fall on flower days under an ascending moon. Cut the main head from below before it gets too big and the flower buds open and become bitter. Leave the sideshoots to develop into spears that can be harvested later. Florets will store in the refrigerator for several days and can be frozen

TROUBLESHOOTING

Protect plants from birds with netting. Spray oak bark 505, *Equisetum arvense* 508 as a fresh tea, and yarrow tea to counter mildew.

Collecting seeds

• Broccoli flowers in its second year. Avoid collecting seed from plants that bolt in their first year, because it will be poor quality.

• Save seed from a minimum of 20 plants to prevent inbreeding. Dry the flower heads indoors and thresh off the seeds.

• Keep broccoli away from other flowering brassicas to prevent it from interbreeding, or cover their blooms.

CATCH CROPS

Broccoli is a slow-growing crop that needs plenty of room to develop. As it grows, make use of the free space around the plants to sow quicker-maturing crops, such as lettuce and radishes. With repeated sowing, you'll reap the rewards of several harvests before the broccoli is ready.

EARTHING UP

Broccoli is a tall crop that is prone to root damage if the stems are rocked by wind on an exposed site. As the plants develop, pile soil around their base and firm it in to provide extra support.

Soil can be mounded around the base of each plant up to the lowest leaves.

	SPRING	SUMMER	FALL	WINTER
Sow				
Harvest				

Time to harvest: **12–16 WEEKS** • Sow ¾in (2cm) deep, 12in (30cm) apart in rows 12–18in (30–45cm) apart.

Rotation information: **ROTATION GROUP 2 • MEDIUM FEEDERS**

Broccoli sprouts

Brassica oleracea
Italica Group

Sometimes called "poor man's asparagus," broccoli sprouts' green or purple flower buds are just as tender and rich in flavor. The plants have a year-round presence in the vegetable patch; choose early and late-maturing varieties for a constant harvest from late winter into spring.

SITE AND SOIL PREPARATION

Broccoli sprouts prefer a sunny site that is open but sheltered. Dig plenty of compost into the soil before planting, ideally with cow manure in the mix. If the soil is too acidic (below pH 6.8), add lime a few months before planting. Work the soil as deep as possible in dry weather, then firm it slightly by walking on it.

SOWING AND PLANTING

On flower days with a descending moon, sow seeds thinly ¾in (2cm) deep indoors from early spring onward, or outside between mid-spring and midsummer. Plant out seedlings slightly deeper so they have firm foundations, on flower days while the moon is descending.

ROUTINE CARE

Water the seedlings regularly while they are establishing; also hoe soil up around the base of the plants when weeding to protect them from wind. Spray horn manure 500 at fall equinox. Tidy up fallen or yellow leaves during fall, and spray barrel compost in late fall, while the moon is descending, to maintain healthy soil microflora.

HARVESTING AND STORING

Pick broccoli sprouts from late winter into late spring. The flowering shoots should be clearly developed but with fairly compact flower heads.

On flower days under an ascending moon, cut the sprouts with a sharp knife, starting with the central shoot, leaving smaller sprouts to grow and be harvested later. Pick early in the morning and store fresh florets, unwashed, in open bags in the refrigerator. Wash before freezing.

TROUBLESHOOTING

In early spring make leaves less appetizing to flea beetles with preemptive sprays of oak bark decoction, and *Equisetum arvense* 508 as a fresh tea, ideally under a descending moon.

Collecting seeds

• Broccoli sprouts flower in their second year. Grow the plant in the usual way and allow the seeds to mature on the plant for as long as possible without letting the pods shatter. Dry the mature flower heads indoors, then pull off the seeds.

• Save seed from a minimum of 20 plants to prevent inbreeding. Avoid collecting seed from plants that bolted in their first year. They will be of poor quality.

• Broccoli sprouts will breed with other members of the brassica family that flower at the same time. Prevent this by stopping other brassicas from flowering; or put a bag over them just before they do.

PEST PROTECTION

Tender, young plants are prone to both attack by birds and damage from the caterpillars of cabbage white butterflies—cover them with fine netting to deter both pests. Growing nasturtiums near broccoli will keep aphids away.

Secure the netting at soil level to prevent pests from creeping underneath it. Weigh it down with soil or rocks.

Support this tall crop by tying it loosely to stakes in fall.

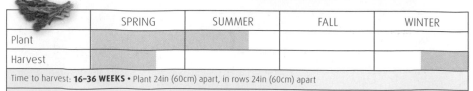

	SPRING	SUMMER	FALL	WINTER
Plant	███	██		
Harvest	█			██

Time to harvest: **16–36 WEEKS** • Plant 24in (60cm) apart, in rows 24in (60cm) apart

Rotation information: **ROTATION GROUP 2 • MEDIUM FEEDERS**

Globe artichokes
Cynara scolymus

Although globe artichokes are related to the thistle family, these statuesque, low maintenance perennials provide a crop that is regarded as a delicacy in their native Italy. The edible parts can be found at the base of the leathery flower petals, and deep within the heart of the flower itself.

SITE AND SOIL PREPARATION
Originating from Sicily, globe artichokes like a sunny, sheltered spot in full sun, and almost any fertile soil that is slightly acidic.

SOWING AND PLANTING
Globe artichokes can be grown from seed sown on flower days, preferably with a descending moon in early spring, but they will take three years to crop. You can achieve the same result in two years by growing sideshoots or offsets divided from existing plants and planted out in late spring. During a descending moon period, plant offsets—or 4in (10cm) high seedlings—in holes no deeper than a trowel blade and backfill with garden soil and compost.

ROUTINE CARE
Cut the main stem in the first year as soon as the flower appears to enable the plant to produce a stronger crop over the next 3–4 years, after which it should again be divided. In early spring when the moon is descending, spray the bed with horn manure 500 before the plants start growing, then mulch with compost covered by straw. Spray horn silica 501 early in the morning when silvery flowering stems appear deep in the base of the leaves.

HARVESTING AND STORING
Each plant produces about 12 heads from late summer to early fall. In an ascending moon period, pick the topmost bud first before the scales open, then work down the plant, harvesting the tight buds. Boil the heads; then remove the petals to eat their tender base dipped in oil or butter. The final delicacy is the center of the flower, often preserved in olive oil.

TROUBLESHOOTING
Backfill newly planted offshoots fully or they will die from lack of water or from frost.

Collecting seeds
- It is exceptionally easy to collect seeds from globe artichokes.
- Grow the plants in the usual way, but instead of harvesting the buds, let the flower heads develop and produce seed.
- Cut the flower heads when mature—they look like thistles—and dry them under cover. Extract the seeds by placing the seed head in a bag, and pounding it until the seeds fall out.

SPACE WELL
These large perennials need plenty of room and time to establish fully, but their silvery sea-green leaves and large thistlelike flowers are highly decorative so are often given space in an ornamental border.

New plants can be grown from offsets cut away from mature plants and planted out in late spring.

Harvesting the uppermost king bud first encourages further buds to develop farther down the plant.

Globe artichokes become inedibly tough once the flowers have opened.

	SPRING	SUMMER	FALL	WINTER
Plant				
Harvest				

Time to harvest: **64-68 WEEKS** • Plant 3–5ft (90cm–1.5m) apart

Rotation information: **ROTATION GROUP 4 • MEDIUM FEEDERS**

Pisces
the Fish

Cancer
the Crab

Leaf days

Leaf days occur when the moon passes the constellations associated with the element of water—Pisces, Cancer, and Scorpius. Water is vital for all life on earth, but in the biodynamic garden it is particularly significant for crops grown for their leaves, whose main constituent is water. They include spinach, cabbage, and aromatic herbs like parsley; trees or shrubs grown as hedges; and even the grass in your lawn. Leaf crops are best cultivated under a descending moon, but the speed at which some develop means that often you won't want to wait for a leaf day to maintain them. Be pragmatic: if work cannot be done on a leaf day, the root day rhythm is the next best option. Aim to harvest when the moon is ascending, ideally on a flower or fruit day, when the forces are concentrated in the upper part of the plant—you'll gain a few days of extra storage.

Leaf days and lunar cycles

☙ The moon passes a water-leaf constellation every 8–9 days, and spends 1½–2½ days in each.

☙ In the northern hemisphere the moon is on its ascending cycle when it travels through Pisces.

☙ The moon's path is descending when it passes in front of the constellations of Cancer and Scorpius.

Scorpius
the Scorpion

Things to do on…

Leaf days

A strong association with water means that these are the optimal days for tending leafy vegetables and stem crops, including lettuce, asparagus, and rhubarb. It is the watery component that makes salad greens so refreshing in salads on hot days—the challenge is to achieve the crispness that helps leaf crops store well and taste best.

• **Sow seeds 2–3 days before full moon** to encourage strong germination for all leaf day crops including greens like arugula.

• **Leaf days leading up to moon–opposition Saturn** are best for transplanting leaf crop seedlings: the moon's watery influences are balanced with the crispness associated with Saturn and silica.

• **Ascending and waxing moon periods** are when the upper part of the plant is most vital, which makes them good times to spray leaf crops with flavor-enhancing teas.

• **Descending or waning moon periods** when the earth is breathing in are the most efficient times to water or spray liquid manures on the soil around leaf day crops.

• **When the moon is at perigee** protect leafy crops from chewing insects by spraying *Equisetum arvense* 508 as a fresh tea. This not only makes the leaves firmer, and less appealing to pests, they will also be more appetizing for you.

Asparagus

Kohlrabi

Water liquid manure feeds onto the on leaf days with a descending moon

Trim vigorous hedges under an ascending moon to help slow down their growth.

Lay sod or sow seed for a lawn—but mow on a leaf day and the grass will grow faster.

Transplant crops like Swiss chard on days with a descending moon.

Birds love to eat up young seedlings, so protect transplants with netting.

Plant hedges and ornamental foliage shrubs on leaf days when the moon is descending.

Sow Florence fennel and other stem crops just before a full moon for good germination.

Apply horn manure 500 and soil sprays in large droplets under a descending moon.

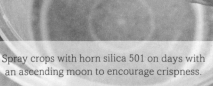

Spray crops with horn silica 501 on days with an ascending moon to encourage crispness.

Thin leaf crops like chicory when the moon is ascending—and enjoy the thinnings in salads.

Cabbage
Brassica oleracea Capitata Group

There are cabbage types of all sorts for every season: spring, summer, fall, and winter. If you sow the appropriate varieties at the right times, you can eat vitamin-rich greens fresh from the garden all year round. All are grown in a similar way.

SITE AND SOIL PREPARATION

Cabbage likes any soil that is humus-rich and slightly alkaline. Dig in cow manure compost the season before planting, adding lime, if needed. To avoid clubroot, do not grow them where other brassicas have grown in the previous three years. Spray barrel compost on the soil during a descending moon before sowing or transplanting.

SOWING AND PLANTING

Sow directly ¾in (2cm) deep and 4in (10cm) apart into furrows 6in (15cm) apart or in pots, under a descending moon. Follow the same lunar rhythm to transplant—spring and summer types in fall, and larger, denser fall and winter varieties in midsummer—once the seedlings have 6–7 leaves. Dip their roots in a sloppy paste of horn manure 500 and clay, for better rooting and greater pest resistance, and plant each out as deep as the first seed leaf, to its final location.

ROUTINE CARE

Weed regularly and earth up around the bases to support the plants and keep the roots moist. Spray horn silica 501 at sunrise over the cabbage tops, once they start putting on leaves, but only if horn manure 500 was previously used. Boost growth of spring, summer, and fall cabbage by spraying them with stinging nettle liquid manure, in the evening under an ascending moon. Remove any yellowing leaves.

HARVESTING AND STORING

Pick under an ascending moon, if possible. You can cut leaves as spring greens before the plants form heads. As soon as the heads of hearting cabbages are firm, pick them, otherwise they may crack. Store whole fall and winter cabbages in a cool cellar or pickle them—sauerkraut is a classic way of preserving cabbage.

TROUBLESHOOTING

Use brassica collars and fabric to protect plants from cabbage root flies and cabbage white caterpillars; grazing chickens are even more effective. Grow lettuce as a catch crop around new cabbage in summer to shade out weeds and keep the soil moist. If cabbage fail to develop hearts, they either lacked food and water early on, or suffered cramped roots at transplanting.

VARIETIES TO TRY

Choose from round or pointed cabbage with compact or loose heads and smooth or crinkled leaves. They come in shades of light, dark, or blue-green, in white, or even in red or purple.

Loose-leaf cabbage forms open heads with no hearts. Cut them off whole at the base or as separate, loose leaves.

Hearting cabbage forms heads of tightly packed leaves. There are different varieties available to grow in summer and winter, so you can harvest them year round.

SPRING AND SUMMER CABBAGE

	SPRING	SUMMER	FALL	WINTER
Sow				
Harvest				

FALL AND WINTER CABBAGE

	SPRING	SUMMER	FALL	WINTER
Sow				
Harvest				

Time to harvest: **14–36 WEEKS** • Plant or thin to 12–20in (30–50cm) apart, depending on variety

Rotation information: **ROTATION GROUP 2 • MEDIUM FEEDERS**

Collecting seeds

• Grow cabbage in the usual way, but instead of cutting them, leave at least 20 plants to flower for the best seed.

• Cut the flower stalks when the first seed pods turn brown; take indoors to thresh, dry, and store the seeds.

• Cabbage may interbreed with nearby brassicas. To prevent this, pinch off flowering stems on the other brassicas or put bags over the plants just before they flower.

Brussels sprouts

Brassica oleracea Gemmifera Group

A quintessential winter vegetable, Brussels sprouts withstand frost and are very nutritious, with especially high levels of vitamin C, and substances that protect against some forms of cancer. Conveniently, you can harvest the sprouts in batches as needed during the darkest, coldest months of the year.

SITE AND SOIL PREPARATION

Brussels sprouts prefer rich loam that is not too acidic—lime the soil if needed. In winter or early spring, under a descending moon, dig the bed fairly deeply, working in plenty of compost or well-rotted manure, cow manure, if possible, and chopped comfrey leaves for potassium. Let the soil settle and become firm. Do not grow Brussels sprouts where brassicas were planted in the last three years. They thrive if planted in a plot after early potatoes and beans.

SOWING AND PLANTING

Sow seed at a descending moon, ¾in (2cm) deep indoors or under cloches, for a crop all through winter. Once seedlings have seven leaves, transplant them, in the afternoon at a descending moon, up to the level of the seed leaves; stagger them in the rows to reduce wind damage. Spray horn manure 500 in the planting holes and firm well to encourage strong roots.

ROUTINE CARE

Keep well weeded and watered until the plants establish and shade out the soil. Feed with a kelp, stinging nettle, or comfrey liquid manure in the evening to deter aphids. In very hot or changeable weather, spray oak bark decoction or chamomile tea on the foliage in the morning to minimize stress to the plants. Buttress tall, overwintering plants against winter winds by tying them in to supporting stakes.

HARVESTING AND STORING

You can start harvesting in late summer, but the flavor improves after winter frost. Twist or slice off a few sprouts at a time from each plant, starting at the bases. When all sprouts are gone, cut the leafy tops. Sprouts freeze well. In severe cold, uproot whole plants and hang in a cool, frost-free place.

TROUBLESHOOTING

Use collars or fabric to protect against root flies and cabbage white caterpillars. Soft sprouts result from a lack of soil potassium; cut off the tops in fall to avoid this. Intercrop seedling sprouts with lettuce and spinach to help keep the soil moist and weed free.

Collecting seeds

• Brussels sprouts flower in their second year. Grow them in the usual way, but leave several sprouts to flower on each plant. Collect from at least 20 plants for the best quality seed.

• The flower heads develop from the sprouts. Cut them when the first pods ripen and take indoors to extract, dry, and store the seeds.

• Brussels sprouts may cross-pollinate with other brassicas. Avoid this by preventing other nearby brassicas from flowering. Another option is to cover their flower heads with paper bags, secured with rubber bands, just before they open.

PROVIDING SUPPORT

Sprouts grow slowly and steadily, but also reach up to 3ft (90cm), so position them somewhere with no prevailing, buffeting winds. Firming soil at planting, and earthing up the plants prevents wind rock.

REMOVING LOWER LEAVES

As they grow taller, the lower leaves of Brussels sprout stems start to turn yellow. This is not a sign of poor health, but the leaves are best removed to allow good airflow between the plants and prevent disease.

Cut or pull yellowing leaves from the stem. Add them to the compost heap.

🌰🌰🌰	SPRING	SUMMER	FALL	WINTER
Sow				
Harvest				

Time to harvest: **20–25 WEEKS** • Plant or thin to 24in (60cm) apart

Rotation information: **ROTATION GROUP 2 • MEDIUM FEEDERS**

Swiss chard
and spinach beet
Beta vulgaris subsp. *cicla* var. *flavescens*

Collectively known as chard, these crops are easy to grow, less prone to bolting than spinach, and very nutritious. They are good sources of vitamins A, C, and K, iron, and calcium. Spinach beet is also called perpetual spinach because it survives over winter to provide a second crop of leaves in spring.

SITE AND SOIL PREPARATION
Chard varieties like an airy site in full sun or dappled shade and rich, moisture-retentive loam. Feed the soil with very well-rotted compost before sowing or planting. Work the soil under a descending moon into a fine tilth to mix the compost evenly and thoroughly into the soil. Spray horn manure 500 in the afternoon on the bed before or soon after sowing.

SOWING AND PLANTING
Start both crops indoors in early spring or sow outdoors under a descending moon from mid-spring to early summer. Make a second, later sowing of spinach beet in mid- to late summer for overwintering. Before sowing, soak seeds in BC overnight or sprinkle them on a clean cloth and drip BC on it until it is sodden. Sow the seed in 1in (2.5cm) deep furrows that are 15in (38cm) apart for spinach beet and 18in (45cm) apart for Swiss chard. Sow spinach beet seed more closely if harvesting as salad greens. Lightly sprinkle compost and soil over the seeds and firm gently. Plant out seedlings when large enough to handle.

ROUTINE CARE
Water regularly. Mulch if necessary to keep the soil moist. Mist horn silica 501 over the tops at sunrise, no sooner than three weeks after transplanting or after the young leaves form on direct-sown plants.

HARVESTING AND STORING
Harvest leaves and midribs with a knife, rather than pulling them off and disturbing the roots. Do not cut too low into the heart, especially on the ribbed types—it discourages new growth.

TROUBLESHOOTING
If the leaves get spotty and tough, or taste bitter and earthy, compost used in the soil may not have rotted fully or too many liquid manures were used. Lettuce (*see p.197*) and spinach (*see p.192*) make good companions for chard crops, because they need similar soils and watering.

Collecting seeds
• Both crops flower in their second year. Leave at least 20 plants over winter; protect Swiss chard with cloches or a deep mulch and it will come back in the spring.
• Spinach beet and Swiss chard cross-pollinate, so cage the plants or allow only one to set seed in alternate years. Once the seed heads mature, cut them off and extract the seeds, which store well.

COLORFUL CHARD
Swiss chard, also known as seakale beet or silverbeet, is a colorful vegetable. Its leaves are larger, curlier, and glossier than spinach and vary in shade from deep green to greenish-yellow and reddish-green.

Varieties with brightly colored midribs retain their vivid hues even when cooked, making for attractive dishes.

The broad stalks may be colored white, yellow, pink, or red and can be cooked in the same way as asparagus.

Swiss chard may develop especially bright coloring in the winter cold.

	SPRING	SUMMER	FALL	WINTER
Sow				
Harvest				

Time to harvest: **8–52 WEEKS** • Thin to 4in (10cm) apart for salad leaves and up to 12in (30cm) for larger leaves and midribs
Rotation information: **ROTATION GROUP 2 • MEDIUM FEEDERS**

Napa cabbage
Brassica rapa Pekinensis Group

Popular in Asian cooking for its hardiness and high vitamin content, napa cabbage has an appealing crunchiness and mild flavor that works well in salads, soups, and stir-fries. There are three main types to choose from: barrel-shaped or hearted cabbages; tall, cylindrical cabbages; and loose leaf varieties.

SITE AND SOIL PREPARATION

Napa cabbage needs humus-rich, moisture-retentive, but free-draining soil. A plot where green beans have grown has the nitrogen-rich soil this crop needs. Dig in some biodynamic compost, made preferably with cow manure, before sowing or planting in the same 13-day, descending moon period. Alternatively, spray BC on the bed the day before sowing.

SOWING AND PLANTING

Napa cabbage needs moderate, cool temperatures when forming its leaves or it will bolt. Sowing in the days leading up to a full moon reduces the risk of bolting. Sow in early spring under cover 4–6 weeks before the last frost to harvest before midsummer heat causes it to bolt. For fall eating, sow after midsummer—the days are shortening and bolting is less likely. Sow seeds ½in (1.5cm) deep and 4in (10cm) apart.

ROUTINE CARE

Keep the plants evenly watered. Spray spring-sown seedlings with 4–6 leaves on successive days, with horn manure 500 on the bed one afternoon to resist bolting, and horn silica 501 over the tops the next morning to improve the flavor. For the same benefits, spray summer-sown seedlings with 500 once in the afternoon under a descending moon, then at an ascending moon with 501, a month before harvesting the leaves. Mulch with compost as the plants mature, to keep the soil moist and at a constant temperature. Shade in sunny or hot weather and spray with chamomile, dandelion, and stinging nettle teas in the early morning or late evening to prevent heat stress, improve flavor, and promote good health.

HARVESTING AND STORING

Harvest leaves or mature heads (*see right*) to eat within a few days. Wrap hearted types in plastic and store upright to keep longer.

TROUBLESHOOTING

Indoor-sown seedlings are less likely to bolt in biodegradable pots. Grow this crop with its fellow brassicas, such as Brussels sprouts, cabbage, and cauliflower, for easy rotation.

Collecting seeds

- Napa cabbage flowers in its second year by early summer. Do not collect seeds from plants that bolt in their first year—they will be of poor quality.

- Overwinter at least 20 plants. Once the seed heads turn brown, pick them, dry them indoors, and thresh out the seeds.

- This crop cross-pollinates with other brassicas. Avoid it by preventing nearby brassicas from flowering or put paper bags over their flower heads before they open.

CUT AND COME AGAIN

Napa cabbage matures within 8–10 weeks, but you can harvest the outer leaves in several passes from tender, young plants well before this, as well as the flowering shoots. If you cut a plant at the base, you can crop it again (*see below*).

Cut adult plants to within 2in (5cm) of the soil, leaving the stumps to reshoot.

Just a few weeks after the first cut, new leaves will be ready to harvest.

	SPRING	SUMMER	FALL	WINTER
Plant				
Harvest				

Time to harvest: **4–10 WEEKS** • Thin to 12–18in (30–45cm) apart, depending on variety

Rotation information: **ROTATION GROUP 2 • MEDIUM FEEDERS**

Bok choy
Brassica rapa Chinensis Group

Easy to grow but prone to bolting, bok choy—or pak choi, as it is sometimes called—is a type of Chinese cabbage that has tangy green leaves and juicy white stems, but no head. Eat on the day of picking, raw in salads, or added to stir-fries and soups.

SITE AND SOIL PREPARATION

Choose a site with full sun and a dark fertile soil—a spot dressed with biodynamic compost for a previous crop is ideal. If the plants lack food or water, they will soon bolt, so hoe the topsoil lightly and incorporate mature compost evenly right across the bed, if necessary. Then spray horn manure 500 when the moon is descending to keep the soil airy and well drained.

SOWING AND PLANTING

Either sow direct under cover in mid-spring to avoid transplanting, or transplant seedlings started indoors. The plants are likely to bolt if sown much later, so wait for the days to shorten in late summer before sowing again, allowing 12in (30cm) between plants so the plants can mature fully before the first frost. Timing sowings to midpoints between lunar apogee and perigee, or to Moon–Saturn oppositions, helps promote balanced growth. Winter hardy varieties sown in late fall can survive outdoors but need the protection of fabric or cloches. A greenhouse is the best option.

ROUTINE CARE

This type of cabbage has shallow roots, so keep the soil moist with light sprinklings rather than heavy drenches, which cause the soil to leech valuable humus. The roots are also sensitive to temperature changes and need water that is at least as warm as the soil. Also the large but gossamerlike leaves dislike being battered and bruised by wind. Spring sowings can be sprayed with horn silica 501, but only in the afternoon to reduce the risk of bolting. Spray late-summer sowings with 501 in the month before fall equinox on a descending moon to help concentrate the flavor.

HARVESTING AND STORING

Bok choy sown in mid-spring provides cut-and-come-again leaves or thinnings within a few weeks of planting. Within 6–8 weeks the plants will have firm, succulent hearts to be cut and used fresh from the plot. Harvest on leaf days when the moon is ascending.

TROUBLESHOOTING

Spray yarrow tea to keep powdery mildew at bay, and dandelion tea to de-stress plants in variable weather and temperatures.

Collecting seeds

• Bok choy flowers in its first year. Grow plants normally, but allow them to flower, rather than harvesting them. When the seed heads are brown, take them inside to harvest the seed.

• Collect seed from at least 20 plants for the best diversity.

• To stop bok choy from crossbreeding, prevent nearby brassicas from flowering or put a bag over their blooms.

SOWING FROM SEED

Choose a site that has been clear of brassicas for at least 3 years, and sow seeds directly into compost-rich soil to avoid transplanting. The first leaves will be ready within weeks.

Sow seeds evenly and thin seedlings to their correct spacing. Water the rows and keep them moist to prevent bolting.

Garden fabric will protect spring-grown bok choy from flea beetles, and winter-grown crops from hard frosts.

Harvest the whole plant by cutting just below the base of the stems.

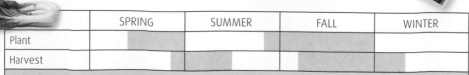

	SPRING	SUMMER	FALL	WINTER
Plant				
Harvest				

Time to harvest: **6-8 WEEKS** • Sow ½in (1.5cm) deep. Plant 8–12in (20–30cm) apart in rows 12–20in (30–50cm) apart

Rotation information: **ROTATION GROUP 2 • MEDIUM FEEDERS**

Chinese broccoli
Brassica oleracea Alboglabra Group

This trouble-free, Asian brassica can be spring-sown in a small plot to produce useful fall harvests, then sown again to overwinter for a spring crop. Grown for its crisp flowering stems and dark, wrinkled leaves that look a bit like kale, Chinese broccoli is also known as Chinese kale, "kai-lan." It has a mustardlike flavor when eaten raw in salads or steamed, and packs a punch in stir-fries.

SITE AND SOIL PREPARATION

A small bed in full sun or partial shade will suit this compact crop, but make sure no other brassicas have been grown there for the previous three years. Chinese broccoli thrives in fertile, well-drained soil, dressed lightly with biodynamic compost that has been dug in well. Rake the soil to a fine tilth, ready for sowing, and spray with horn manure 500, ideally on a leaf day under the descending moon, to safeguard the kind of humus development that allows plants to produce fine feeder roots.

SOWING AND PLANTING

For a crop at the beginning of summer, you can try sowing seeds from early spring onward in soil that has been warmed under cloches; however, if the soil is too cold, the seedlings will bolt. For most varieties—and there are many—it is better to sow in late spring after the last frost, or to sow from late summer onward for an early to late fall harvest.Sown in early fall, Chinese broccoli will crop in spring but needs protection from winter cold. Sow seeds shallowly, about ¼in (0.5cm) deep, 1–2in (2.5–5cm) apart on a leaf day when the moon is descending. Thin the seedlings 6–10in (15–25cm) apart, in rows 14–20 in (35–50cm) apart.

ROUTINE CARE

The most important task is to prevent plants from bolting by keeping them well watered throughout their growing season. Spring-sown seedlings can be given a morning spray of horn silica 501 without risk of bolting, but if the flower heads are starting to form, spray with chamomile instead. Late-summer sowings can be given horn silica 501 around fall equinox, whatever their stage of development. Comfrey liquid manure will provide plenty of essential potassium for leafy greens. Apply all of these biodynamic preparations on leaf days when the moon is descending.

HARVESTING AND STORING

Chinese broccoli is ready to pick within 6–10 weeks. Harvest the plants successionally when the moon is ascending, either by cutting the main stem when two or three flowers are open (these are considered a delicacy); or by clipping the top of the main stem to encourage side growth and an extended harvest.

TROUBLESHOOTING

Chinese broccoli beds are generally trouble-free as long as you keep on top of weeds. Try interplanting with basil, beans, and garlic.

Collecting seeds

• Chinese broccoli flowers in its second year. Grow the plants in the usual way, but allow at least 20 to overwinter and flower. When the seed heads are brown, take them indoors to harvest the seeds.

• It is not worthwhile to collect seeds from plants that bolted in their first year; they will be of poor quality.

• Chinese broccoli is a brassica, and will cross-pollinate with other family members. Prevent this by stopping nearby brassicas from flowering, or by placing a bag over their flowers just before they open.

	SPRING	SUMMER	FALL	WINTER
Plant				
Harvest				

Time to harvest: **6–10 WEEKS** • Thin to 6–10in (15–25cm) apart in rows 14–20 in (35–50cm) apart

Rotation information: **ROTATION GROUP 2 • MEDIUM FEEDERS**

Kohlrabi
Brassica oleracea
Gongylodes Group

This northern European member of the brassica family produces a surprising turniplike ball, which is prized for its sweet, nutty taste. The pale green, white, or purple swellings at the base of the leaf stem are not roots—they sit on the ground at soil level. Try hardier purple types of kohlrabi for a beautiful fall harvest.

SITE AND SOIL PREPARATION

Prepare the ground in the fall before you plant with compost made at least in part from well-rotted cow manure. A non-acidic soil is best to avoid clubroot. Work the compost in on either a leaf or root day when the moon is descending.

SOWING AND PLANTING

Sowing under a descending moon, early kohlrabi can be started inside from late winter, and planted out under a descending moon when large enough to handle. Alternatively, wait until the soil has warmed above 50°F (10°C) and sow outside from early spring, under cloches if needed. For later sowing and fall harvesting, choose a slower-growing purple variety. Watering is essential for kohlrabi and can be made more efficient by spraying horn manure 500 during sowing or transplanting, followed by a light mulch, especially on lighter, sandy-loam soils.

ROUTINE CARE

When the plants start to form bulbs, spray horn silica 501 in the morning, under a descending moon, to boost flavor. Spray *Equisetum arvense* 508 liquid manure in wet summers; stinging nettle liquid manure in hot ones; and comfrey in an average summer. Ideally, time sprays to a descending moon on leaf days.

HARVESTING AND STORING

For tender kohlrabi, harvest when they are between golf ball and tennis ball size, when the moon is ascending. Both summer and fall crops are at their best freshly picked, although fall kohlrabi can be stored in a box of sand.

TROUBLESHOOTING

Interplant later sowings of kohlrabi with lettuce: the leaves act as a living mulch, keeping the soil around the plants cool in summer.

Collecting seeds

• For the best seeds, save them from a plot of at least 20 plants of the same variety.

• Grow kohlrabi in the usual way, without letting the plants flower, and leave them to overwinter, mulching if necessary. In very cold regions, dig up the roots in fall, store under cover, and plant them out in spring.

• Allow the plants to flower in summer. Collect the seed as each flower head ripens, usually the central one first, then the sideshoots.

• Kohlrabi will cross-pollinate with other brassicas if they flower nearby at the same time.

SOWING UNDER COVER

In milder areas, sow early crops under cover in small pots in late winter to give them a head start. Harden the plants off before planting out with protection from frost. Sow every two weeks for a continuous supply.

Sow 3–4 seeds into each small pot of compost. Water and keep them under cover. Germination takes 1–2 weeks.

Thin overcrowded seedlings and plant out the strongest when each plant has three or four true leaves.

To harvest, lift the whole plant or cut the bulbs just above the roots.

	SPRING	SUMMER	FALL	WINTER
Sow				
Harvest				

Time to harvest: **20–24 WEEKS** • Plant 8–12in (20–30cm) apart in rows spaced 12–15in (30–38cm) apart

Rotation information: **ROTATION GROUP 2 • MEDIUM FEEDERS**

Mustard greens

Brassica juncea

These vitamin-packed, cabbagelike greens have distinctive mustard and pepper flavors—hot and spicy in salads, mild and tangy when cooked. Harvest in summer or grow this useful winter-hardy crop from fall onward.

SITE AND SOIL PREPARATION

Mustard greens like dark, fertile soil, ideally where biodynamic compost was added for a previous crop. Choose a bright location with some shade to reduce the risk of bolting. Before sowing, spray horn manure 500 when the moon is descending.

SOWING AND PLANTING

Warm the soil using cloches, then sow seed after the last frost, and under a descending moon. Sow midsummer to early fall for plants that overwinter in the ground.

ROUTINE CARE

Keep the bed well watered throughout summer. For spring sowings, wait until the first leaves have formed and spray horn silica 501 in the afternoon to increase flavor. For sowings after midsummer, it is safe to spray horn silica 501 in the morning without increasing the risk of bolting. Spray under a descending moon.

HARVESTING AND STORING

Harvest young leaves and flowering shoots as a cut-and-come-again crop but avoid overstripping plants destined to stay in the ground through winter.

TROUBLESHOOTING

Applied under a descending moon, yarrow, chamomile, and stinging nettle teas help spring-sown seeds stay healthy and stress-free in inclement or unsettled weather. Oak bark decoction provides extra protection for plants intended for overwintering, especially those intended to be saved as seeds (*see below*).

Mustard greens are brassicas, so bear this in mind for crop rotation. Spray yarrow tea to keep powdery mildew at bay. Spray dandelion tea to destress plants if the weather and ambient temperatures are variable.

Collecting seeds

• Start plants for seeds in late spring to allow them one full year in the ground. Keep them moist to prevent them from bolting in the first year.

• Leave the plants in the soil over the winter, and let them flower and set seed.

• Cut the whole plant and hang it indoors to dry with a paper bag over the seed heads.

• To prevent cross-pollination, allow just one type of mustard green (*Brassica juncea* family) to flower if intending to save seed.

Oak bark is a simple decoction made from finely crumbled oak bark (*see p.36*), which helps protect mustard greens from gray mold, powdery and downy mildew, and pests.

Break oak bark down into small pieces before boiling it in water.

COLORFUL CROP

There are many varieties of mustard greens with different textures and colors but the same distinctive peppery flavor. Some have attractive leaves that are veined or tinged with red and purple.

	SPRING	SUMMER	FALL	WINTER
Sow				
Harvest				
Time to harvest: **20–36 WEEKS** • Plant out 4–6in (10–15cm) apart in rows 24–30in (60–75cm) apart				
Rotation information: **ROTATION GROUP 2 • MEDIUM FEEDERS**				

Spinach
Spinacia oleracea

Spinach is a superfood, loaded with vitamins, fiber, and nutrients, especially if eaten raw. It is easy to overcook, and not just in the home kitchen, where it can turn soggy. In the garden, too, spinach bolts in high summer temperatures, or if left unwatered for more than a day. As an alternative in summer, try New Zealand spinach (*Tetragonia tetragonoides*), which is less prone to bolting in hot spells.

SITE AND SOIL PREPARATION
Spinach likes good soil that drains well but retains moisture. Add well-rotted manure or biodynamic compost during a descending moon, well before sowing. To maintain soil sponginess, spray horn manure 500 before and after sowing.

SOWING AND PLANTING
Sow seeds under cover from mid-spring, on leaf days during a descending moon, and harden them off and plant out when the moon is descending. Sprinkle a handful of undiluted BC in the base of the hole when planting out. Spinach can be sown outdoors from early spring to reach maturity before the summer temperatures rise. Large-leaf, winter-hardy varieties can be sown in late summer to overwinter. Sow New Zealand spinach at double the spacing, and soften its hard seeds in barrel compost overnight before sowing.

ROUTINE CARE
Before thinning the seedlings, spray with horn silica 501 early one morning on a leaf day, once the young leaves are unfolded. Mulch lightly with mature compost, covered with straw to reflect heat and light, and to retain soil moisture. That evening, spray the bed with chamomile tea, and the next day, apply kelp or stinging nettle liquid manure.

HARVESTING AND STORING
Harvest as a cut-and-come-again crop until hot weather arrives, then cut plants whole before they bolt. Pinch rather than pull the leaves off to avoid rocking the sensitive roots.

TROUBLESHOOTING
To avoid downy mildew, keep the bed weed free, and harvest only the largest leaves to promote good airflow.

Collecting seeds

• Spinach plants are male or female, so allow several to flower to ensure you have enough seed-bearing female plants.

• As soon as the plants begin to die off after flowering, pull up the seed-bearing plants whole. Hang them under cover for a few weeks until the seeds start to turn brown.

• Once the seeds change color, harvest them from the pods, and store them in paper envelopes.

• To ensure pure seeds, only collect them from one type.

SOWING DIRECT
Spinach is prone to bolting if transplanted, so is best sown directly where it is to grow. Sow the seeds in furrows 1in (2.5cm) deep, spaced 8–12in (20–30cm) apart. Keep the seedlings moist.

Spinach seedlings are prone to attack from birds, which tear at their leaves. Protect the plants with plastic netting.

When harvesting the leaves, only take a few from each plant at a time to avoid sapping the plant's strength.

NEW ZEALAND SPINACH
Heat tolerant, grow it as an alternative to normal spinach during the hot summer weeks.

	SPRING	SUMMER	FALL	WINTER
Sow				
Harvest				

Time to harvest: **6–12 WEEKS** • Plant 3–6in (7–15cm) apart

Rotation information: **ROTATION GROUP 3 • MEDIUM FEEDERS**

Kale
Brassica oleracea Acephala Group

Kale is the hardiest of the winter brassicas, and can withstand temperatures down to -5°F (-15°C). It is a type of cabbage with a very tough stem but no heart. The only edible parts are its large leaves, which can be smooth or curled (Scotch), green or purple—or in the case of Cavolo Nero, Tuscan black cabbage, dark greenish-black. Cooked like cabbage, kale leaves are more strongly flavored, and are rich in calcium. Their flavor sweetens after a frost.

SITE AND SOIL PREPARATION
Kale grows best in well-cultivated, well-drained soil that is not too acidic, and into which well-rotted cow manure has been worked during the fall before planting.

SOWING AND PLANTING
Sow seed directly when the moon is descending from mid-spring, or in cold weather, inside in pots. Thin the seedlings, then spray horn silica 501 on the morning of a leaf day, at least once, for taste. Plant out when the moon is descending in early summer, replacing nitrogen-fixing broad beans or early peas, or early potatoes. Spray horn manure 500 before and at sowing or planting on a leaf day afternoon.

ROUTINE CARE
Water deeply in the evenings to ensure the soil is not dry or compacted. In dry years an *Equisetum arvense* 508 spray will give the plants a boost if applied one evening across the whole plot, soil, and plants. Keep the bed weed free and remove any yellowing leaves from the plants.

HARVESTING AND STORING
Depending on when it was sown or planted, tender young leaves can be harvested two months after sowing when the moon is ascending. Mature leaves can be picked from early fall and into spring. Harvest from the base of the plants upward, without stripping them bare. Plants form sideshoots if the crown is trimmed in early winter. When left to grow, kale bears edible florets in spring.

TROUBLESHOOTING
Kale has good resistance to downy mildew, but in very wet years, keep the leaves healthy by spraying *Equisetum arvense* 508 as a fresh tea. In early winter, protect plants from frost and wind rock by earthing up around the roots to just below the lowest leaves.

Collecting seeds
• For the best seed, save them from a plot of 20 kale plants, all of the same type. Grow them in the normal way without letting them flower.

• Leave the plants outside over winter, let them flower the following summer, and collect the seeds. The plants will benefit from being staked, because the flower heads are tall.

• Kale will cross-pollinate with other brassicas if they are allowed to flower nearby at the same time, which should be avoided.

TRANSPLANTING
If you don't have space for a seedbed in which to sow and then transplant your seedlings, raise them in small pots instead. Sow two seeds in each pot in mid-spring, ½in (1cm) deep. Thin and grow, then plant out.

LONG-TERM HARVEST
Kale is harvested as individual leaves taken from the outside of the plant. They can be picked two months from sowing, and all the way through winter. Allow the plants time to regrow after picking leaves.

	SPRING	SUMMER	FALL	WINTER
Sow				
Harvest				

Time to harvest: **24–28 WEEKS** • Plant out 50cm (20in) apart

Rotation information: **ROTATION GROUP 2 • MEDIUM FEEDERS**

Celery
Apium graveolens var. *dulce*

Celery is a valuable addition to winter dishes—its crunchy stems and tasty leaves enliven salads, stocks, and stews, while its seeds have a fennel-like flavor. There are two types to grow. Trench celery, which is earthed up as it grows to stop the stems from turning green in the light (called blanching), and the self-blanching types that are grown in tightly packed blocks.

SITE AND SOIL PREPARATION

Celery needs well-composted, spongy soil that retains moisture without being boggy. Add lots of biodynamic compost and spray with horn manure 500 two weeks later, under a descending moon, to keep it airy.

SOWING AND PLANTING

Sow indoors under a descending moon. Chamomile and stinging nettle tea can be applied as a fine mist to plants and soil while the moon descends. Also, while the moon is descending, plant self-blanching celery in blocks so the plants shade each other. For trench celery, dig trenches under a descending moon, fork well-rotted compost into the base, and ridge the excavated soil between. With the base of the trench 12in (30cm) deep, plant then water the celery, and spray them with horn manure 500 or BC.

ROUTINE CARE

Mulch plants with straw to retain moisture, and mix in either comfrey, stinging nettle, and kelp liquid manures while watering. To blanch the stems, gradually earth up around trench celery, drawing it from the ridges. For self-blanching types, wrap collars around the outermost plants of each block. To help plants grow vertically, spray horn silica once in the morning 2–3 weeks after planting, again in midsummer in the morning, then on the afternoon of the fall equinox.

HARVESTING AND STORING

Water well before picking to prevent stringiness, and harvest under an ascending moon so that vitality remains in the stems.

TROUBLESHOOTING

To prevent bolting, keep plants well watered and cover newly planted celery with fabric to protect against low temperatures. Grow celery near cabbage and cauliflower to deter cabbage white butterflies from them.

Collecting seeds

• Save seed from a plot of 12 plants of the same variety. Grow them in the normal way, without allowing them to flower in their first year.

• Leave them in the ground over winter. Or, in cold areas lift the roots in fall, store inside, and replant in spring.

• Allow them to flower in summer and collect the seeds. Celery will interbreed with celeriac if both are allowed to flower at the same time.

SOWING SEEDS INDOORS

Celery requires a long growing season, so it is best sown under cover in early spring. The plants are then grown indoors until the risk of frost has passed, when they can be hardened off and planted outside.

Sow the seeds into flats, and prick out the seedlings once they are large enough, giving them more space.

When the risk of frost has passed, plant celery outside 10in (25cm) apart. Keep the plants moist at all times.

Self-blanching celery is planted in blocks to keep the light from the stems.

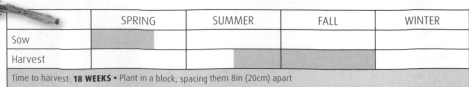

	SPRING	SUMMER	FALL	WINTER
Sow	■			
Harvest		■		

Time to harvest: **18 WEEKS** • Plant in a block, spacing them 8in (20cm) apart

Rotation information: **ROTATION GROUP 3 • MEDIUM FEEDERS**

Florence fennel
Foeniculum vulgare var. *azoricum*

Florence fennel's edible overlapping leaf stems—sometimes described as bulbs—swell just above ground level, and are similar to celery stalks in appearance. In its native Italy, it is eaten raw or as pinzimonio—sprinkled with salt and dipped in olive oil. Florence fennel is distinct from garden fennel, whose fine green, anise-flavored fronds are grown as a herb, and are often used to season fish dishes.

SITE AND SOIL PREPARATION

Florence fennel prefers a sheltered site in full sun or very light shade. It needs fertile sandy-loam soil, richly dressed with biodynamic compost. Plant it after early potatoes or peas, adding extra biodynamic compost first. Mound the soil into furrows to help drainage, if needed, and to give the fine roots something friable and humus-filled to anchor them. Spray horn manure 500 on the soil while the moon descends at or before sowing.

SOWING AND PLANTING

Sow indoors or out under a descending moon when temperatures are above 59°F (15°C). Germination can be patchy if the weather is changeable—sow new batches on successive leaf days, nine days or so apart.

ROUTINE CARE

Hoe regularly, and keep the plants well watered to prevent bolting. As the bulbs start to expand, earth up or mulch them halfway up for support and to blanch the bulbs. Collars can be used for blanching but are less convenient. Once the bulbs are too plump for your thumb and forefinger to meet around, spray horn silica 501, ideally on a clear, sunny, still morning.

HARVESTING AND STORING

Harvest the bulbs when the size of a cooking apple under an ascending moon, cutting them just above the soil. Bulbs will store in the refrigerator for a week if left uncovered.

TROUBLESHOOTING

Pick slugs off young plants, with those that have been mulched being most at risk. Protect plants from frost by covering them with fabric, and by spraying valerian 507 the night before frost is expected.

Collecting seeds

• Let plants mature to form their bulbs, and a tall flower stem will develop in summer.

• After flowering, this stem will droop under the weight of seed. Cut the seed head before the seeds fall to the ground.

• Dry the seed head indoors and in a paper bag to catch the seeds, ready to store.

• Florence fennel may cross-pollinate with garden fennel, coriander, dill, or with any wild fennel growing nearby if they are allowed to flower.

AN EARLY START

Florence fennel can be started under cover for an earlier harvest. The plants are prone to bolting, which can be triggered by root disturbance and dry soil, which you can take simple steps to avoid.

Sow seeds under cover into biodegradable pots to avoid root disturbance when planting out.

The plants should be mulched with biodynamic compost to help retain soil moisture during summer.

If the stump is left in the soil and kept moist, it will commonly reshoot.

	SPRING	SUMMER	FALL	WINTER
Sow				
Harvest				

Time to harvest: **12–22 WEEKS** • Plant 12in (30cm) apart

Rotation information: **ROTATION GROUP 3 • MEDIUM FEEDERS**

Arugula

Eruca vesicaria subsp. *sativa*

Anybody can grow arugula—whether in a wide open garden or a tiny window box—for its long, mustardy leaves. But anybody who does, however, will learn how a quick-growing salad leaf like this can trip up even experienced gardeners. Give it the right amount of heat, light, and water, and it is the perfect ingredient to spice up late spring and early fall salads, soups, and sandwiches.

SITE AND SOIL PREPARATION

Like the equally pungent radish, arugula grows very quickly from seed. Its lobed, luminous green leaves can be ready to eat within 4 weeks of sowing. The soil must be rich, well composted, and moisture retentive. It bolts very quickly in thin soils that dry out in bright sun, so choose somewhere more shaded.

SOWING AND PLANTING

Sow under a descending moon; inside from late winter; outdoors from early spring. To prevent the risk of bolting, avoid sowing near lunar apogee, and stop sowing altogether in midsummer. Resume sowing from late summer into early fall, protecting later batches from cold using fabric or cloches. Sow seed every 10 days or so for a constant supply of leaves and thinnings. Water the soil first, using either barrel compost or horn manure 500 as a soil and seed soak.

ROUTINE CARE

Arugula leaves are at their tenderest and mildest if the soil is cool and earthy smelling. With such a quick-growing crop, and one that can be being sown every other week or so, don't worry about spraying horn manure 500 or horn silica 501. This is especially so if the plot in particular, or the rest of the garden, is being sprayed regularly with these anyway.

HARVESTING AND STORING

Leaves can be picked when the moon is ascending, once large enough to handle, and as closely to the base as it is possible. Picking the leaves small helps to prevent bolting, and means plants keep producing tender leaves. Ensure the soil remains rich and is not allowed to dry out.

TROUBLESHOOTING

A type of wild arugula, *Eruca vesicaria*, is slower growing, less likely to bolt, and hardier than the annual form. Its jagged leaves are more intensely flavored, which they retain for longer after harvesting.

Collecting seeds

• Sow arugula for seed saving as early as possible in spring. Keep it well watered so that it flowers, and thus sets seed, as late as possible.

• Do not save seeds from plants that set seed or bolt quickly—they are of poor quality.

• Collect the seed heads after they and the leaves have turned darkish yellow. Dry the seed heads inside before collecting the seeds.

SOWING SEEDS DIRECTLY

Sow arugula outside, ½in (1cm) deep, in furrows or blocks, from early spring. Since it is very quick growing, sow in regular batches, 10 days apart for a constant supply all summer. Keep moist.

Thin out seedlings as they develop, leaving them 8in (20cm) apart.

PREVENTING BOLTING

Arugula is prone to bolting if it becomes too warm, dry, and hungry. Avoid sowing in full sun, ensure the soil is fertile, and keep plants well watered at all times.

Plants that have bolted can still be harvested until they die off.

	SPRING	SUMMER	FALL	WINTER
Sow				
Harvest				
Time to harvest: **4–6 WEEKS** • Sow and thin to 4in (10cm) apart				
Rotation information: **ROTATION GROUP 2 • MEDIUM FEEDERS**				

Lettuce
Lactuca sativa

Lettuce is commonly shipped hundreds of miles to supermarkets each day, where it has to be thrown away within 48 hours if it is unsold, because it keeps so poorly. However, it is a very easy crop to grow, requiring little more than some light initial digging and basic watering. It is also very quick to grow and can be harvested as individual leaves, cut-and-come-again style, or as large, crunchy heads.

SITE AND SOIL PREPARATION
Lettuce needs a sunny or part-shaded site, on good friable soil that was dressed with biodynamic compost or well-rotted manure, possibly for a previous crop. Try to leave three years between planting it in the same place.

SOWING AND PLANTING
Lettuce needs to grow quickly to be at its best, and will bolt if it lacks food or water. It is best sown late-winter to early fall under a descending moon, and needs temperatures of 50–68°F (10–20°C) to germinate. Start early sowings inside or outside under cloches. Before sowing, spray the bed with horn manure 500, and sow seed every 2–3 weeks. Avoid the lunar apogee, which increases the risk of bolting.

ROUTINE CARE
Spray the seedlings with horn manure 500 as they sprout, or any spare stinging nettle, dandelion, or chamomile teas to maintain balance. Thin the seedlings, using the thinnings as baby greens. Spray horn silica 501 only once the plants have started to form hearts to avoid the risk of bolting. Keep the bed well watered, taking care not to fill the heads of the lettuce, which encourages gray mold and slugs.

HARVESTING AND STORING
Lettuce is best cropped under an ascending moon, early in the morning or in the evening to avoid bitterness and wilt. Plants grown closely in blocks should be cut, rather than pulled, to avoid disturbing nearby plants.

TROUBLESHOOTING
To avoid slugs, cutworms, and gray mold, do not plant lettuce too closely together, and do not overfeed or overwater them. Also be sure to only dress them with biodynamic compost that is fully fermented.

Collecting seeds
• Sow as early as possible, since the plants need a long growing season in order to bear seeds.

• Maintain the plants as for normal harvesting but let about 20 of the best ones run to seed.

• Once the seed head has turned yellow, cut the main stem and take it inside to dry the seeds before they fall to the ground.

• Store the seeds in paper envelopes.

TYPES TO TRY
Lettuce either forms dense hearts that are cut whole, or open heads that are picked as loose leaves. Some have smooth leaves, others uneven edges, but all are grown in the same way.

Lettuce with hearts are cut off at the base, although single leaves can also be picked, if that is preferred.

Many lettuces have textured leaves, such as the oak-leaf type above. Use them to add interest to salads.

Dark-leaf types can scorch in full sun, so given them a little shade.

	SPRING	SUMMER	FALL	WINTER
Sow				
Harvest				
Time to harvest: **6–8 WEEKS** • Plant 6–14in (15–35cm) apart				
Rotation information: **ROTATION GROUP 3 • MEDIUM FEEDERS**				

Corn salad
(Lamb's lettuce)
Valerianella locusta

Corn salad is an easy-to-grow salad crop. It flourishes wild in northern European pastures, where it has acquired the affectionate nickname, lamb's lettuce. Its rounded, sometimes velvety, leaves are no bigger than the palm of a hand, and form in rosettes just above soil level. Eaten raw, they add a cool, rather than spicy, nuttiness to both summer and winter salads.

SITE AND SOIL PREPARATION

Any rich, well-composted soil, in sun or part shade, is ideal for corn salad. Weed the area thoroughly before sowing, then spray the soil with horn manure 500 under a descending moon. Remove any weed seedlings from the bed before sowing, and follow this with a BC spray.

SOWING AND PLANTING

Corn salad is sown directly under a descending moon from mid-spring to early fall. If sown before midsummer, choose bolt-resistant types. It germinates slowly, taking 1–2 weeks, but is then ready to harvest 4–5 weeks after that. Sowings made in early fall are more useful than those made before midsummer, since they do not bolt and are ready to eat when the supply of summer salad is declining. Crucially, plants sown in fall will also survive over winter and into the following spring if kept covered with cloches.

ROUTINE CARE

Keep the bed well weeded, especially early on, otherwise corn salad's low, broad leaves will get crowded out. Pat or lightly tread down disturbed or hoed soil to prevent the soil and the corn salad roots from drying out. Keep the soil fairly moist by watering slowly, and by using a sprinkler head with a fine nozzle. This prevents the leaves from accumulating muddy splashback, which make them more difficult to clean when they arrive in the kitchen. When the moon is descending, give the young plants a boost with stinging nettle liquid manure one afternoon, either sprayed on the plants or mixed in their water. The following morning, apply horn silica 501. Do this anytime midway between the perigee and apogee moon to help stimulate both flavor and yield, while maintaining the plant's balance.

HARVESTING AND STORING

Each plant can be cropped repeatedly under an ascending moon, from spring to fall. Either pick off the larger leaves to let the smaller ones grow, or snap or cut the plant's central stem, which stimulates new growth. Regular harvesting keeps the plant in check, and prevents the leaves from becoming too large and flavorless.

TROUBLESHOOTING

Plants that have stayed in the ground over winter will set seed and spread. Pull them up before this occurs, otherwise the plant can become an invasive and annoying weed.

CLEAN AND WEED-FREE

Corn salad forms a low rosette of leaves that is easily obscured by weeds if they are left to grow, so weed around your plants often. To keep soil from accumulating in their crowns, water plants lightly so the soil isn't splashed up.

Leave enough space between the rows and individual plants, so these low-growers don't crowd each other out.

Collecting seeds

• Leave some fall-sown plants to overwinter in the ground. They are very hardy, so there is no need to mulch them.

• The plants will then flower in mid-spring.

• Collect the seed during midsummer, before it falls from the seed heads, and store.

	SPRING	SUMMER	FALL	WINTER
Sow				
Harvest				

Time to harvest: **4–6 WEEKS** • Sow and thin to 4in (10cm) apart

Rotation information: **ROTATION GROUP 3 • MEDIUM FEEDERS**

Endive
Cichorium endivia

Endive is an agreeably bitter-tasting green salad that is hardy enough to crop from fall into early winter. It is related to chicory, which can cause confusion. There are two main types to grow. Curly or frisée, which has curly outer leaves, and sweeter-tasting, broadleaf escarole or Batavian, which has a more upright head.

SITE AND SOIL PREPARATION

Endive enjoys fertile, well-drained soil with a loose texture. It can be grown following a previous crop that was well composted before planting, such as early or main potatoes, or nitrogen-fixing peas and beans.

SOWING AND PLANTING

Before sowing under a descending moon, add biodynamic compost to the furrows. Thin the seedlings as they develop, spraying them with horn manure 500 anytime under a descending moon. Sow curly types in batches from late spring to midsummer; hardier Batavian types are sown late summer and early fall.

ROUTINE CARE

Keep plants well watered, and encourage their growth by applying dandelion tea before thinning, and yarrow tea afterward, when the moon is descending. Weed plants regularly.

HARVESTING AND STORING

Harvest under an ascending moon, picking young leaves as a cut-and-come-again crop and mature heads whole. Batavian types can be protected from light frost using cloches or straw mulch. Heavy frost will kill them, so place them under cover for blanching.

TROUBLESHOOTING

Endive is fairly disease resistant, but if conditions are wet and humid, spray *Equisteum arvense* 508 liquid manure on the bed at seedling stage, then as a tea as they mature. Do this under an ascending moon. Deter slugs with pine needle mulch, a sprinkling of sage leaves, or sprays made from absinthe and fern, or pine nut extract. Avoid wetting the plants when watering to prevent root maggots. If the tips are scored in hot weather, spray horn silica 501 very early one morning, high above the plants, in a fine mist.

Collecting seeds

- Prevent endive from bolting in the year it is sown, and leave it to overwinter.
- In the second season, let the plants flower and collect the pods.
- Dry pods indoors, separate out the seeds, and store.
- For pure seeds, only save them from one variety of endive. If two types flower near each other they will interbreed. To prevent this, either cage plants, or only allow one type to flower.

SOWING DIRECT

Endive is best sown directly in furrows, ½in (1cm) deep, where it is to grow. Sow from late spring to early fall, depending on the type you are growing. Keep the seedlings moist.

Water the base of the seed furrow before sowing to encourage the seeds to germinate more quickly.

Thin out the seedlings as they develop, leaving the remaining plants 9–12in (23–30cm) apart.

BLANCHING ENDIVE

Endive is grown for its bitter flavor, which, if preferred, can be made sweeter by blanching the leaves. This means covering the plant with a saucer, or tying its leaves closed to exclude the light for about 2–3 weeks.

When revealed, the blanched leaves are a pale yellow-green color.

	SPRING	SUMMER	FALL	WINTER
Sow				
Harvest				

Time to harvest: **10–12 WEEKS** • Plant 10–16in (25–40cm) apart

Rotation information: **ROTATION GROUP 3 • MEDIUM FEEDERS**

Chicory
Cichorium intybus

Chicory can be sown as a cover crop, since its deep roots help to break up compacted soil. However, in the garden it is more often grown for its distinctively bitter leaves, which can be eaten fresh in salads, or oven-baked. Belgium chicory, or witloof chicory, is grown for forcing and blanching during fall to produce dense white heads known as chicons. This is a connoisseur crop that rewards the effort taken.

SITE AND SOIL PREPARATION
Chicory needs full sun or part shade, and fertile soil that has been improved with mature biodynamic compost or well-rotted manure.

SOWING AND PLANTING
Spray horn manure 500 on the bed one afternoon a few days before sowing to encourage root growth. Rake the soil to a fine tilth before sowing under a descending moon. Sow seed indoors in mid-spring to plant out during a descending moon, or sow outside in late spring.

ROUTINE CARE
Keep plants well watered in the early stages, watering regularly rather than excessively thereafter. Avoid getting water or soil in the leafy heads, since it encourages decay and slugs. Spray stinging nettle liquid manure on the soil around the plants to keep it friable. Dandelion tea can be applied as a very fine mist over young plants to help them establish, then spray horn silica 501 before thinning to promote firm leaves and upright growth, which helps deter slugs.

HARVESTING AND STORING
The earliest chicory will be ready in summer, while later sowings are harvested from late fall to late winter. Healthy leaves feel firm rather than rigid. Pick them before the heads grow too tall and lose their compact shape. Loose-headed sugarloaf types can be used for cut-and-come-again salad, or blanched by tying the heads closed a week before harvesting. Belgian chicory is used for forcing (*see right*).

TROUBLESHOOTING
Discourage caterpillars and cutworms by spraying *Equisetum arvense* 508 as a fresh tea, or tansy decoction.

Collecting seeds
• Prevent chicory from bolting in the year it is sown and leave the plants to overwinter.

• In the second season, let it flower and collect the seed, drying the pods indoors.

• Only save seed from one variety of chicory. If two different types flower near each other—including wild varieties, such as coneflowers—they will crossbreed.

• Prevent this using cages, if necessary.

SOWING DIRECTLY
Seeds can be sown directly where they are to grow in late spring, once the last frost has passed. Sow seed into furrows ½in (1cm) deep, in rows spaced 18in (45cm) apart, and keep the seedlings moist. As they grow, thin the plants to 8–18in (20–45cm) apart, depending on the type. Add the thinnings to your salads.

FORCING CHICORY
In fall lift the roots, trim off the lower half, and cut the tops to 1in (2.5cm) above the crown. Pot the roots, cover with soil mix, and place a soil-filled pot upside-down over the top. In 3–4 weeks, at 45–61°F (7–16°C), the blanched chicons will be ready to cut.

The chicons should be harvested once they reach about 6in (15cm) tall.

	SPRING	SUMMER	FALL	WINTER
Sow				
Harvest				

Time to harvest: **14–16 WEEKS** • Plant or thin to 8–18in (20–45cm) apart

Rotation information: **ROTATION GROUP 3 • MEDIUM FEEDERS**

Red orach
Atriplex hortensis var. *rubra*

Red orach is a larger, colorful alternative to spinach, with similar levels of protein, but much higher levels of vitamin C. It is grown in a similar way to spinach but is much taller, reaching up to 6ft (1.8m). It can also be grown in a sunnier site than spinach, where it is less prone to bolting. As well as red, the leaves can also be yellow or green, and vary in texture from smooth to slightly crinkly.

SITE AND SOIL PREPARATION

Orach likes rich, moisture-retentive soil. Thin, dry, sandy soil can be dressed with mature compost before or at planting. Soil that is dark and loamy will just need a spray of horn manure 500 or barrel compost. Spray and add compost while the moon is descending.

SOWING AND PLANTING

Soak the seeds overnight in a cup of dynamized horn manure 500 or BC, and sow during the following afternoon where the soil was sprayed. Sow directly in furrows every few weeks under a descending moon from early spring, water them in, and keep them moist.

ROUTINE CARE

Once the seedlings have 2–4 leaves, spray horn silica 501 one morning, avoiding node days, to promote firm, upward growth. Spraying them with 501 when they are any taller, or if the soil is dry, may encourage bolting. Thin out the seedlings and keep plants well watered. For sweet and crunchy leaves, spray with *Equisetum arvense* 508 as a fresh tea. Don't apply 508 as a liquid manure; this risks encouraging too much vigor—these are already naturally tall plants.

HARVESTING AND STORING

Pick larger leaves to cook like spinach. The flower heads can also be harvested while young and tender to eat lightly steamed.

TROUBLESHOOTING

To avoid a forest of plants, and future self-seeding, sow in batches, cut baby leaves for salad, and remove plants before they seed.

Collecting seeds

• Red orach flowers and sets seeds in its first year, and will spread freely if the seeds are naturally allowed to fall to the ground.

• Grow the plants in the normal way, allowing them to flower. Taller plants may need support.

• As seed heads start to yellow, cut them off, take them inside to dry, then collect the seeds. Store them in paper envelopes.

• For pure seeds, only collect them from one type of orach, and don't allow others to flower.

ATTRACT ALLIES

Red orach flowers are very attractive to bees, so plant it near crops where good pollination is essential, such as green and runner beans. The flowers also attract lacewings, which feed avidly on aphids. Grow it near crops most vulnerable to attack, such as broad beans and most brassicas.

HARVESTING THE LEAVES

The leaves vary in color and texture. Red leaves taste the spiciest, green ones are milder, and the yellow leaves have the sweetest flavor. Use a mix of colors to brighten salads, visually and flavorwise.

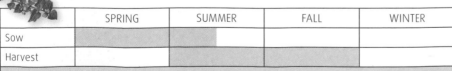

	SPRING	SUMMER	FALL	WINTER
Sow				
Harvest				

Time to harvest: **6–12 WEEKS** • Thin and plant out 10–20in (25–50cm) apart

Rotation information: **ROTATION GROUP 3 • MEDIUM FEEDERS**

Radicchio
Cichorium intybus

Radicchio is a type of hearting chicory. Its crisp leaves redden and become less bitter as the weather cools in late fall. The leaves enliven mixed salads and pasta dishes; temper the slightly bitter taste with a drizzle of olive oil and a pinch of salt or enjoy with pancetta. You can also grill or oven bake the hearts, with parmesan, for example.

SITE AND SOIL PREPARATION
Radicchio prefers an open site on friable, well-drained, well-composted soil—in full sun in cool weather, but in heat it likes afternoon shade. Dress the soil with biodynamic compost before planting, or backfill with it when transplanting, under a descending moon.

SOWING AND PLANTING
Sow indoors in mid-spring or outdoors from late spring. Overwinter later sowings under cover to harvest the next spring; transplant them before severe frost. Before planting, spray the bed with horn manure 500 and then BC a month later, both in the afternoon under a descending moon.

ROUTINE CARE
Water carefully so plants develop tasty, full-sized leaves. For good leaf growth in the early stages, spray them with comfrey liquid manure in the afternoon. Mist horn silica 501 over the tops, just before fall equinox in the morning, to ripen the leaves to a bittersweet, not just a bitter, flavor. Mulch with straw just before cold weather arrives or cover with cloches or garden fabric.

HARVESTING AND STORING
From late summer onward, pick off outer leaves from spring-sown plants as they begin to firm up; older leaves are more bitter. You can also cut entire plants (*see right, bottom*). In fall, lift plants, with their roots, from later sowings to force indoors. Remove the crown for eating and replant the roots in pots filled with soil mix. Keep them at 50–59°F (10–15°C) in the dark (or cover with another pot) to stimulate blanched, tender, new crowns. Store crowns in the refrigerator in a perforated plastic bag. You can use individual, frozen leaves if you thaw them slowly.

TROUBLESHOOTING
Radicchio is fairly trouble free. Pluck off any wilted or browned outer leaves. Use only fully mature compost when preparing soil to decrease risk of attack by wireworms, slugs, and snails.

Collecting seeds

• Radicchio flowers in its second year. Do not collect seed from plants that bolted in their first year—they will be of poor quality. Try to grow at least 20 plants for seeds.

• Radicchio will cross-pollinate with other forms of chicory. To prevent this, allow only one type to flower at a given time or cover the blooms of other chicories with paper bags before they open and release pollen.

• Allow the seed plants to flower in summer. When the pods are brown, cut them from the plant to harvest the seeds under cover.

GROWING THE CROP
Sow seeds thinly or transplant seedlings into rows that are 12in (30cm) apart. Add a tiny sprinkling of very finely chopped comfrey leaves to planting holes to provide an early food source.

Radicchio is frost hardy, but its shallow roots perish if any air gaps are left at thinning or transplanting, so firm it in.

Radicchio bolts in hot or dry weather. Keep plants well watered, especially early on and just before the heads form.

Harvest an entire head by slicing it off at the base; it will grow back next year.

	SPRING	SUMMER	FALL	WINTER
Sow				
Harvest				

Time to harvest: **14–16 WEEKS** • Plant or thin to 8-12in (20-30cm) apart

Rotation information: **ROTATION GROUP 3 • MEDIUM FEEDERS**

Asparagus
Asparagus officinalis

For many, asparagus is an expensive luxury, yet a permanent bed of it is relatively easy to establish from seed or rooted crowns, and will provide you with nutritious white, green, or purple-pink spears for around 20 years. Asparagus is a natural diuretic, helping to cleanse excess salt from the body.

SITE AND SOIL PREPARATION
Asparagus needs sun and shelter on well-drained, sandy loam. Raised beds are vital on heavy soils and make maintenance easier. Dig in lots of mature compost, ideally from cows, seasoned with nutrient-rich kelp, comfrey, or both, under a descending moon. On acidic soils, sprinkle a little neutralizing wood ash, if you can.

SOWING AND PLANTING
Sow seed in shallow furrows in a seed bed in early spring; thin the seedlings and let grow; plant out in a permanent bed in mid-spring the next year—all under a descending moon. It is easier to transplant one-year-old rather than two- or three-year-old crowns: you are less likely to damage the roots. A 4ft- (1.2m-) wide bed takes two staggered rows of established crowns. Plant them 6in (15cm) deep in trenches; spread out the roots, even if they overlap, and lightly cover them with soil. Gradually fill the trenches as the crowns start into growth to encourage stronger roots and a longer, more productive life.

ROUTINE CARE
Over winter, replace weathered or dried mulch with fresh biodynamic compost. For firm, upright spears, mist over the bed with horn silica 501 at spring equinox, at an ascending moon at sunrise. Spray the bed with horn manure 500,

under a descending moon in the afternoon near fall equinox, for strong roots. Apply BC on the bed the month after fall equinox, in the evening at a descending moon, to deter disease.

HARVESTING AND STORING
Harvest spears once they are 8in (20cm) tall (*see right, bottom*). You can eat the spears raw, steamed, or in soups and stews.

TROUBLESHOOTING
Asparagus is trouble free in good soil, topped off regularly with high-quality, properly matured compost. Take care not to damage the roots when weeding, mulching, and topdressing, otherwise they rot. Let chickens graze dormant beds to peck out any asparagus beetle larvae.

Collecting seeds
• To get viable asparagus seeds, you need a male and female plant.
• Allow the stems of a female plant to grow and flower, and produce its red berries.
• Collect the ripe berries; rub their seeds through a colander; remove any remaining flesh under running water.
• Allow the seeds to dry for several hours, then store them in glass jars.

COMPANION PLANTS
Asparagus and tomatoes (*see p.219*) may grow near each other in the same place for several years to their mutual benefit. While tomatoes deter asparagus beetles, asparagus is said to release a chemical that encourages the growth of tomato plants.

HARVESTING SPEARS
Harvest nothing in the first year and just one stalk per crown in the second. From the third year, harvest any spears that grow between mid-spring and early summer—usually a couple of dozen spears per crown.

Cut off spears just below the soil surface, with a sharp, curved knife.

	SPRING	SUMMER	FALL	WINTER
Sow or plant				
Harvest				
Time to harvest: **3 YEARS** • Plant out 18in (45cm) apart				
Rotation information: **ROTATION GROUP 4 • MEDIUM FEEDERS**				

Rhubarb
Rheum × hybridum

Rhubarb is much underrated: it is probably the most cost-effective food in the garden, being easy to grow and needing little attention. It gives the first dessert crop of the year, and can be harvested for three years before it has to be divided and replanted. Last but not least, the stalks make delicious, tart desserts, and a very palatable wine.

SITE AND SOIL PREPARATION

Rhubarb thrives in sun or part shade on free-draining soil. It is hardy, but struggles in frost pockets or poorly drained hollows. Dig in a lot of compost before planting, at a descending moon.

SOWING AND PLANTING

It is easiest to grow root cuttings, called crowns or sets: an average family needs 1–4 sets. Plant under a descending moon. Dig a wide hole 18in (45cm) deep: keep the topsoil separate, then dig out the subsoil. Backfill with 1:4 parts crumbled subsoil to rich, manure-based compost. Firm the set in gently and replace the topsoil, leaving the bud poking out of the top.

ROUTINE CARE

Spray BC in spring, in the evening under a descending moon, to keep the topsoil healthy. Mist horn silica 501 over the plants at sunrise soon after spring equinox, then twice monthly on an ascending moon, for crisper shoots. Compost any flowering stalks in summer. In fall, mulch with leaf mold mixed with chopped comfrey leaves, leaving crowns uncovered, otherwise they may rot. Spray the bed with horn manure 500 in fall, in the afternoon under a descending moon, to keep nutrients moving underground.

HARVESTING AND STORING

Harvest only stalks from plants that are at least two years old. The leaves should not be eaten. Freshly picked stalks freeze well.

TROUBLESHOOTING

Spray comfrey, kelp, or stinging nettle liquid manure as a feed once or twice a season on the bed and both sides of the leaves. Intersow a new rhubarb bed with lettuce and spinach to suppress weeds and shade the soil. Replace any crowns that show signs of rot.

Collecting seeds

• Rhubarb is self-pollinating, so seeds from one plant may be resown the following year. Let the plant flower in midsummer and form papery seed heads, then collect and dry the seeds.

• The seeds rarely produce plants that come true to type, which is why rhubarb is usually propagated from cuttings. So sow as many seeds as possible and eliminate any seedlings that are atypical.

• Allowing rhubarb to flower can weaken it—avoid doing this by collecting seeds only from plants that are over three years old.

FORCING EARLY STEMS
The first shoots emerge between midwinter and the first spring frost and may be forced. Keep them artificially in the dark, under a pot, bucket, or terra-cotta forcing pot, for several weeks.

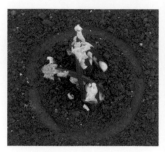

Forcing shoots blanches them, making them paler, sweeter, and more tender. Force only the first flush of stems.

HARVESTING RHUBARB
When harvesting, pull only firm, crisp, and juicy stems with fully open leaves. Rather than cutting off the shoots, twist them off from the base to avoid leaving stumps that might decay.

Harvest one-third of each plant before midsummer, then leave it to recover.

	SPRING	SUMMER	FALL	WINTER
Plant				
Harvest				

Time to harvest: **16–25 MONTHS** • Plant 3–4ft (90–120cm) apart

Rotation information: **ROTATION GROUP 4 • LIGHT FEEDERS**

Sea kale
Crambe maritima

Sea kale's natural habitat is the beach, but it will be quite happy in any garden. This handsome plant is treated in a similar way to rhubarb, but all parts are edible—leaves, shoots, flower buds, and even the roots. Sea kale was traditionally eaten by sailors because its high vitamin C content prevented scurvy.

SITE AND SOIL PREPARATION
Sea kale grows in full sun or part shade, and does not mind the wind. It prefers rich, well-composted, sandy, free-draining soil bolstered with light loam and a sprinkling of finely milled oak bark chips, which add slow-release calcium.

SOWING AND PLANTING
It is simpler to grow sea kale from root cuttings, called thongs, or divisions from a dormant plant. In early spring or early fall, bury each thong or division with its bud at soil level and lightly sprinkle soil over the bud. Sow seed shallowly outdoors in early spring after the last frost. Thin seedlings to 1–2ft (30–60cm) apart and transplant to their final bed around fall equinox. Sow, plant, and transplant under a descending moon, if possible.

ROUTINE CARE
Water new plants well; established ones are less thirsty. To maintain a healthy soil balance, spray BC under a descending moon closest to spring equinox. Mist horn silica 501 over the tops, at sunrise at summer solstice, to reinforce the plants' upper parts (for leaf texture and flavor). Spray the bed with horn manure 500 in the afternoon at fall equinox for strong roots. After the leafy growth has died back to almost nothing in late fall, remove and compost any leafy debris. Fork lightly and dress the bed, under a descending moon, with fresh biodynamic compost, chopped comfrey leaves, leaf mold, or a combination of all three.

HARVESTING AND STORING
Harvest only forced shoots (*see right and facing page*); mature leaves are too bitter. Cut the shoots off at soil level. New plants take time to establish. Take only a few shoots and leaves from each plant in the second year, then harvest for about ten years before renewing the plants.

TROUBLESHOOTING
Sea kale's crinkly leaves thrive if you spray the plant in the evening with leftover fresh plant teas or decoctions that you have used on other crops—especially chamomile and stinging nettle teas, and oak bark decoction.

Collecting seeds

- Sea kale will pollinate its own summer flowers.
- Leave the seed pods to mature on the plant and collect them in early fall, when the pods have hardened and turned brown.
- Gently crack the outer shells to reveal the seeds, make sure that they are dry, then store them in glass jars for up to a year.

FLOWERS AND FRUIT
The edible flowers are best eaten raw, and can be added to salads for color. Leave some blooms to mature, however, since the pealike fruit that follow can also be eaten, and taste similar to cabbage.

LONG-SEASON HARVEST
From the second year, you can force the new young shoots from midwinter as for rhubarb (*see facing page*) to obtain a crop of blanched 10in (25cm) leaves up to mid-spring.

Once you remove the forcing pots, allow plants to build up strength over summer, ready to harvest next spring.

	SPRING	SUMMER	FALL	WINTER
Sow or plant				
Harvest				

Time to harvest: **26–56 WEEKS** • Thin and plant out 2–3ft (60–90cm) apart

Rotation information: **ROTATION GROUP 2 • LIGHT FEEDERS**

Sagittarius
the Archer

Aries
the Ram

Leo
the Lion

Fruit days

Fruit days are the periods when the moon is in front of the constellations of Sagittarius, Aries, and Leo. They relate to the element of fire, or warmth, which fruit and seeds need to ripen, whether apples, tomatoes, sweet corn, or peas. It's relatively easy to keep to the fruit day cycle for perennials like pears and blueberries—plant them once and they'll often outlive their owners! Strong roots are essential, so aim to plant trees and bushes on fruit days under a descending moon, ideally in the afternoon. This is also the best time to sow or transplant seedlings of other fruit day crops, but if you miss this opportunity the moon will move on into an earth-root constellation—the perfect backup option. Harvest on fruit days with an ascending moon to enjoy the best taste and maximum storage time.

Fruit days and lunar cycles

❧ The moon visits a fire-fruit constellation roughly every 8–9 days, and spends 2–2½ days in each.

❧ In the northern hemisphere the moon's ascending cycle begins in Sagittarius and travels through Aries.

❧ The moon's descending path runs through Leo, and it is still descending as it returns to Sagittarius.

Things to do on…
Fruit days

GREAT · FRUIT DAY TASK

The element of fire associated with fruit days provides ideal conditions for cultivating a wide range of fruiting crops, from peas and beans to blackberries and apples. They depend on warmth and light for their ripeness, flavor, and ability to store well—whether freshly picked, or preserved as jam, chutney, sauce, or even as wine.

• **Fruit days leading up to moon–opposition Saturn** are the best times for preparing the ground and planting fruit trees for a long and healthy life.

• **Sow fruit crops in the 2–3 days before full moon** for stronger germination, and to grow robust plants suitable for transplanting.

• **Fruit days with an ascending moon** are good times to take cuttings of soft fruit like black currants, and to lift strawberries for replanting the following year. These—and waxing moon periods—are also optimal days for spring-pruning fruit trees.

• **Choose descending moon periods** for pruning fruit trees in fall: this gives nourishing sap time to descend into the root system before branches are removed.

• **In damp weather, especially during perigee**, leave fruit crops alone to avoid encouraging disease.

Tomatoes

Zucchini

Sow fruiting crops like squash on fruit days with a descending moon.

Harvest fruiting crops like beans on fruit days for the best storage and flavor.

Cut thick stems to pick crops like pepper to avoid rocking and damaging their root

Replant strawberry runners every year on fruit days with a descending moon.

Fruit days are a great time to take on bad weeds like bindweed before they get a stranglehold.

Hoe to stimulate weed germination; remove weeds on the next root day.

Choose fruit days with an ascending moon to prune fruit trees in late spring: the sap pushing up from below helps keep diseases out.

Fruits like red currants picked on fruit days will be at their sweetest and full of flavor.

Plant fruit trees under a descending moon for stronger rooting and a longer life.

Apply tree paste—a compost for tree trunks—to keep your fruit trees healthy.

Spray silica-rich *Equisetum arvense* 508 tea or liquid manure to keep pests and diseases at bay.

Peas
Pisum sativum

Freshly harvested peas are at their succulent and nutritious best the moment you pick them. Whether you grow podded, snow, or sugar snap varieties, dwarf forms or climbers, treat the plants well and they will keep you in delicious, crunchy peas from mid-spring until late fall.

SITE AND SOIL PREPARATION

Peas like sun and fertile, medium-textured soil that warms quickly in spring. They dislike heavy clay, and very sandy or acidic soil: add lime well before planting, if necessary. Dig in compost in the fall before planting under a descending moon (not at the same time as lime), or use a plot where compost was used for a previous crop.

SOWING AND PLANTING

Start sowing in late winter under cover, ideally under a descending moon. Once harsh frost has passed, sow direct in batches: start with hardier, smooth seeds; sow wrinkly peas until early summer. Soak the seeds (*see right*), then sow 1½–3in (4–8cm) deep. Space the rows as far apart as the height of the crop—snow peas and sugar snap peas grow tallest, to 6ft (1.8m).

ROUTINE CARE

Support climbing peas with netting and wooden sticks from local hedges or trees, rather than bamboo. Peas are slow starters: help them by weeding and mulching. To boost yields, spray soil and plants with valerian 507 when plants are knee high, and spray horn silica 501 over the tops at sunrise under an ascending moon as flowering starts. For best results apply the sprays on fruit days. Water well at flowering to ensure a good crop. Pinch off the growing tips from each plant once the first pods form to encourage more pods.

HARVESTING AND STORING

Pick peas daily as needed and cook or freeze immediately to stop the sugar from turning to starch. Pick snow and sugar snap peas as whole pods when the peas are just formed.

TROUBLESHOOTING

Prevent mildew on summer sowings by spraying *Equisetum arvense* 508: use as a fresh tea in the morning on young shoots or, when they are taller, as a liquid manure in late afternoon on the soil. Peas prefer not to have members of the onion family nearby. Use pine nut spray to discourage slugs and snails.

Collecting seeds

• Save seed from one variety of peas that flowered when no others were in bloom at the same time.

• When the pea pods bulge and are about to split open, cut the whole plant off at the root on a dry day.

• Dry the pods indoors on a cloth-covered table, or by hanging them in a burlap bag, and collect the seeds that drop out.

• Store the seeds in batches in sturdy, labeled paper envelopes.

BONUS HARVEST

Tender new pea shoots make a delicious addition to salads: their fine leaves and tendrils taste a bit like snow peas. For the best and sweetest flavor, pick the young shoots on leaf days when the plants are 4–6in (10–15cm) tall. Save the thinnings and pinched-off growing tips from the main crop for salads, too.

SOAKING PEA SEEDS

Peas have tough skins: soaking dry seeds immediately before sowing ensures that they are fully hydrated and germinate quickly. Chamomile tea also helps seeds to form baby roots.

Soak peas in a seed bath of chamomile tea for 36 hours before sowing.

	SPRING	SUMMER	FALL	WINTER
Sow				
Harvest				

Time to harvest: **11–14 WEEKS** • Sow 2–3in (5–8cm) apart, depending on variety

Rotation information: **ROTATION GROUP 1 • LIGHT FEEDERS**

Runner beans
Phaseolus coccineus

These climbers are one of the most ornamental plants in the vegetable garden, with pretty scarlet or white flowers all summer. They are easy to grow, producing a steady, abundant supply of tasty beans.

SITE AND SOIL PREPARATION

Choose a sunny, sheltered site. Prepare the soil under a descending moon in the previous fall: dig in plenty of compost, ideally with chopped comfrey leaves and wood ash to provide potassium. Lime the soil if it is acidic. Lay the compost in 2in (5cm) deep and 32in (80cm) wide trenches or in 3in (8cm) high and 6in (15cm) wide hills, spaced 36–40in (90–105cm) apart.

SOWING AND PLANTING

Erect supports for the beans before planting (*see right*). Sow direct from late spring and successively to early summer, under a descending moon. To help them germinate, soak seeds just before sowing for a few hours in warm chamomile or nettle tea. Sow seeds 2in (5cm) deep in furrows with 2–3 seeds per station. If a late, unexpected frost threatens, spray valerian 507 over the soil the night before sowing. Protect seedlings from birds and rabbits, if necessary.

ROUTINE CARE

Control weeds, and earth up the bases of the plants to help them grow. Water plants well with tepid water; cold water inhibits growth and encourages bean aphids. Mulch with straw in hot weather to keep roots moist and stop soil from crusting. Once the beans reach the top of the support, pinch off their growing tips. Spray horn silica 501 over the tops, in the morning under an ascending moon and just before flowering, to prompt the flowers to open for pollinating bees.

HARVESTING AND STORING

Harvest beans every other day or so to stop pods from becoming tough and stringy. Always cut them off; pulling them off can damage the supports and the roots.

TROUBLESHOOTING

Do not work or harvest runner beans if it is wet, which encourages disease. If the air is very dry at flowering, spray diluted, fresh nettle, chamomile, or comfrey tea all over the vines, in the evening, to help the flowers open. Radishes are good companions for this crop, but kohlrabi and beets seem to suffer near runner beans.

Collecting seeds

• For pure seed, save only from a single variety that is a good distance away from any other runner bean varieties flowering at the same time.

• Leave pods to mature on the plants; collect them once the beans inside have swollen and the pods are brown and crisp.

• Cut the pods on a dry day and and extract the beans. Store them in large, labeled paper envelopes or bags.

SOWING IN POTS

Runner beans are frost tender, so early sowings may be started off in late spring indoors in pots, before being transplanted once they have two true leaves. Harden off seedlings and plant out after risk of frost is past.

Sow two seeds per pot, 2in (5cm) deep, and thin the resulting seedlings to leave the strongest one in each.

PROVIDING SUPPORT

You can leave runner beans to trail along the ground, but training them up supports saves space, makes harvesting easier, and reduces the risk of pests and diseases. Bend tall stakes into a tepees or use in parallel rows for better airflow.

	SPRING	SUMMER	FALL	WINTER
Sow				
Harvest				

Time to harvest: **8–12 WEEKS** • Sow or plant out in stations 9in (23cm) apart and rows 32in (80cm) apart

Rotation information: **ROTATION GROUP 1 • LIGHT FEEDERS**

Green beans
Phaseolus vulgaris

These versatile beans may be dwarf bush or climbing plants, with flattened or tubular pods that may be green, red, purple, golden-yellow, or multicolored. You can eat the pods whole or leave the pods to mature on the plant and eat just the beans, called flageolet or cannellini beans, while they are still tender. If you dry the shelled beans, you can even store or can them as haricot and kidney beans.

SITE AND SOIL PREPARATION
Green beans need full sun, warmth, shelter from wind, and light but fertile soil. Dig in mature compost made partly from comfrey leaves if you have not done so already for a previous crop. Spray horn manure 500 on the bed, in the afternoon under a descending moon, two weeks before sowing or planting. If needed, warm the soil to 55°F (13°C) by covering it with cloches.

SOWING AND PLANTING
Start seeds indoors in early or mid-spring (*see right*) or sow direct from late spring onward. Space rows 18in (45cm) apart. Sow 4–5 seeds of climbing beans at each post; stagger seeds around tepees for balanced light and airflow.

ROUTINE CARE
Pinch off growing tips of climbing beans as they reach the top of the support to stimulate more pods to form lower down. Mulch and water the plants well throughout flowering. Spray horn silica 501 over the tops, at sunrise under an ascending moon, once the first flowers set.

HARVESTING AND STORING
Climbing green beans are harvested later than dwarf types. Pick tender pods regularly to keep the plant flowering; snap them off cleanly. Harvest haricot beans as for seeds (*see box, right*).

TROUBLESHOOTING
Irregular watering causes pods that are well filled at one end but shriveled at the other. Discourage aphids by spraying transplants with stinging nettle cold extract. Spray an *Equisetum arvense* 508 fresh tea over the plants before tying them in to ward off fungal diseases. If conditions become overcast or humid, spray it again, as a liquid manure, or with an oak bark decoction, in the air over the foliage in the morning. Touching the plants when wet increases the risk of disease.

Collecting seeds
- It is fairly easy to save seed from green beans, but select plants that grow true to type—they can cross with other types of beans in the garden.
- Sow seed crops of green beans as early as possible, indoors if necessary (*see right*). Space the plants farther apart than usual, to improve flowering, bean formation, and ripening and to reduce the risk of disease.
- When the pods turn dry and brown, cut each plant at ground level and then hang upside down indoors to dry, leaving plenty of space between plants. Extract the seeds from the dried pods, and store in paper bags.

SOWING UNDER COVER
Green beans are not frost-hardy, so in cooler climates start them indoors in pots or flats deep enough for the long taproots to develop fully before the green shoots emerge. Biodegradable cardboard tubes filled with potting mix are good for this.

Push two seeds 2in (5cm) deep into each tube and keep them moist. Thin each pair of seedlings to leave the strongest.

When all risk of frost is past, harden off the seedlings for about two weeks, ready to plant out in early summer.

Plant each tube into the soil: it will soon decay, leaving the roots undisturbed.

	SPRING	SUMMER	FALL	WINTER
Sow	███			
Harvest		███		

Time to harvest: **8–12 WEEKS** • Sow or plant out dwarf beans 4in (10cm) apart and climbing beans 12in (30cm) apart

Rotation information: **ROTATION GROUP 1 • LIGHT FEEDERS**

Broad beans
Vicia faba

No vegetable garden is complete without a few rows of broad beans standing over winter and through summer for an abundant crop of protein-rich food. Also called fava beans, they taste best when they are just starting to push against the insides of the pods—when bean and pods can be eaten whole.

SITE AND SOIL PREPARATION
These deep-rooted beans need light, fertile, well-drained, and well-dug soil in a sunny, frost-free site. Dig in lots of biodynamic compost or well-rotted manure, seasoned with potassium-rich, chopped comfrey leaves or wood ash, under a descending moon. Sprinkle lime on acidic soil.

SOWING AND PLANTING
Broad beans are best sown in late fall or early spring. Soak seeds for two hours in BC before planting. Start hardy varieties in indoors in pots (*see facing page*) in late winter. Beans in pots grow quickly: prepare the planting area before the second pairs of leaves appear.

ROUTINE CARE
If the weather is unsuitable, keep the plants from becoming stressed with a light dose of liquid manure (nettle, comfrey, or kelp) when watering. Spray horn silica 501 over the bed, under an ascending moon in the morning and as flowering is ending, to keep the leaves active and the pods firm.

HARVESTING AND STORING
Fall-sown crops mature in seven months; spring-sown ones in three. Cut, rather than pull, off pods.

TROUBLESHOOTING
Blackflies (black bean aphids) appear on the growing tips in late spring; spray stinging nettle or kelp liquid manure on the bed and on both sides of the leaves; repeat spray if you spot more blackflies. You could also intersow in late autumn with lupines, which attract hoverflies to feed off the aphids. Lupine roots bring up potassium from deep in the subsoil; if beans lack this mineral their leaves get brown blotches, or chocolate spot. If necessary, dig in every other intersown row of lupines to release more potassium to the beans. Broad beans also are good companions for early potatoes.

Collecting seeds
- You can grow broad beans for seed in the same way as green beans (*see facing page*).
- Like green beans, broad beans breed with other types of beans, so choose seed for saving from plants that grow true to type.
- Harvest the whole plant once the pods turn brown, and finish drying and store them as for green beans.

SOWING SEED DIRECT
Use a dibber to sow the large beans singly, 2–3in (5–8cm) deep in two rows 8in (20cm) apart; stagger the seed in the rows but fill any gaps at the ends. Leave at least 30in (75cm) between each pair of rows.

GETTING A GOOD CROP
Broad beans are easy to grow, but regular watering makes the difference between an abundant harvest or no crop at all.

After flowering, when the pods begin to form, pinch off the growing tip of each plant to help the pods to swell.

Beans need support with stakes and twine, unless they are the dwarf types sown for late summer picking.

	SPRING		SUMMER		FALL		WINTER	
Sow								
Harvest								
Time to harvest: **12–28 WEEKS** • Sow direct or plant out 6–8in (15–20cm) apart								
Rotation information: **ROTATION GROUP 1 • LIGHT FEEDERS**								

Lima beans
and soybeans
Phaseolus lunatus,
Glycine max

Lima beans are large and white or green, and are also known as butter beans. Soybeans can be either yellow, black, brown, or green. The beans are rich in protein and can be eaten fresh or dried for cooking later. Fresh soybeans are known as edamame.

SITE AND SOIL PREPARATION
Lima beans and soybeans need a sheltered site in full sun, with warm, fertile, well-drained soil. In fall, dig in plenty of well-rotted biodynamic compost, made in part with potassium-rich comfrey leaves. Break up any hard soil that might restrict the plant's root, which would affect growth.

SOWING AND PLANTING
Lima beans and soybeans can be grown as bushes, while some types of lima beans climb, so need tall supports. All are tender, and need a growing season of about 100 days. Sow directly during a descending moon into soil warmed with cloches to at least 64°F (18°C). When the moon is descending, spray the bed with horn manure 500 before sowing, then once the seeds have come up.

ROUTINE CARE
Protect plants on cold nights with fabric, and stake any that blow or topple over. Pinch off the growing tips of climbing beans when they reach the top of their stakes. Mulch around the plants, and water them regularly from the start of flowering and throughout its duration. Spray horn silica 501 when the first flowers have set.

HARVESTING AND STORING
Harvest under an ascending moon and eat the beans like peas. Beans can also be dried on the plants to use during winter.

TROUBLESHOOTING
To prevent fungal diseases during warm, humid spells, spray with *Equisetum arvense* 508 as a fresh tea and avoid touching the plants.

Collecting seeds
• Beans make gathering seed a relatively easy process. Start plants intended to produce seed as early as possible.

• Space them wider than normal outside to improve flowering, bean set, ripening, and to reduce the risk of disease.

• Select seed for saving from plants that grow true to type—they can crossbreed with other types of beans in the garden.

• Harvest the whole plant when the pods start drying and turning color.

• Continue drying indoors, shell, and store.

SOWING FROM SEED
Lima beans and soybeans require warm and sheltered conditions to grow well, and need to be pampered at first. As conditions improve in summer, however, they become less demanding.

Before sowing or planting out, warm the soil where they are to grow by using cloches for a few weeks.

As the seedlings emerge or are planted out, cover them with a bottle cloche to keep them warm and sheltered.

Ensure plants are well watered once they are flowering and producing pods.

	SPRING	SUMMER	FALL	WINTER
Sow				
Harvest				

Time to harvest: **14–16 WEEKS** • Sow bush beans 3in (8cm) apart; climbing beans 3ft (90cm) apart

Rotation information: **ROTATION GROUP 1 • LIGHT FEEDERS**

Zucchini
and summer squash
Cucurbita pepo

Zucchini and summer squash are among the most prolific crops to grow, and just a few plants will keep you in their produce all summer. They also require plenty of space, so don't grow more plants than you really need. Zucchini, in particular, should be picked when young, but are easily missed in the sea of green leaves, so consider types with easier-to-spot yellow fruit.

SITE AND SOIL PREPARATION
These crops need fertile, generously composted soil. Dig plenty of compost deeply into the soil before sowing or planting, or grow them on the low side of a compost heap. Provide shelter to protect the fragile leaves and stems.

SOWING AND PLANTING
When the moon is descending, spray the bed with horn manure 500. Sow seeds when the moon is descending, indoors 2–3 weeks before the last frost; outside in warmed soil after the last frost. Soak the seeds in BC for an hour or so before sowing. Plants raised indoors should be planted out when the moon is descending.

ROUTINE CARE
In hot weather, water plants thoroughly but not daily. Mulching is not required. Where space is limited, train the stems up stakes or a trellis, pinching off the tips when the support is covered. Apply horn silica 501 early one morning when plants start to grow rapidly. As flowers appear, spray diluted liquid manure feeds, ideally kelp and comfrey sprays, to maintain plant health. Spray horn silica 501 again as the fruit begin to develop.

HARVESTING AND STORING
Harvest when the moon is ascending once the fruit are as long as your hand. Pick daily, cutting them from the plant with a knife.

TROUBLESHOOTING
Deter slugs and snails with pine needle mulch. Spray yarrow tea on seedlings and again as the plants flower to prevent powdery mildew.

Collecting seeds
• Zucchini and summer squash can interbreed, so don't allow different types to flower at the same time.

• When the first female flower is due to open, cover it the night before with a paper bag.

• The next morning, take a male flower, remove its petals, and insert it into the female bloom, transferring the pollen.

• Put the bag back over the female flower for 2 days, then remove it.

• Harvest the fruit when the plant has died back and clean the seeds as for tomatoes (*see p.219*).

TRAINING STEMS
Zucchini and summer squash are large, vigorous plants, and many types have trailing stems. These can be left to sprawl, although that makes them more vulnerable to pests.

Make a tepee of stakes, at least 6ft (1.8m) tall, and plant a trailing plant at the base, training it upward.

If stems are allowed to trail, guide them along the ground so they don't overwhelm neighboring plants.

Summer squash can become heavy, and should be tied in for extra support.

	SPRING	SUMMER	FALL	WINTER
Sow				
Harvest				

Time to harvest: **14–20 WEEKS** • Thin and plant out 3ft (90cm) apart

Rotation information: **ROTATION GROUP 4 • HEAVY FEEDERS**

Cucumbers
and gherkins
Cucumis sativus

Eating a juicy cucumber is a great way to rehydrate during a hot day in the garden, since they are packed with water. There are two main types to grow: the long, smooth Dutch or frame type, which needs the warmth of a greenhouse to ripen, and the rougher-skinned, more rugged outdoor or ridge varieties that tolerate cooler temperatures. Baby cucumbers are eaten as gherkins.

SITE AND SOIL PREPARATION

Outdoor cucumbers need a sheltered, sunny site, and deep, well-drained, mineral-rich soil. Pile horse manure compost into a ridge and cover with soil, ready for sowing or planting.

SOWING AND PLANTING

Cucumbers are sown when the moon is descending. Sow plants for outdoors under cover, at 68°F (20°C), a month before the last frost. Spray and water the plants moderately with fresh *Equisetum arvense* 508 tea to deter disease. Seed can be sown outside in early summer under cloches, midsummer without. To prevent slug damage, and to make picking easier, train the plants vertically up suitable supports.

ROUTINE CARE

Encourage plants to produce fruiting stems by pinching off the growing tips when they have 4–5 leaves, then again when they outgrow their supports. Remove any nonfruiting shoots. Water infrequently but thoroughly, and early on, use BC stirred for 20 minutes in warm water, at least once. Balance this by applying horn silica 501 over the plants. To prevent the fruit from flagging and to deter mildew, spray the leaves with comfrey or nettle liquid manure. Plants should also be mulched with straw to retain

moisture and protect the shallow roots. Spray horn manure 500 before laying the mulch.

HARVESTING AND STORING

Regularly harvest the fruit under an ascending moon before they become large and bitter tasting. Cut the stems, don't pull them, to avoid damaging the plants.

TROUBLESHOOTING

Keep the plants moist and avoid working with them on leaf days, or when they are wet, to lower the risk of disease. Sow radishes around the base of the plants to repel cucumber beetles.

Collecting seeds

• Save seed from only one variety of cucumber or gherkin each year to avoid cross-pollination, or keep different varieties caged.

• Grow cucumbers and gherkins in the normal way, letting the fruit ripen on the vine for as long as possible. Harvest the fruit before the first frost.

• Scrape out the seeds and soak them in water. When this froths up, wash the seeds in a strainer, then dry them on paper towels.

• Store the dry seeds in paper envelopes.

PROTECTING THE ROOTS

Cucumbers dislike root disturbance, which can check their growth. Avoid it by sowing the seeds into biodegradable pots or cardboard tubes, which can be planted whole. They soon decay, leaving the roots undisturbed.

Keep plants grown in biodegradable pots moist after planting to encourage the pot to break down more quickly.

Female flowers are essential for fruiting. They have small fruitlets behind their petals.

	SPRING	SUMMER	FALL	WINTER
Sow				
Harvest				
Time to harvest: **16–20 WEEKS** • Thin or plant out 2–3ft (60–90cm) apart				
Rotation information: **ROTATION GROUP 4 • HEAVY FEEDERS**				

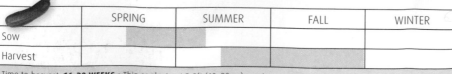

After initial training, cucumber plants cling to their supports using tendrils.

Marrows
Cucurbita pepo

Marrows are a favorite for children, and can be enormous and highly decorative. Although they are the same plant, there are specific seeds for zucchini and marrows, and one crop cannot be grown in the hope of harvesting it as the other. There are two types of marrows: those that trail, which, if left unchecked, can reach corners of the garden you'd long since forgotten, or the climbing bush types. These work better if space is tight and you have a sturdy enough vertical growing frame for them to scale.

SITE AND SOIL PREPARATION
Marrows need a sunny, sheltered site, warm and fertile soil, space, and lots of water. Dig in plenty of compost or well-rotted manure before planting, or grow trailing types at the base of a compost heap. Weed before planting, and spray horn manure 500 to seal the soil.

SOWING AND PLANTING
Sow seeds indoors during a descending moon in mid-spring, or outside under cloches in late spring. Soak the seed in BC for an hour first. Plants raised indoors can be planted out after the last frost under a descending moon.

ROUTINE CARE
Pinch off the growing tips of trailing marrows when they have 4–5 leaves to promote fruiting sideshoots to form. If a single large fruit is the aim, thin all but one so it can utilize all of the food and water. Keep the plants well watered with lukewarm, rather than cold, water. In cool, cloudy, or wet spells, pollinate the flowers by hand (*see right*). To enhance their flavor, spray horn silica 501 in the morning as the first baby marrows are developing, then again one afternoon 3–4 weeks before harvesting. Spray *Equisetum arvense* 508 as a fresh tea on the leaves and fruit to prevent fungal diseases.

HARVESTING AND STORING
Fruit are harvested regularly while the moon is ascending. If their skins were cured in the sun while growing, they store well indoors in a dry, airy spot at 45–50°F (7–10°C).

TROUBLESHOOTING
Deter slugs by spraying pine nut extract and laying wood chips. To prevent rot, ensure the fruit have not formed in small dips in the soil, where moisture could accumulate, encouraging disease. Overfeeding encourages excess leaf growth, not more fruit.

Collecting seeds
- Marrows can crossbreed with zucchini, pumpkins, and summer squash. For pure seeds, don't allow these to flower.
- When the first female flower is due to open, cover it with a paper bag the night before. Next day, remove the petals from a male flower and insert it into the female bloom to transfer pollen. Remove the paper bag after two days.
- Pick the fruit when the plant dies and store it indoors for two weeks before saving the seeds.
- Clean the seeds as for tomatoes (*see p.219*), and store them in an airtight container.

RETAINING MOISTURE
Marrows are thirsty plants and should be kept well watered all summer. To help retain soil moisture, mulch around plants with compost or bark. Mulch can also be used to keep the fruit off the damp soil surface.

HARVESTING
Marrows reach maturity in about two months, when they should be harvested using a knife—the stems are very tough. Wear gloves to do this since the stems are covered with many fine, sharp prickles.

Marrow fruit can be thinned if you want to grow especially large ones.

	SPRING	SUMMER	FALL	WINTER
Sow				
Harvest				

Time to harvest: **14–16 WEEKS** • Thin or plant out 3ft (90cm) apart

Rotation information: **ROTATION GROUP 4 • HEAVY FEEDERS**

Pumpkins
and winter squash
Cucurbita maxima, C. moschata, C. pepo

Pumpkins and winter squash are similar in flavor to marrows and summer squash, but can be stored over winter. Their flesh is rich in fiber and vitamin A, and great for hearty winter soups and pies. You can transform the gourds, once emptied, into Halloween jack-o'-lanterns.

SITE AND SOIL PREPARATION

These deep-rooted crops grow in full sun or light shade in rich soil with plenty of well-rotted manure or compost; dig the compost in as deep as possible, under a descending moon. You can also grow them like zucchini (*see p.215*) at the base of a compost heap.

SOWING AND PLANTING

Soak seeds in BC for two hours and sow indoors in pots 4–6 weeks before risk of frost is past, or outdoors under cover. An upturned glass jar creates a warmer microclimate than a cloche. Harden off seedlings before transplanting them.

ROUTINE CARE

Water each plant well early on; make a shallow watering basin. Spray the area around the planting hole with horn manure 500 or stinging nettle liquid manure. If the weather is unsettled, mist the young leaves with *Equisetum arvense* 508, yarrow, or dandelion fresh teas to prevent any powdery mildew. In normal to hot weather, spray the plant with comfrey and 508 as liquid manures, in the evening after pinching off the main stem and sideshoots. Spray horn silica 501, at sunrise over the plant tops under an ascending moon, after the first fruit sets or a month before cutting the fruit.

HARVESTING AND STORING

Fruit are ripe when their stems start to wither and crack. Cut each fruit with as long a stem as possible, turn it upside down, and leave in the sun for 7–10 days to harden the skin—to cure. Protect it from night frost with fabric. Unbruised fruit stores into early winter in a cool, dry area.

TROUBLESHOOTING

Clear organic matter that encourages slugs from beneath young fruit. Pumpkins and sweet corn (*see p.222*) make good companions.

Collecting seeds

• Pumpkins and winter squash may cross-pollinate if allowed to flower at the same time.

• Cover the first female flower with a paper bag on the night before it opens.

• The next day, take a male flower, remove its petals, and insert it into a female bloom to transfer the pollen.

• Replace the bag for two more days, then remove it. Label the fruit that forms and harvest it when plant starts to die off.

• Clean the seeds as for tomatoes (*see right*).

GROWING THE PLANTS

Pumpkins and winter squash are large and productive plants, so do not grow more than you really need or have space for. To obtain the largest fruit, thin the fruitlets to 2–3 per plant.

A female flower can be identified by the embryonic fruit beneath its petals.

To deter slugs and keep the fruits clear of damp soil, place them on a mulch of dry straw or on a wooden board.

Once their skins are cured, the fruit can be stored under cover for many months.

	SPRING	SUMMER	FALL	WINTER
Sow				
Harvest				

Time to harvest: **14–22 WEEKS** • Sow or plant 3–5ft (1–1.5m) apart for bush 4–6ft, (1.2–1.8m) apart for trailing varieties

Rotation information: **ROTATION GROUP 4 • HEAVY FEEDERS**

Tomatoes

Solanum lycopersicum

Tomatoes are a very satisfying crop to grow. The fruit range from huge beefsteak to tiny cherry tomatoes, in hues from green, orange, yellow, red, and purple to black and even striped. The vine or bush types thrive in containers, as well as in the same soil as last year, if it is refreshed.

Site and soil preparation

Tomatoes need shelter, full sun, and rich, well-drained soil with pH 5.5 or above. In fall, under a descending moon, prepare the soil with well-rotted biodynamic compost and manure. Chicken manure, chopped comfrey leaves dried from last year, and wood ash all provide potassium. Another option is a 3:2:1 compost of tomato shoots and leaves, manure, and comfrey. Ten days before planting, warm the soil by covering it with a layer of compost.

Sowing and planting

Sow at a descending moon, indoors in pots in late winter or early spring, and repot as soon as two leaves unfold. After the last frost, spray with horn manure 500, in the afternoon under a descending moon, then plant outdoors, just after the first flowers trusses form. Rows 2–3ft (60–90cm) apart allow airflow and light.

Routine care

To keep plants stable, earth up or mulch with compost or mature manure topped with straw. Pinch off water shoots between the main stem and sideshoots to focus light, heat, and energy on ripening fruit. Feed every 10–14 days, spraying foliage and soil with comfrey, kelp, or stinging nettle liquid manure. Spray *Equisetum arvense* 508 fresh tea on leaves to fight fungal disease. Once fruit sets, mist over the tops with horn silica 501, at sunrise under an ascending moon, for riper flavors and better storage.

Harvesting and storing

Twist each fruit off to eat fresh, cook, or preserve. Before the first frost in fall, gather all the last green tomatoes (*see right, below*).

Troubleshooting

Tomatoes are sensitive and antagonistic: keep them away from potatoes to avoid blight, and zucchini, dill, all fennel, kohlrabi, and peppers. Spray new plants and the area around with stinging nettle cold extract to deter aphids.

Collecting seeds

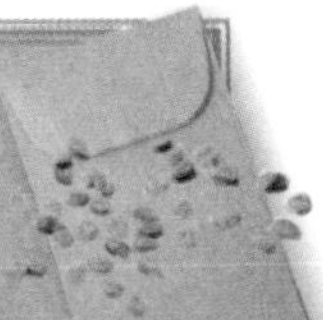

- Select fully ripe fruit, avoiding any that are still green on trusses in the middle of the plant.
- Slice the tomato open and squeeze the seeds out of the watery pulp, and into a strainer.
- Rinse under running water, rubbing the seeds gently to remove the pulp. Mix them with fine sand to make it easier.
- Dry the cleaned seeds and store in paper towels. They should keep for several years.

Providing support

Tomatoes are high yielding and become laden with heavy trusses of fruit. Support bush types by inserting a stake for each stem and tie them in, and train vine types up a single tall stake or a vertical string.

Green tomatoes

Use unripe tomatoes in chutney or fried as vegetables. You can also pull up the entire plant with its roots and hang it to ripen upside down in a warm, dry place, such as a greenhouse. Picked fruit will also ripen if placed in a bag with a banana.

	SPRING	SUMMER	FALL	WINTER
Sow				
Harvest				
Time to harvest: **12–20 WEEKS** • Plant 18-36in (45-90cm) apart, depending on variety				
Rotation information: **ROTATION GROUP 4 • HEAVY FEEDERS**				

Sweet peppers
and chili peppers
Capsicum annuum

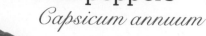

Confusing a sweet, or bell, pepper with a chili pepper is an eye-watering mistake for those not used to spicy food. Bell peppers are usually larger and rounder than chili peppers, but all have green leaf (*Capsicum*) aromas when cut. They are subtropical, so perform best if grown inside in all but the warmest climates.

GROWING FROM SEED
Sow seed ¼in (1cm) deep in flats or pots. Transplant seedlings grown in flats into pots, when the first true leaves appear after two weeks, into a 3:2:5 mix of soil, sand, and compost to grow.

If sowing direct into small pots, thin the seedlings when their true leaves appear to leave the strongest in each pot.

SITE AND SOIL PREPARATION
Peppers need dry, desert heat in full sun: add very mature compost to well-drained, friable soil, topped with coarse sand and rocks. Peppers thrive at the edges of raised beds where paving reflects heat and light. Spray the soil with horn manure 500, in the afternoon under a descending moon, before planting, then warm under cloches. to sprawl from within an open, chicken-wire cage lets more air, light, and heat onto the fruit.

HARVESTING AND STORING
Peppers ripen to green and then to hues such as red, yellow, or orange, depending on the variety. Cut, rather than pull, off each fruit, with as much stem as possible so it stores longer.

SOWING AND PLANTING
In most areas, sow peppers indoors (*see right*) from late winter onward, about 2 months before the last spring frost. They need 68°F (20°C) to germinate, in 10–15 days: cover the seed flat with glass or leave near an oven or on a sunny windowsill. Plant peppers under a descending moon in rows that are 3ft (90cm) apart.

TROUBLESHOOTING
Avoid buildup of fungal disease in soil by waiting four years before planting peppers where potatoes, tomatoes, and eggplant grew. Peppers prefer not to be near zucchini or tomatoes.

Harden off the plants and plant them out two weeks after all frost has passed. Insert stakes to provide support.

ROUTINE CARE
After planting, water with lukewarm water to avoid shocking the roots. Hoe off weeds, but do not mulch, so the topsoil stays dry. Water every 5–7 days, mixing in compost tea or liquid manure as a food source—comfrey is best. Spray horn silica 501 over the plant tops, in the morning under an ascending moon, once the first fruit forms and again during the four weeks before harvesting. Allowing half-grown plants

Collecting seeds
• Grow all types of peppers in the usual way, but allow fruit grown for seeds to ripen fully on the plants.

• Remove the ripe fruit and dry under cover in a warm, bright area. Chili peppers dry out, while peppers just shrivel.

• Halve them to extract the seeds. Wear gloves to keep from burning your skin. Leave to dry for a few hours; store in sealed jars.

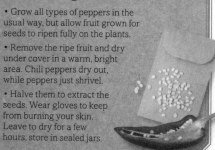

Picking the first fruit while still green encourages others to be produced.

	SPRING	SUMMER	FALL	WINTER
Sow				
Harvest				

Time to harvest: **18–26 WEEKS** • Plant out 12in (30cm) apart

Rotation information: **ROTATION GROUP 4 • MEDIUM FEEDERS**

Eggplant
Solanum melongena

The lavender-purple, black, and creamy white eggplant, also called aubergine, originated in India and is a staple of the vegetarian diet, providing a calorific energy boost with no fat. It soaks up different flavors in dishes such as moussaka and ratatouille and makes a great grilling vegetable.

SITE AND SOIL PREPARATION

Eggplant need plenty of heat, light, and humidity over their long growing season to mature. They grow best in very fertile, dark, composted soil that holds both heat and water. Only a sheltered site in full sun will do.

SOWING AND PLANTING

In temperate climates, sow indoors or in a warm greenhouse at least a month before the last expected frost. Soak the seeds overnight in a BC seed bath before sowing. Germination takes 2–3 weeks at 68°F (20°C). Pot seedlings up or plant out once the first true leaves appear; cover if the temperature drops below 59°F (15°C) at night. The roots are sensitive, so put in support stakes at planting. Leave 24in (60cm) between rows. Spray valerian 507 around eggplant growing outdoors to warm the site if late spring or early summer nights become cool.

ROUTINE CARE

Water regularly. At flowering, lightly tap the plants to mobilize the pollen or make sure bees and other pollinators can get in and out of the greenhouse or outdoor site. Spray this hungry plant and the bed with a range of liquid manures, ideally comfrey alternated with stinging nettle and kelp, every 10–14 days at any time of day. Spray *Equisetum*

arvense 508 as a fresh tea at least once after flowering to keep fungal diseases at bay.

HARVESTING AND STORING

Pick fruit when the skins are shiny and firm. The stems are tough, prickly, and thick, so wear gloves to cut, rather than twist, them off. When the skin color starts to dull, the fruit become tough and bitter even for chickens, so slice them and add them to the compost heap.

TROUBLESHOOTING

Grow eggplant next to runner beans (*see p.211*); the beans help to repel Colorado potato beetles in the areas where they occur.

Collecting seeds

• Grow only one variety of eggplant if saving seed, to prevent cross-pollination.

• Collect seeds from fruit that has been left to ripen after the main crop has been harvested.

• Cut the fruit open and remove as much of the flesh surrounding the seeds as possible.

• Place the remaining flesh in water to separate the seeds, which will sink. Collect the seeds, then dry and store them.

MULCHING

In warmer regions, after planting out eggplant in early summer, mulch around them with a thick layer of well-rotted compost, and cover it with straw. This will help to keep the soil moist and feed the plants.

PINCHING OFF

Nip off the growing tips once the plants have settled in after transplanting or are knee high. Spray horn silica 501 over the tops the next morning. This encourages more flowering and fruiting sideshoots.

	SPRING	SUMMER	FALL	WINTER
Sow				
Harvest				
Time to harvest: **24–28 WEEKS** • Plant 30–36in (60–75cm) apart				
Rotation information: **ROTATION GROUP 4 • HEAVY FEEDERS**				

Sweet corn
Zea mays

There are two types of sweet corn: corn grown for animal feed and the food industry, and the juicy corn on the cob, which we can grow at home and eat steaming hot and dripping with butter. Pick it just before eating: the sugar starts turning to starch immediately.

SITE AND SOIL PREPARATION

Sweet corn needs a long, warm growing season in full sun to ripen, ideally in slightly acidic, moisture-retentive, rich soil. Prepare the bed in late fall under a descending moon with plenty of composted manure or rich compost. If the compost is limited, lay it into furrows 4in (10cm) wide and 2in (5cm) deep, then cover with soil. Mark the furrows with sticks and sow directly into them the following spring.

SOWING AND PLANTING

In warm climates in mid-spring, sow 2–3 seeds per station in furrows 1in (2.5cm) deep and 15in (40cm) apart. Thin out the weaker seedlings. In cool regions, start the plants under cover in mid- to late spring in biodegradable pots and harden off the seedlings before planting them out in late spring or early summer, after the last frost. Sowing outdoors under protection may be a better option, because sweet corn does not do well with any root disturbance. Spray the soil with horn manure 500 just before or soon after sowing, in the afternoon under a descending moon.

ROUTINE CARE

Keep the newly sown rows weed free, but take care not to disturb the shallow roots. Earth a little soil up around the stem bases to protect them and prevent the stems from rocking in the wind. Water sweet corn well, especially while it is establishing and in summer.

HARVESTING AND STORING

Harvest cobs when their hair, or silk, withers and turns brown. Ripe kernels are plump enough to make the cob feel firm and bumpy. Pop open a kernel: if the juice is milky, the cob is ripe. Steady each stalk with one hand, then pull and slightly twist off the cob. Peel back the cob's papery outer sheath to reveal the kernels inside.

TROUBLESHOOTING

For a sweeter-tasting crop, spray horn silica 501 over the tops of the plants at sunrise just before the tassels are ready to emerge or later when the cobs are swelling. Sow only one type of sweet corn each year to avoid cross-pollination and starchy, less tasty kernels.

Collecting seeds

• Leave the best cobs to ripen for one or two months longer on the stalks, after the others in the patch have been harvested. Pick them before the first frost.

• Peel back the bleached, papery outer sheath to expose the kernels and make them easier to dry.

• Tie several cobs together, using the outer husks to save space, and hang them indoors to dry.

• In early spring, twist off the kernels, discarding any that are brown or shriveled. Store only the good ones in a glass jar.

HAND POLLINATION

Sweet corn is pollinated by the wind, so grow the plants in square blocks or patches to enable pollen to blow from the pointed male tassels to the floppy female silk on the cobs.

If it is wet or windless at the 10-day flowering time, brush a male flower over female ones to pollinate them.

COMPANION PLANTS

Sweet corn is a tall plant and requires plenty of space, which creates useful areas around its base that you can use to grow other crops—intercropping. Plant climbing green and runner beans to scale the sweet corn, which also provides support, and underplant it with trailing squash or zucchini.

	SPRING	SUMMER	FALL	WINTER
Sow				
Harvest				

Time to harvest: **20–28 WEEKS** • Sow, plant or thin 12in (30cm) apart

Rotation information: **ROTATION GROUP 4 • HEAVY FEEDERS**

Okra
Abelmoschus esculentus

Okra's edible, pointed seed pods are usually green, but may be pink or white. You can eat them raw, fried, pickled, or in a stew, such as gumbo or creole. Gumbo refers to the plant's name in its native East Africa, where it thrives in humid, warm conditions. However, okra can also be grown in temperate climates under cover, such as in a greenhouse.

SITE AND SOIL PREPARATION

Okra needs full sun, humidity, and steady daytime temperatures of 68–86°F (20–30°C) in sun. The soil should also be warm, as well as fertile, well drained, and moisture retentive. Dig in plenty of biodynamic compost or well-rotted manure—horse or sheep manure is best, since it is warmer and less dense than cow dung. Spray the bed with horn manure 500 before sowing or transplanting, just after hoeing any weeds, ideally in the afternoon under a descending moon.

SOWING AND PLANTING

Before sowing, lightly smooth the rough, rounded seeds with fine sandpaper, then soak overnight in BC or some horn manure 500 left over from an afternoon's spraying to help germination. In cool climates, use a propagator to maintain the 61°F (16°C) needed for germination. A month before the last frost date, sow seeds under a descending moon, ½–1in (1–2cm) deep in rows 2–3ft (60–90cm) apart.

ROUTINE CARE

Water okra regularly as it establishes and mulch with compost. In an afternoon, spray the foliage with kelp, comfrey, or stinging nettle liquid manure or diluted vermicompost, all of which are rich in nitrogen and nutrients okra needs. Then spray the entire plant in the morning with chamomile tea to stabilize the nitrogen.

HARVESTING AND STORING

Start cutting immature pods from midsummer, every other day, once they are 2–4in (5–10cm) long. The more you pick, the more the plant will produce. Longer, mature pods are woody and stringy. Use a knife and wear gloves—the hairy leaves can irritate the skin. You can store unwashed pods for several days if you keep them whole and cool. Pull old plants and chop up the stems before composting them to help them decompose more easily.

TROUBLESHOOTING

Avoid overwatering okra because it causes overly lush foliage and watery pods. To help the plant get settled after being transplanted, when it is at risk of attack from aphids, spray the foliage with 24-hour stinging nettle cold extract.

Collecting seeds

• Grow only one variety of okra for seed saving to avoid cross-pollination. Allow the pods to grow as large as possible.

• Dry the pods on the plant or indoors. Split the pods open, collect the seeds, and dry them for several days before storing them in glass jars.

• Collect new seeds every year: they do not store well for long.

PROVIDING SUPPORT

Okra are tall plants, and with enough heat, soil fertility, and water, they can easily reach 6ft (1.8m) tall by the end of summer. However, even young plants that are half this height can become top heavy. To keep them from collapsing, insert tall stakes when the plants reach 2ft (60cm), and regularly tie them in, using soft string.

	SPRING	SUMMER	FALL	WINTER
Sow				
Harvest				

Time to harvest: **18–23 WEEKS** • Sow and plant out 12–18in (30–45cm) apart

Rotation information: **ROTATION GROUP 4 • HEAVY FEEDERS**

Tomatillos
Physalis ixocarpa

Tomatillos are native to Mexico, where their tart flavor provides the basis for salsa verde. Although its name suggests otherwise, tomatillo is not a green version of the traditional red garden tomato. It is, in fact, related to the cape gooseberry, and because the fruit is enclosed in a papery outer husk, the plant is also commonly called the husk tomato or husk cherry. Tomatillos are self-pollinating, but growing at least two plants ensures good pollination and fruit set.

SITE AND SOIL PREPARATION
Tomatillos need fertile, well-drained soil, and plenty of sun. They grow well in raised beds, or pots, if the garden soil is unsuitable. Aerate the soil to a spade's depth, and fork in some mature biodynamic compost. Avoid planting in beds where potatoes, tomatoes, okra, eggplant, or peppers have grown in the last three years.

SOWING AND PLANTING
Tomatillos need hot weather and a long growing season. They are sown indoors in early spring, while the moon is descending, at between 68–80°F (20–26°C), 6–8 weeks before the last frost. Sow into small pots, and plant out under an ascending moon once hardened off. Plant them more deeply in the soil than in their pots to keep them moist. Water well, but ensure the soil does not become rinsed of nutrients.

ROUTINE CARE
Keep plants well watered, and mulch with compost covered with straw to help retain moisture. Support them with stakes or trellis so the fruit is easier to pick and less likely to attract pests and diseases. Before flowering, spray with comfrey liquid manure under a descending moon. Once in flower, pinch off the growing tips to keep the plants compact and to concentrate

nutrients and flavors. Then spray horn silica 501 on the next fruit day in the morning and late afternoon. Follow this with stinging nettle or kelp liquid manure.

HARVESTING AND STORING
Harvest the fruit when the moon is ascending. Wash before storing in the refrigerator, where they will last several weeks, or freeze them. Avoid storing them in airtight containers.

TROUBLESHOOTING
Tomatillos dislike dry soil in summer and cannot handle frost. Keep aphids and beetles at bay with stinging nettle 24-hour cold extract.

Collecting seeds
- Collect several fruit with their husks intact and let them ripen further in the sun for a few days after picking.
- Remove the husks, cut the fruit open, and soak in water for a few days. Stir and remove the scum.
- The best seeds will sink in the water. Collect and dry them, then store in an airtight container.

Tomatillos flower and fruit over a long period, although the fruit can be slow to ripen unless grown in warm, sheltered conditions. In cool regions, they may be best grown in large containers that are kept under cover.

Tomatillos are ripe when their husks start to change color and split from the plump fruit inside.

To keep well, only remove the husk when the fruit is about to be eaten.

	SPRING	SUMMER	FALL	WINTER
Sow	▮			
Harvest		▮	▮	

Time to harvest: **28–23 WEEKS** • Plant out 3ft (1m) apart

Rotation information: **ROTATION GROUP 4 • MEDIUM FEEDERS**

Strawberries
Fragaria × *ananassa*

Strawberries can be costly to buy but easy to grow, and there are two types. Flavorful summer-fruiting strawberries are planted in fall to crop once in early summer. Everbearing types have milder tasting berries but fruit repeatedly from midsummer into fall, and are planted in spring.

SITE AND SOIL PREPARATION
Strawberries have shallow roots and need plenty of biodynamic compost, well-rotted manure, or leaf mold dug into the bed before planting. They like warm, sandy, and slightly acidic soil that never dries. Give them plenty of sun, air, and warmth to produce a good crop.

SOWING AND PLANTING
Start by buying certified virus-free, organically-raised plants, planting them out in rows when the moon is descending. Leave the crown, where the roots join the leaves, at soil level, exposed to light. Water the plants in.

ROUTINE CARE
Mulch around plants after planting, keeping it away from the leaves. The next spring, weed the soil, and mulch beneath the strawberry plants with straw, or better still, aged spruce or pine needles. This keeps the plants firm and healthy, and also discourages slugs. When the moon is descending, spray the bed with horn manure in early spring. Spray horn silica 501 when the berries start to form. Keep the soil moist and net against birds. Strawberry beds should be moved every three years, but the best fruit comes from two-year-old plants, grown from runners (*see right*) taken from the previous year's bed. In the very first year of planting, pick the flowers off to make for better runners long-term. The runners are taken in midsummer and planted out in fall in a separate bed ready for next year. After the first year this means there will always be two beds of strawberries in the garden: this year's crop, and one planted, ready for the following year.

HARVESTING AND STORING
Pick the berries when dark red and firm, pinching them off at the stalk to avoid bruising. Eat the fruit fresh or freeze them.

TROUBLESHOOTING
Water plants from below to prevent dirt and disease spores from splashing on the leaves and fruit. In damp weather spray *Equisetum arvense* 508 as a fresh tea before and after flowering, and as the fruit ripens. In fall clear away the old leaves and spray with BC. Keep beds mulched for tastier and healthier fruit.

Planting runners
• New strawberry plants are raised from runners—small plantlets—produced by the parent plant, not from seeds.

• In midsummer extend the runners from the best plants, and pin the plantlets down into small pots of potting mix buried into the soil.

• Cut off the runner beyond the first plantlet. Keep the plantlet well watered until it develops roots. The stem between the parent strawberry and the rooted plantlet can then be cut.

• The new strawberry plant can now be planted directly into the soil, ready to fruit next year.

PROTECTING THE FRUIT
Ripe strawberries are as desirable to birds and many other pests as they are to us, so it is important to protect them as soon as they start to show color in early summer.

Placing dry straw beneath the fruit deters slugs and keeps them off the moist soil, where they could decay.

Cover plants with nets or cages to protect the fruit from birds. Ensure birds cannot sneak in underneath.

Strawberries grow well in baskets, which keep them away from slugs.

	SPRING	SUMMER	FALL	WINTER
Plant				
Harvest				

Time to harvest: **2–4 WEEKS AFTER FLOWERING** • Plant 12in (30cm) apart, 18in (45cm) between rows

Rotation information: **ROTATION GROUP 4 • MEDIUM FEEDERS**

Raspberries

Rubus idaeus

Firm, juicy raspberries with fruit in a range of jewel-like colors can be picked from early summer through fall if you plant both summer- and fall-fruiting varieties.

SITE AND SOIL PREPARATION

Choose a permanent site for your raspberries in full sun or partial shade, and clear perennial weeds before spraying horn manure 500 on the soil under a descending moon. Raspberries need fertile, well-drained, slightly acidic soil, but will settle for a slightly alkaline soil if plenty of well-rotted manure and biodynamic compost is dug in before planting. Add finely chopped comfrey leaves to provide potassium.

SOWING AND PLANTING

Buy certified disease-free, virus-resistant, bare-root, one-year-old canes for planting in fall or spring. Choose a fruit day under a descending moon and plant canes with their tops finishing 1in (2.5cm) below the surface of the soil. Over time, develop the bed with root cuttings from red varieties taken in spring on fruit days at the end of the moon's ascent and planted on a descending moon. Or guide the growing tips of black and purple varieties down to the soil, peg them, and separate them from the mother plant once rooted.

ROUTINE CARE

After planting, cut the first green shoots off summer-fruiting raspberries before they flower to make the plants stronger long term. They will crop from their second year onward.

Fall raspberries can crop in their first year. Before the shoots reach the first wire, encourage erect growth by spraying horn silica 501 early in the morning on a fruit day.

HARVESTING AND STORING

Choose a dry day, ideally when the moon is ascending, and gently twist off the fruit, leaving the core on the plant. The berries are best eaten fresh, but, unlike many soft fruits, freeze well, too.

TROUBLESHOOTING

Smother summer weeds with a mulch of leaf mold or compost. In hot weather, water thoroughly every few days; avoid short daily splashes that leave the topsoil wet and promote fungus diseases such as gray mold (*Botrytis*).

Pruning raspberries

- Summer raspberries canes that grew and produced fruit in one year will die the next. Prune these out shortly after harvesting under a descending moon.

- For each plant choose up to four strong new shoots that will fruit next year and cut them back to four buds. Prune out the remaining new shoots.

- For fall raspberries, cut all stems down to the ground in fall in their first year, ready to reshoot in spring. In subsequent years, leave canes to overwinter and cut down in spring.

TRAINING RASPBERRIES

Erect a support system with stout posts at the end of each row with one or two wires strung between them. Position shoots between the wires as they grow, and cut them when they reach the top.

RAINBOW FRUIT

Golden raspberries are said to be the sweetest, but along with black and purple varieties, have the distinctive flavor and appearance of the species.

EQUISETUM MANURE

To protect fruit from disease, spray *Equisetum arvense* 508 liquid manure on the soil before the plants get too tall, ideally on a fruit day with a descending moon.

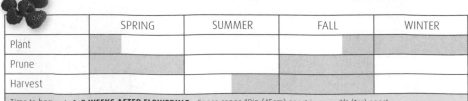

	SPRING	SUMMER	FALL	WINTER
Plant	▓		▓	
Prune	▓		▓	
Harvest		▓	▓	

Time to harvest: **6–8 WEEKS AFTER FLOWERING** • Space canes 18in (45cm) apart in rows 3ft (1m) apart

Rotation information: **NOT ROTATED • MEDIUM FEEDER**

Blackberries
and hybrid berries
Rubus fruticosus

There are few better wild harvests than blackberries picked from bramble-filled hedgerows. But homegrown blackberries are simple to grow, easier to pick than their wild counterparts—and unlikely to be covered in roadside dust. Even sweeter tasting are hybrid crosses between raspberries and blackberries, such as tayberries, boysenberries, and loganberries.

SITE AND SOIL PREPARATION

Blackberries and hybrid berries need plenty of space and similar soil: slightly acidic, fertile, and enriched with plenty of biodynamic compost. Blackberries enjoy full sun or partial shade, while hybrid berries need full sun. Start by clearing perennial weeds; this can be made easier by spraying BC and horn manure 500, which have a loosening effect on the soil.

SOWING AND PLANTING

Plant container-grown plants in late fall or early spring under a descending moon. Install a post-and-wire trellis for the plants to climb. Plant with the top of the root ball 4in (10cm) below the soil.

ROUTINE CARE

Boost the soil while the moon is descending: in early spring spray BC and mulch with biodynamic compost. Then spray horn silica 501 just before flowering. When the fruit has set, tie the fruiting canes in to their supports—good spacing

ensures healthier fruit that is easier to pick. In late fall, spray horn manure 500, turn in the existing mulch, and dress with new compost. Protect the turned soil with straw.

HARVESTING AND STORING

Pick ripe, firm berries in dry weather, trying to leave the stalks attached. Eat them fresh or freeze without washing. Wash as they defrost.

TROUBLESHOOTING

Net against birds, which are their main pest. Use a diluted tree paste on pruning wounds.

Pruning blackberries

• After fruiting, under a descending moon, cut out old, stiff woody canes that have produced a crop of berries.

• Leave this year's tender new green shoots to grow upward and then weave them onto the horizontal wires, ready to bear fruit next year.

PROPAGATING

To increase your blackberry patch, propagate under a descending moon by guiding the growing tips of strong, new shoots down to the soil, and pegging them into the ground until they are rooted. They can then be separated from the mother plant and replanted.

YARROW AND NETTLE TEA SPRAY

Collect yarrow flowers to make a yarrow tea (*see p.30*), and add some stinging nettles as the water is boiling. Remove from the heat, and strain once cool. Spray the blackberries before and after flowering to keep fungal diseases at bay. Then spray comfrey liquid manure for a ripe, abundant crop.

	SPRING	SUMMER	FALL	WINTER
Plant				
Prune				
Harvest				

Time to harvest: **6–8 WEEKS AFTER FLOWERING** • Space plants 6ft (1.8m) apart in rows 12ft (3.6m) apart.

Rotation information: **NOT ROTATED • MEDIUM FEEDER**

Gooseberries
Ribes uva-crispa

The relentlessly prickly, wiry stems of these shrubs protect tangy, tart-tasting berries that are ideal for jam-making, chutneys, tarts, fruit salads, and taste superb in gooseberry pie. The long-lived bushes are really very easy to grow as bushes or upright cordons once you get the hang of pruning them.

SITE AND SOIL PREPARATION

Gooseberries grow in most soils in sun or part shade, but beware of planting them in frost pockets: their flowers may be decimated by early spring frost. Prepare the soil under a descending moon by digging an oblong hole a little deeper than your spade; overfill it with 60:40 good soil to biodynamic compost to create a mound 4–6in (10–15cm) above soil level. This increases airflow around the plant and helps prevent mildew.

SOWING AND PLANTING

For a crop the next summer, the best time to plant two-year-old bushes is 1 month after the fall equinox, ideally under a descending moon. Alternatively, plant a strong shoot, or leg, removing all buds below the soil and leaving 6in (15cm) above ground—enough for 4–5 buds—for a crop in the second year.

ROUTINE CARE

Mulch in spring to keep weeds away from bushes. Water in late spring when the berries swell.

HARVESTING AND STORING

Ideally, pick berries when the moon is ascending. Leave the stalk attached to keep the skin intact so the fruit is less likely to oxidize and spoil before use.

TROUBLESHOOTING

Mix finely chopped comfrey leaves and oak bark into the soil-compost mix to add the slow-release potassium and calcium gooseberries often lack. Spray the plant with dandelion, yarrow and *Equisetum arvense* 508 teas before and after flowering to avoid fungal disease, and with elder decoction to discourage aphids, which cause leaf curl. Slow sap movement caused by changeable early spring weather attracts saw flies: keep sap moving with nettle or chamomile tea. If the blockage was caused by frost lifting and disturbing the roots, tread them down gently.

Pruning gooseberries

- In late fall, prune off any dead wood and most of the previous year's growth, leaving two buds to provide the new season's growth.
- Keep the centers of bushes open to air and light by removing a few of the oldest stems at the base. Cut back the other main stems at the tips to shape the bush.
- The berries start to swell in late spring: at the next ascending moon, cut the new sideshoots back to the fifth leaf, leaving the main stems untouched. This reduces the risk of mildew and encourages fruiting spurs to form for the following year.

FALL PRUNING

Perform late-fall pruning on sunny afternoons that are crisp, but are definitely not freezing. Pruning sideshoots to two buds prompts the formation of plenty of fruiting shoots while keeping the plant open to light and air.

Use clean, sharp pruners to cut just above an outward-facing bud.

RIPE HARVEST

Berries are ripe when plump and slightly translucent if backlit by the sun. Birds also appreciate the buds and berries, so net the crop at bud burst and as it ripens.

Red or reddish-pink gooseberries are usually the sweetest of all.

Yellow gooseberries range in hue from very pale to amber or golden yellow.

	SPRING	SUMMER	FALL	WINTER
Plant				
Prune				
Harvest				

Time to harvest: **10 WEEKS AFTER FLOWERING** · Plant bushes 5ft (1.5m) apart

Rotation information: **NOT ROTATED · MEDIUM FEEDERS**

Black currants

Ribes nigrum

Of all the soft fruits, black currants are the richest in vitamin C. Eat them fresh from the bush or make them into juices, jellies and jams, not to mention wine. They are self-pollinating, so one plant can provide a crop.

SITE AND SOIL PREPARATION

Black currants need fertile, well-drained soil that is not too acidic (above pH 6) in full sun or part shade. Avoid frost pockets—flowers may not set fruit. Prepare the soil under a descending moon: dig as deep as you can; backfill with 4in (10cm) of good soil mixed with sand; fill with a mix of good soil, very finely chopped comfrey leaves, and well-rotted biodynamic compost with bird or chicken manure for extra potassium.

SOWING AND PLANTING

Plant a two-year-old, bare-root bush or stool (*see right*). You can also take 10in (25cm) hardwood cuttings under an ascending moon in late fall: bury them with just the top two buds above ground. A year later, transplant them under a descending moon to a permanent bed.

ROUTINE CARE

Mulch to suppress weeds, add fertility, and keep the soil moist. *Equisetum arvense* 508, yarrow or chamomile tea, sprayed on all green parts from early spring onward, keeps mildew at bay. At every Moon–Saturn opposition between spring equinox and harvest, spray kelp, seaweed, or comfrey liquid manure on and around the bushes to keep them balanced and strong. Spray horn silica 501 in the air above the plant just before flowering and after harvest. Apply horn manure 500 to the soil one evening near the fall equinox.

HARVESTING AND STORING

Snip off fruit trusses, or sprigs, with scissors when the fruit is dark, shiny, and ripe.

TROUBLESHOOTING

Net buds and berries against birds. Spray cold-extract or fresh nettle over the plant early in the season to discourage aphids and mites.

Pruning black currants

- Avoid pruning just after harvest: wait until a descending moon just after the fall equinox to allow sap to return to and replenish the roots.

- Prune back fruited stems, to leave the one-year-old, new stems—they will produce next year's fruit. This also creates an open-centered bush to help it resist pests and diseases.

- Mature bushes grow up to 5–6ft (1.5–1.8m) tall.

PLANTING A STOOL

The easy way to start growing black currants is to plant bare-root plants, or stools, that have been certified disease-free. Do this under a descending moon: between fall and spring is best. Plant the stool about 2in (5cm) deeper than the level of the soil mark on the stem to encourage new shoots to emerge directly from soil.

Prepare the soil before planting by digging as deep as you can.

Check the depth against a post laid across the planting hole.

Once the stool is planted, firm in gently and water thoroughly.

	SPRING	SUMMER	FALL	WINTER
Plant				
Prune				
Harvest				

Time to harvest: **10–12 WEEKS AFTER FLOWERING** • Thin and plant out 5ft (1.5m) apart

Rotation information: **NOT ROTATED • HEAVY FEEDERS**

Red currants
and white currants
Ribes rubrum

Red currants and their close but sweeter-tasting cousins, white currants, are used for jams, jellies, home wine-making, and desserts. They also freeze well, so you can enjoy them at any time of year. Currants are grown in a similar way to gooseberries (*see p.228*).

(*see p.228*)

SITE AND SOIL PREPARATION

To crop well, red and white currants need a sunny or part-shaded site that is cold enough in winter to prompt dormancy, yet frost-free during early spring flowering. They need well-drained soil—do not plant in dips in the land, which may get waterlogged. Dig plenty of biodynamic compost into the soil before planting. Add large amounts of comfrey leaves to the compost when making it, or sprinkle finely chopped comfrey leaves into the hole at planting (comfrey provides potassium for healthy shoots and steady yields).

SOWING AND PLANTING

Plant currants bought as container-grown bushes from a nursery at any time of year, preferably under a descending moon. You could also grow them from hardwood cuttings taken in late fall.

ROUTINE CARE

Mulch in spring with compost and chopped comfrey leaves covered by straw to combat weeds. Water in spring just before the berries start to swell. Spray horn manure 500 at or before planting and at fall equinox, ideally under a descending moon,

to encourage worm activity. Spray the soil with BC at spring equinox to cleanse it of winter fungal pathogens. Spray horn silica 501 between bud burst and flowering.

HARVESTING AND STORING

Use scissors to snip off ripe clusters, or strigs, ideally when the moon is ascending. Be careful—the fruits explode if held too firmly.

TROUBLESHOOTING

Maintain plant health between bud burst and harvest with a spray each of *Equisetum arvense* 508 tea, and kelp liquid manure.

Pruning red and white currants

- In late fall, prune off any dead wood and most of the previous year's growth. Cut one or two of the oldest stems almost to their bases.
- Fruit is borne on both old and young wood, so leave two outward-facing buds on the remaining fruiting shoots.
- Keep the centers of bush currants open to air and light.

TRAINING CURRANTS

Red and white currants may be grown as freestanding bushes or as cordons (single stem with fruiting spurs) along a wall or trellis. Plant currant bushes 4–5ft (1.2–1.5m) apart.

You can space currants grown as cordons just 12–18in (30–45cm) apart.

Use figure-eight knots to tie in cordons to support stakes or wires.

PROTECTING THE CROP

Protect the new buds in spring and summer berries from birds with netting. Do not overwater: too much will burst the berries.

	SPRING	SUMMER	FALL	WINTER
Plant				
Prune				
Harvest				

Time to harvest: **10–14 WEEKS AFTER FLOWERING** · Plant cordons 12-18in (30–45cm), bushes 4-5ft (1.2-1.5m) apart

Rotation information: **NOT ROTATED • MEDIUM FEEDERS**

Blueberries
Vaccinium corymbosum

The blueberry has been hailed as a superfood that can reduce the risk of cancer, heart disease, and some chronic illnesses—and fortunately they taste great, too. Blueberry plants are low maintenance and cold tolerant, but only in very acidic soil with a pH of 4.5–5.5; if this rules out your garden soil, try growing them in pots.

SITE AND SOIL PREPARATION

Blueberries need sun, perhaps with afternoon shade, and well-drained soil. Most soils—especially soils with lime added for brassicas—are too alkaline or not acidic enough. You can grow blueberries in pots or dedicated beds filled with acidic (lime-free) compost or create acidic soil by adding pine-needle leaf mold, pine bark, wood chips, coffee grounds, and composted sawdust.

SOWING AND PLANTING

Plant under a descending moon, either two- or three-year-old container-grown bushes, from late fall to early spring, or rooted suckers from existing plants in early spring.

ROUTINE CARE

Mulch well with acidic mulches and water with rainwater, rather than alkaline (hard) tapwater. Spray the soil with horn manure 500 at the fall and spring equinoxes, in the morning. During the first two barren years of plants grown from cuttings, spray horn silica 501 just before removing the flowers (*see box, right*). Spray 501 over fruiting plants in beds and container-grown plants under an ascending moon, once either side of flowering, to enhance fruit flavor and ripeness.

HARVESTING AND STORING

Pick berries when they are blue-black, plump, and slightly soft with white blooms; any that do not pull away easily have little flavor. Berries store for up to a week in the refrigerator; wash them in vinegar water to keep away mold.

TROUBLESHOOTING

Net the fruit to deter birds. Keep the soil cool and moist by mulching and watering.

Pruning blueberries

- If you have raised plants from suckers, remove the flowers in the first two years to divert energy into forming strong roots below ground and a bushy shape above it.
- Remove suckers growing from the roots of young plants, and branches blocking light in the center.
- As the plants mature, allow a couple of root suckers to grow each year and regenerate the plants, if necessary.
- Prune established plants—four years and over—when dormant by cutting out any dead or damaged wood, under a descending moon. Cut down the oldest shoots (*see right*).

POLLINATION

Blueberries are self-pollinating, but it is best to grow at least two or three to aid pollination and provide enough fruit for an average family. The best pollinators are butterflies and bumblebees, so entice them with companion plants, such as crocuses and cherry trees.

These attractive shrubs produce beautiful little flowers in spring.

PRUNING OLDER BUSHES

When pruning bushes that are at least four years old, cut the thickest, oldest shoots down to the base, if possible to a strong new shoot at or near soil level.

	SPRING	SUMMER	FALL	WINTER
Plant				
Prune				
Harvest				
Time to harvest: **8–10 WEEKS AFTER FLOWERING** • Plant 5ft (1.5m) apart				
Rotation information: **NOT ROTATED • MEDIUM FEEDERS**				

Cranberries
Vaccinium macrocarpon

Cranberries are high in vitamin C and antioxidants, and mouthwateringly sweet, whether you eat them fresh, crushed as juice, or as cranberry sauce. They are North American natives, where they enjoy acidic soils in bogs, so if you want them to thrive and fruit well, give them similar conditions in your garden, and lots of care.

SITE AND SOIL PREPARATION

Cranberries need cold winters to produce fruiting buds, a long growing season from mid-spring to late fall to ripen the fruit, and a wet but well-drained soil with pH 4.0–5.5. Wet soil by a pond is an option; use pine mulch to acidify the soil; or create an 8in (20cm) deep bed (*see p.231*) with acidic soil, under a decending moon.

SOWING AND PLANTING

Plant rooted cuttings or container-grown plants under a descending moon in spring, in the soil, pots, or hanging baskets. Dip the roots of this shallow-rooting shrub in BC to colonize them with mycorrhizal fungi, which help roots to feed.

ROUTINE CARE

Water regularly, especially young plants, with rainwater, which is more acidic than tapwater, to keep roots moist. Constantly flooding soil washes it of nutrients until plants succumb to disease, so spray horn manure 500 in the afternoon at spring and fall equinox on the plants and soil. Spray horn silica 501 above the bush, at sunrise under an ascending moon, when flowering ends in midsummer. Topdress hanging baskets with acidic compost every year and spray the foliage with kelp liquid manure after pruning and fruit set.

HARVESTING AND STORING

Rooted cuttings crop from the third year; mature plants crop in the first year after planting. Pick berries when dark red and seeds are brown, before the first frost. Freeze the fruit or keep in a container for several weeks in the refrigerator.

TROUBLESHOOTING

To maintain soil acidity, protect the plants from extreme winter cold, keep the soil moist and weed-free in summer, and top up beds each year after harvest with sand and a pine-needle mulch.

Pruning cranberries

• Cranberries need only light pruning to shape the plant, stop its long runners from taking over the garden, and make harvesting much easier.

• Prune only once plants are three years old, in early spring before new green growth starts.

• Comb each bush with a hand fork or rake to identify the longest runners and cut them back to shape. New fruiting sideshoots or uprights will grow from the pruned runners.

NETTLE MANURE

Cranberries are self pollinating, so only one is needed to produce a crop. Just before flowering, give plants a boost by spraying them with stinging nettle liquid manure (*see below and p.38*).

Cut nettle stems and leaves—they are highest in nutrients when just in flower.

Pack the stems into a net sack before macerating in rainwater for 4–10 days.

Soak 2–4oz (50–100g) nettles per 1¾ pints (1 liter) of water.

	SPRING	SUMMER	FALL	WINTER
Plant	▨			
Prune	▨			
Harvest			▨	

Time to harvest: **20–26 WEEKS AFTER FLOWERING** • Plant 3ft (90cm) apart

Rotation information: **NOT ROTATED • LIGHT FEEDERS**

Melons
Cucumis melo

Although melons are warm-climate plants, you can still grow them in cooler climates—use hardy varieties and give them the best chance of ripening by sowing seed early and keeping the plants warm either in a greenhouse or outdoors in a poly house. Cantaloupes (muskmelons) are most likely to succeed.

SITE AND SOIL PREPARATION

Full sun is vital; the long taproots need moisture-retentive, humus-rich subsoil. Before sowing, dig in plenty of well-rotted manure or biodynamic compost, under a descending moon. Weed the bed with a couple of passes two weeks apart and spray a 7:3 mixture of horn manure 500 and stinging nettle liquid manure, over it once in the afternoon to keep the soil friable.

SOWING AND PLANTING

In warm climates, sow in late spring under an ascending moon, ideally at opposition to Saturn. Soak seeds in BC for an hour before sowing sideways into well-drained hills (*see right*), to speed germination and avoid stems rotting at the bases. Sow six seeds per hill; thin to 3–4 seedlings. In cool regions, sow indoors at 70–75°F (21–24°C), singly in biodegradable pots, in mid-spring. Spray valerian 507 on the soil in the evening and cover to warm it before planting. Plant seedlings, removing pot bases, two weeks after the last frost; keep at 61°F (16°C) or more.

ROUTINE CARE

Mulch with compost or straw in warm climates to keep the soil moist and obtain the most benefit from twice-weekly watering. Use tepid, not cold, water to avoid checks in growth. Feed by watering the soil or foliage with kelp, comfrey, or stinging nettle liquid manure.

Hand-pollinate each plant under cover once it has four female flowers—one male flower will pollinate four females. Mist 501 over plants at sunrise after flowering and pinch sideshoots to 2–3 leaves to keep the plants airy. Stop watering as the melons swell and pinch off any really small fruit so that the largest ones ripen fully.

HARVESTING AND STORING

Melons are ripe when the skin is soft and plump, and fruit comes off as you twist and pull the stalk gently. Muskmelons also smell musky. Eat them fresh or freeze as melon sorbet.

TROUBLESHOOTING

Melons suffer if overwatered, underfed, or exposed to cold. Keep the plants tidy by pinching back sideshoots.

Collecting seeds

- Melon seeds can be scooped out from healthy, disease-free, ripe fruit after harvesting them for eating.
- Rub the seeds in sand or ash first to make cleaning off the pulp easier, then rinse the seeds well in running water.
- Dry the seeds and store in labeled paper envelopes. They will last for several years.

MAKING A HILL

Make 6in (15cm) tall hills from a 4:1:5 mixture of lightly packed topsoil, sand, and compost. Space them 6–8ft (1.8–2.5m) apart. Alternatively, sink single pots or terra-cotta pipe sections into growing bags or beds.

PROVIDING SUPPORT

Melons ripen better if trained up trellis rather than over soil, but they are heavy, so need support.

Raise melons off the soil to stop them from rotting: an upturned pot is ideal.

Support melons on trellis with slings, to prevent falling and bruising.

	SPRING	SUMMER	FALL	WINTER
Sow				
Harvest				

Time to harvest: **12 WEEKS** • Sow batches of seed or plant out seedlings 6–8ft (1.8–2.5m) apart

Rotation information: **ROTATION GROUP 4 • HEAVY FEEDERS**

Apples
Malus domestica

Apples are the most widely grown hardy fruit in the world. They come in a huge variety of textures and tastes and are delicious eaten raw or cooked. You can train them all sorts of ways, from large trees to fans or single-stemmed cordons.

SITE AND SOIL PREPARATION

Choose a sunny, airy, but sheltered site. Apples prefer well-drained, clay-loam soil that is neutral or slightly alkaline. Well before planting, clear all weeds in several passes, spraying barrel compost after each weeding, under a descending moon in the evening, for healthy soil. Spray horn manure 500 in the evening at the last descending moon before planting to settle the soil.

SOWING AND PLANTING

Plant trees when dormant, between late fall and early spring, under a descending moon, ideally at moon-opposition Saturn.

ROUTINE CARE

Spray BC in late afternoon at spring equinox on the trunk and soil to ward off fungal diseases. Spray horn silica 501 in the early morning over treetops, either side of flowering, to boost growth. If heavy crops set, thin clusters after the June drop (*see facing page*). Cut out the central fruit and any damaged ones. Thin again at midsummer to leave one fruit per cluster. Apply tree paste in mid-fall. Spray 500 under the tree in late afternoon at fall equinox for healthy roots.

HARVESTING AND STORING

Eat early season apples soon after harvest. Midseason apples keep for up to eight weeks; late-season ones last over winter. Store them in slatted flats in a cool, dry place.

TROUBLESHOOTING

Most apple trees need another tree nearby that flowers at the same time to pollinate it. Plant several trees or choose one to flower at the same time as a neighbor's tree.

Pruning apples

• Prune in early spring when the plant is pushing sap out, rather than sucking in potentially harmful organisms. The best time to do this is when the moon is ascending, ideally on a fruit day.

• Remove damaged, congested, or unproductive growth.

• On spur-bearing apple trees, which produce fruit on short sideshoots from branches at least two years old, lightly shorten the current year's growth on the main branches, reducing weak stems by up to half. Cut back sideshoots on what remains to 4–6 buds.

• For tip-bearing apples, which bear fruit at the ends of stems produced the previous year, cut back a few of the older stems.

APPLE BUDS

Spray *Equisetum arvense* 508 and fresh teas of chamomile, stinging nettle, dandelion, oak bark, or yarrow, on buds from bud burst onward, to increase the tree's resistance to pests and fungal diseases. Apply at a time of high humidity or in the days leading up to a full or perigee moon.

COMPANION PLANTS

Wildflower meadows around apple trees will encourage beneficial insects, but keep the soil under the trees free of weeds and perennial grasses. Spray the area with horn manure 500 in the afternoon and horn silica 501 in the morning.

	SPRING	SUMMER	FALL	WINTER
Plant				
Prune				
Harvest				

Time to harvest: **14–20 WEEKS AFTER FLOWERING** • Plant 2½–32ft (0.75–10.5m) apart, depending on type and variety

Rotation information: **NOT ROTATED • MEDIUM FEEDERS**

Pears
Pyrus communis

The pear is often called the queen of fruit, owing to its shapely form and refined taste. Pears are juicier and less tart than apples and have a distinctive, gritty texture. The trees grow much like apples, but are vulnerable to frost as they flower earlier.

SITE AND SOIL PREPARATION

Pears need sun, warmth, and shelter. The best soil is slightly acidic (pH6.5). Avoid heavy soil that warms up slowly in early spring. Weed and prepare the soil as for apples (*see facing page*).

SOWING AND PLANTING

Dwarf and semidwarf varieties, often grown as cordons, are most suited to gardens. Plant under a descending moon, when trees are dormant: dig a hole wider than it is deep; spread the roots downward from the trunk; backfill with mature biodynamic compost and good soil.

ROUTINE CARE

Spray horn manure 500, in the afternoon under a descending moon, in spring and fall after routine weeding to restore the soil. Spray *Equisetum arvense* 508 as a tea over the whole tree before flowering to prevent fungal diseases. Spray horn silica 501 above the tree, in the very early morning at an ascending moon, after fruit set and again in the weeks leading up to harvest, for ripeness and flavor.

HARVESTING AND STORING

Eat the ripe fruit of summer varieties in midsummer, soon after picking. The main season is from early fall to late winter: harvest unblemished, slightly unripe fruit to ripen indoors and for storing. Pears keep for up to three months, if stored in cool, dry conditions—slatted boxes aid airflow.

TROUBLESHOOTING

For consistent fruiting, plant at least two trees that flower at the same time. If growth is poor, spray comfrey or kelp liquid manure before flowering and after fruit set to prevent mineral deficiencies. Spray stinging nettle and chamomile teas alternately, twice each season on the leaves to prevent stress. If the site is prone to spring frost, protect the trees with garden fabric during flowering.

Pruning pears

• The best time to prune is on a fruit day under an ascending moon.

  • In early summer, shorten side stems and fruit-bearing sideshoots (spurs) and cut out nonfruiting sideshoots.

  • Prune hard in winter to keep the tree open to light and air: remove crossing, congested, and a few older stems. Cut back strongly upright stems to shape. Thin congested spurs.

Apply tree paste in fall on summer-cropping trees before pruning; apply it on later varieties after pruning.

THINNING FRUITLETS

Thin out any substandard fruitlets in the month after they form, especially any that are unusually small or in some way damaged. Thinning allows the best fruit to mature to full size and lets in more air and light, needed for healthy ripening.

CLEARING FALLEN FRUIT

Pears (and apples) naturally drop fruitlets in early summer, but be diligent about collecting and composting them to avoid attracting flies, wasps, and disease-causing organisms.

	SPRING	SUMMER	FALL	WINTER
Plant				
Prune				
Harvest				

Time to harvest: **16–20 WEEKS AFTER FLOWERING** • Plant 30in (75cm) to 20ft (6m) apart, depending on type and variety

Rotation information: **NOT ROTATED • MEDIUM FEEDERS**

Sweet cherries
Prunus avium

Grown as large trees or as fans on a sun-drenched wall, juicy sweet cherries are plucked and enjoyed straight from the tree. To crop well, most need at least one partner for essential cross-pollination; if you have limited space, choose a self-pollinating type. Birds will feast on sweet cherries, so use nets or accept that most trees will produce enough to share.

CROSS-POLLINATION
Two sweet cherries of the same variety may not be enough for cross-pollination, even if they flower together. Ask your nursery for advice on combinations that produce the best crops. A frost-free spring and a healthy bee population ensure a good harvest.

SITE AND SOIL PREPARATION
Choose a sheltered, frost-free site with deep soil and plenty of sun. Spray the planting area with horn manure 500, then dig a deep planting hole and fill with an equal mix of rich biodynamic garden compost and soil that has been lightly sprinkled with handfuls of coarse sand and pebbles.

SOWING AND PLANTING
Plant when trees are dormant in late fall or in very early spring when the moon is descending. Space trees that will grow to full size 23ft (7m) apart and those on dwarfing rootstocks for fan training 8–9ft (2.5–2.7m) apart. Apply a fine spray of tree paste to roots before planting.

ROUTINE CARE
Keep the ground fertile and moist with a light compost mulch and applications of horn manure 500 at the spring equinox, and at the next descending moon period. Spray comfrey liquid manure just before or after flowering for consistent cropping. Cold snaps in spring can decimate the crop. The evening before frost is forecast apply valerian 507 up to the height of the trunk—do not spray the emerging blossoms. In a wet spring when the risk of fungus disease is high, mix horn silica

501 and valerian 507 in a single spray and aim it up into the air around and on the trees at first light.

HARVESTING AND STORING
Pick the cherries in midsummer on fruit days with an ascending moon. Snip the fruit from the branch, leaving a piece of stalk to harden over and protect the tree. Eat within a few days.

TROUBLESHOOTING
Spray horn silica 501 after harvest and at least a month before fall equinox during the afternoon to "put the tree to sleep." Brush tree paste on the uncleaned trunk in late fall.

Pruning sweet cherries
• Prune under a descending moon in warm, dry spells in summer to reduce risk of silver leaf, a fungal disease that infects pruning cuts and destroys leaves and branches.

• In the first two years, prune single trees to create an open-centered crown with a balanced framework of branches.

• After two years, prune only to remove damaged or diseased wood—nothing further because cherries fruit on old wood.

• On fans, cut back branches that are unproductive and tie in vigorous replacements.

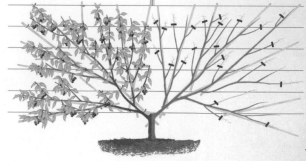

	SPRING	SUMMER	FALL	WINTER
Plant				
Prune				
Harvest				

Time to harvest: **10–14 WEEKS AFTER FLOWERING** • Plant trees 8ft (2.5m) apart, depending on rootstock and type

Rotation information: **NOT ROTATED • MEDIUM FEEDER**

Tart cherries
Prunus cerasus

Robust tart or sour cherries are generally easy to grow and well suited to a small garden, especially the dwarf varieties. The fruit is challengingly tart when eaten by itself, but its taste is transformed when it is cooked or baked to create wonderful jams, pies, cobblers, and sauces.

SITE AND SOIL PREPARATION

Tart cherries need a free-draining, moderately fertile soil with sufficient depth for the tree to put down a strong root system. These trees will tolerate a site with part sun.

SOWING AND PLANTING

Plant when there is a descending moon on fruit or root days, spacing these slow-growing and compact trees 15–18ft (4.5–5.5m) apart. They can also be grown as bushes or as fans against a wall. Although most trees are self-pollinating, the crop will be more reliable if more than one tree is planted.

ROUTINE CARE

Enrich the soil with a light compost mulch and applications of horn manure 500 at the spring equinox, and at the next descending moon period. Tart cherries need to be pruned to produce fruit regularly. Netting these short trees will keep birds from the crop.

HARVESTING AND STORING

Pick tart cherries in dry weather in late summer and early fall, on fruit days when the moon is ascending.

TROUBLESHOOTING

Spray chive infusion (*see p.31*) and nettle tea (*see p.38*) from bud burst—more than once, if necessary—to prevent cherry blackfly aphids from causing leaf curl early in the growing season. Aphids may be a sign of overly compact soil, or soil that has become too dry if the trees are being trained next to a wall. Scrape away as much dry, leeched soil as possible and spray stinging nettle manure or horn manure 500—or both. Repair the area with a compost and topsoil mix and mulch with hay or straw.

Pruning tart cherries

- Prune in the early years in spring and summer, during an ascending moon, to let light and air into the center of the tree. Cut back unruly growth on fans and train in new vigorous new growth.

- In subsequent years thin out woody side branches or spurs growing off the main branches, leaving those growing directly from the central trunk. Thin under an ascending moon in spring or summer.

- After harvesting, shorten overlong branches, retaining most of the new growth for fruiting the following year.

TREE PASTE

After harvesting tart cherries, brush the trunk of the tree with tree paste (*see pp.132–135*). The best time to apply tree paste is under a descending moon, during the afternoon, ideally on a fruit day.

CHERRY PICKING

Use scissors to snip the fruit from the tree, leaving a tiny piece of stalk, which will harden over to protect the branch through winter. Leaving the stalks attached to the cherries until you are ready to use them will allow them to age and mature for a few more days before cooking.

	SPRING	SUMMER	FALL	WINTER
Plant				
Prune				
Harvest				

Time to harvest: **10–12 WEEKS AFTER FLOWERING** • Plant trees 15–18ft (4.5–5.5m) apart, depending on rootstock

Rotation information: **NOT ROTATED • MEDIUM FEEDER**

Plums
gages and damsons
Prunus domestica, P. insititia

These related fruits vary in size, color, and taste. Plums and gages are delicious fresh, or cooked, while smaller, tarter damsons are at their best puréed, baked, or preserved. Not all plums and gages are self-pollinating, so choose plants that flower together, or match your choice to trees in neighboring yards.

SITE AND SOIL PREPARATION

An ideal site has well-drained soil and shelter from wind and cold during flowering. Greengages are the most frost-sensitive; damsons the least. Damsons are also self-pollinating, which is useful if there is space for only one tree. Trees trained lower to fans or cordons are more space-efficient and easier to protect.

SOWING AND PLANTING

Plant the trees when they are dormant and the soil is workable between late fall and late winter under a descending moon, ideally at moon-opposition Saturn, on a fruit or root day. Dig a deep hole and backfill it with a mix of good soil, well-rotted biodynamic compost, and finely chopped comfrey leaves. Firm gently but avoid creating a hard surface.

ROUTINE CARE

Spray horn manure 500 at fall equinox to stimulate the roots, and BC at spring equinox to clean up any disease pathogens in the top soil. Use a series of tea sprays following bud burst (*see right*). Thin young, overcrowded fruit, and support low stems heavy with fruit to keep them from splitting away from the trunk.

HARVESTING AND STORING

Plums and gages ripen from late summer to early fall; damsons ripen in early fall. Harvest on fruit days with an ascending moon.

TROUBLESHOOTING

Rub flaky bark off gently by hand (not with a wire brush) in late fall during the afternoon and cut out stems showing signs of dieback. Then apply tree paste as a general strengthener and protector, working under a descending moon, and ideally on a fruit day.

Pruning plums

- Hold back from pruning for the first three years to build reserves in the trunk and main shoots.
- Prune older trees in warm, dry periods, in spring under an ascending moon, just as growth is starting.
- When the shape is established, remove congested or crossing stems, or branches that have died back within the crown to maintain an open framework of branches.
- On fans, remove awkwardly growing older stems and tie in vigorous new growth.

USING TEAS

Plums and gages benefit from sprays of strengthening dandelion tea after bud burst; cleansing yarrow tea as leaves form; boosting stinging nettle tea as buds form; and stress-relieving chamomile tea after fruit has set.

Spray horseradish tea during April, May, and again in late August to prevent against fungal brown rot.

Try an early evening spray of comfrey liquid manure on the underside of the leaves before and after flowering.

Apply a chamomile spray for trees in fruit to help destress them.

	SPRING	SUMMER	FALL	WINTER
Plant				
Prune				
Harvest				

Time to harvest: **14–16 WEEKS AFTER FLOWERING** • Plant trees at least 8ft (2.5m) apart, depending on rootstock and type

Rotation information: **NOT ROTATED • MEDIUM FEEDERS**

Peaches
and nectarines
Prunus persica

Velvety peaches and smooth-skinned nectarines have a taste beyond compare when freshly picked from the garden. Peach trees can be grown as bushes or fans, while nectarines are best grown as fans—they are less hardy and need a little more warmth.

SITE AND SOIL PREPARATION

The ideal soil is a light, well-drained but moisture-retentive, sandy or rocky loam that is slightly acidic. Before planting, fork the soil over, incorporating plenty of mature biodynamic compost, then spray horn manure 500 a week later; do both tasks under a descending moon. The trees need cold winters to go into dormancy but appreciate the shelter of a sunny wall or fence to protect them from wind.

SOWING AND PLANTING

When the moon is descending, plant the trees while they are dormant, from mid- to late fall, or in early spring before they start to come out of winter hibernation.

ROUTINE CARE

Just before bud burst spray the soil with stinging nettle liquid manure, preferably on a fruit day. After bud burst spray the soil again, this time with BC. Redress with fresh compost if necessary. Keep watering, especially just before fruiting, and mulch, keeping the trunk clear. Thin tiny set fruit a hand's width apart. In early fall an afternoon spray of horn silica 501 will seal the plant and send sugars to feed the roots in winter.

HARVESTING AND STORING

Pick peaches and nectarines under an ascending moon, ideally on fruit days, when the ripe fruit can be twisted easily from the stems.

TROUBLESHOOTING

Nectarines split if they lack water when the fruit are starting to swell. Net ripening fruit to protect it from birds and squirrels.

Pruning peaches

- Prune trees within a couple of weeks of harvest or in early spring, during a descending moon period. Avoid cold spells.
- Fruit appears on shoots grown in the previous season, so prune to replace fruited wood with plenty of new, young wood and to maintain the shape of fans.
- Paint the trees thoroughly with tree paste after pruning to enliven and protect the bark.

BUD BURST

Both peaches and nectarines are self-pollinating, but because they bloom early in spring when the weather is usually cool, there are few pollinating insects around to do the job. Hand-pollinate the flowers with a soft paintbrush, and protect the blossoms from frost to maximize the crop.

TANSY

Discourage fruit tree moths from laying their eggs on your peach trees by siting a potted tansy plant around each one, or spray them with tansy tea early in the season. Before or after the trees bloom, feed them during an ascending moon on fruit days, with a spray of liquid manures made from comfrey or kelp.

	SPRING	SUMMER	FALL	WINTER
Plant				
Prune				
Harvest				

Time to harvest: **16–20 WEEKS AFTER FLOWERING** • Plant 14–16ft (4–5m) apart, according to rootstock and type

Rotation information: **NOT ROTATED • MEDIUM FEEDERS**

Apricots
Prunus armeniaca

You can grow apricots even in temperate regions: treat them right and they will reward you with juicy, sweet, fragrant fruit that cannot be matched by store-bought fruit. The blossoms are pretty, too.

SITE AND SOIL PREPARATION

Apricots need a sunny site that is shielded from cold winds and away from frost pockets. They prefer well-drained, gravelly or sandy loam with a neutral pH. Before planting, dig in plenty of biodynamic compost, at the start of a 13-day descending moon period, then spray the site with horn manure 500 in the evening a week or so later. Root days, fruit days, and cloudy, overcast days are best for this. Then, if possible, plant before the end of that descending moon period.

SOWING AND PLANTING

Apricots can self-pollinate, so you need only one tree for a crop. Plant a one-year-old tree when it is dormant, in fall or spring, or in winter if the weather is unusually mild, at the start of a descending moon. Carefully clean the trunk and branches of any flaky bark. Spray or dip the root ball in BC when planting the tree, but without washing all the soil off its roots, to help the roots establish in the soil. Prune the tree as soon as it is planted to shape it into a wall-trained or bush form. Then paint the cleaned trunk and pruned wood with pruning paste *(see pp.132–135)*.

ROUTINE CARE

Mulch with fresh compost after pruning to feed the soil. Spray horn manure 500, in the late afternoon under a descending moon before flowering, and horn silica 501, in the very early morning under an ascending moon, over the top of the tree before and after flowering.

HARVESTING AND STORING

The fruit usually ripens in late summer. Eat or preserve bruised fruit immediately. Healthy fruit should keep for a week to ten days.

TROUBLESHOOTING

To avoid rot, thin heavy crops, but only after fruit starts to swell. Prevent mites by again cleaning off flaky bark and sealing with pruning paste, on frost-free days at a descending moon.

Pruning an apricot

• Prune wall-trained trees in spring at the start of an ascending moon. At this time the roots will have absorbed sugars from the previous season and rising sap will repel disease organisms from the pruning cuts. Prune bush apricots only if necessary.

• Do not prune in wet weather because it encourages silver leaf disease and canker.

• Aim to retain 3–4 main stems with an airy, open center on bushes. On fans, cut back fruited shoots to new growth.

• In summer, remove any leafy growth shading the fruit and thin fruit, if needed.

FROM FLOWER TO FRUIT

Apricots flower very early in spring; when in cool climates few insects are about. Train the tree as a fan or a bush, so you can protect its blooms from spring frost and hand-pollinate them.

As soon as the flower buds open, lightly brush them to aid pollination, if needed.

Fabric protects apricots from spring frost, but blocks out pollinating insects.

A fruit is ripe when a rich gold and it falls off with a half-twist of its stalk.

	SPRING	SUMMER	FALL	WINTER
Plant				
Prune				
Harvest				

Time to harvest: **14–18 WEEKS AFTER FLOWERING** • Plant bush forms 11–18ft (3.5–5.5m) apart and fans 15ft (5m) apart

Rotation information: **NOT ROTATED • LIGHT FEEDERS**

Figs
Ficus carica

As well as fruit with green or deep purple skins and vibrant deep pink flesh, figs have handsome foliage. They make lovely garden plants both grown as standards, or against a wall.

SITE AND SOIL PREPARATION

Figs need very well-drained soil and warm sun. In cool climates, you may need to train them on a wall or fence and protect them in winter with fabric. Growing figs in the ground in cooler, wetter conditions can result in too much growth and little fruit. To avoid it, confine the roots (*see right*) or grow figs in large pots in a sunny, sheltered site and move them into cool, frost-free conditions over winter. Grow figs in light, sandy soil mixed with well-rotted compost.

SOWING AND PLANTING

Plant one-year-old trees after the last frost so that they have the summer to establish. Plant on a descending moon day, avoiding nodes.

ROUTINE CARE

Spray figs in pots soon after placing them outdoors in spring, with horn manure 500 mixed with stinging nettle tea; spray the plant and compost for steady, not-too-rapid, growth. On all figs, alternate applying leftover chamomile and *Equisetum arvense* 508 fresh teas, for overall health, with kelp and comfrey liquid manures as feed. Mist the tree with horn silica 501, at sunrise before summer solstice, to boost next year's buds, and again before fall equinox for ripening. Mulch in fall against winter cold; top off in early summer to keep the soil moist and help it to retain nutrients.

HARVESTING AND STORING

Ripe figs (*see right*) are rich in fiber and calcium: eat them fresh, as jam, or dry in the sun and store on trays covered with netting to keep wasps off. Turn them every day for a week or so.

TROUBLESHOOTING

Spray young trees with 501 at leaf fall in the afternoon, then with a diluted pruning paste, to help sap flow to the leaves, fruit, and roots. Check the roots of garden trees have not escaped their enclosures every couple of years; chop back with a spade or replant, if necessary.

Pruning figs

• Prune in summer under an ascending moon. Wear gloves since the sap can irritate.

• Open up the center of the tree by light pruning, removing any old or obviously weak canes and dead, diseased, or damaged growth.

• For wall-trained figs, follow the same principle and shorten overvigorous or badly placed stems. Tie in new shoots to the supports.

• Cut back any leafy growth that shades the swelling figs.

RIPENING FRUIT

Ripe figs are soft, with soft, droopy stems, and a powdery bloom on the skins. In cool climates, remove any tiny, hard fruit once the figs ripen: leave them to produce a second crop in warmer regions. Fruit that forms at the end of the season will produce next year's crop.

CONFINING THE ROOTS

Plant figs in a pit to restrict the roots and keep them fruiting. Make the pit about 3ft (90cm) square and line the sides with paving stones or drainage tiles. If planting against a wall, leave a gap the length of your hand and train the plant onto horizontal wires or netting.

	SPRING	SUMMER	FALL	WINTER
Plant				
Prune				
Harvest				

Time to harvest: **32–40 WEEKS AFTER FLOWERING** • Plant 12–15ft (4–5m) apart

Rotation information: **NOT ROTATED • LIGHT FEEDERS**

Citrus fruits
lemons, oranges, & limes
Citrus species

Citrus fruit originate from the subtropical climates of Asia and are evergreen. Grow these trees in cooler climates in large containers so that you can move them under cover and away from fatal frost—they do make wonderfully ornamental plants for the patio and porch.

Kumquat

SITE AND SOIL PREPARATION
Citrus fruit need an open, sunny site and shelter from strong winds. A slightly acidic, sandy loam (pH 6), which warms quickly and drains well but retains nutrients, is best. For pots, use a 3:2:1 mix of good soil, mature compost, and grit sand.

SOWING AND PLANTING
Citrus fruits self-pollinate, so you need only one tree for a crop. Plant container-grown trees in spring and bare-root trees at any time, under a descending moon. Spray the planting hole and tree roots with BC. Water well after planting.

ROUTINE CARE
Between bud burst and flowering, spray foliage and trunks with stinging nettle or kelp liquid manure to boost shoot growth. Spray 501 in the morning over plant tops just before flowering to improve fruit taste and for successful flowering next year. After flowering, spray with comfrey at any time to help form the leaves that plants need to ripen fruit. Water with rainwater after spraying. Every 3–4 years, renew the compost in pots.

HARVESTING AND STORING
Citrus fruit can generally be left on the tree until needed. Pick only when the weather is dry. They store well if kept at 45–48°F (7–9°C).

TROUBLESHOOTING
Poor, dry soils encourage mites, but avoid overwatering and overfeeding. If it is humid, spray fresh *Equisetum arvense* 508 tea on all green parts of the tree to ward off fungal diseases.

Pruning citrus fruit
- On planting, cut off any suckers growing from the base, taking care not to damage the bark.
- Prune the tree just before bud burst under a descending moon. Make as few cuts as possible: remove dead and diseased wood, as well as any water shoots crowding the tree. Prune out branches growing too close to the soil; they restrict airflow, drain the tree of energy, and later may be difficult to remove without killing the tree.
- After pruning, on the same day, spray the woody parts with diluted pruning paste (*see pp.132–135*).
- Thin any overcrowded fruit.

TYPES OF CITRUS
The citrus species include many types of delicious fruit, for example kumquats, mandarins, and oranges. Unlike most cool-climate fruit trees, they flower and fruit at the same time.

The commonest lemon is Citrus limon, but there are other species and hybrids.

Limes such as C. x aurantiifolia *may have green or greenish-yellow fruit.*

The flesh of grapefruit may be colored yellow, pink, or red.

	SPRING	SUMMER	FALL	WINTER
Plant				
Prune				
Harvest				

Time to harvest: **9–11 MONTHS AFTER FLOWERING** · Plant 15–30ft (5–10m) apart, depending on variety

Rotation information: **NOT ROTATED · HEAVY FEEDERS**

Grapevines

Vitis species

Be sure to choose the type of vine you grow according to whether you want to eat grapes fresh or make jam or wine. Table grapes often make flavorless wines, but grapes for preserving make wine that tastes oddly "foxy," and wine grapes are generally not juicy enough for eating.

SITE AND SOIL PREPARATION

Vines need sun and a well-drained soil that warms quickly to fruit and ripen well. Good airflow keeps disease at bay and aids ripening, so train on walls, pergolas, or posts and wire.

SOWING AND PLANTING

Dig lots of mature biodynamic compost into the planting hole and loosen compacted soil when planting, under a descending moon.

ROUTINE CARE

Spray soil in fall with horn manure 500 and BC in spring to encourage strong rooting and overall soil health. Spray horn silica 501, before or after flowering, into the air over the plants to aid ripeness and flavor, and again in late summer if ripening is slow. Apply *Equisetum arvense* 508 tea, oak bark decoction, or yarrow tea on the foliage in the morning, between spring and summer, to improve plant health. Spray stinging nettle or chamomile tea to prevent heat stress. Use comfrey or kelp liquid manures on foliage, in the evening, just before or after flowering to keep your plants well fed and vigorous.

HARVESTING AND STORING

Cut bunches under an ascending moon. Process wine grapes as soon as they are picked.

TROUBLESHOOTING

Net against birds, if needed. Pests and crowding cause vinegar-scented bunches and split, windblown fruits attract vinegar flies: remove any affected bunches promptly.

GROWING TIPS

Overcrowding and overshading of bunches reduces light and airflow, leading to smaller fruit and problems such as mildew or pests. To avoid this, thin embryonic bunches to one per sideshoot on dessert vines or one every 12in (30cm) on wine vines.

Thin the grapes within each new bunch, snipping out about one third.

Pruning grapevines

• In late winter or early spring, cut back the leader to keep it to size and encourage more sideshoots to form. Grape trusses form from nodes left on last year's wood, so prune the rest of the vine to ensure a balance of energy-rich fruit and energy-collecting shoots and leaves.

• Cut off any suckers growing from the base. Paint larger pruning wounds with pruning paste (*see pp.132–135*).

• In early summer, remove lateral or water shoots around the young grape bunches to aid airflow.

• In late summer, pinch out some leafy shoots to increase light and airflow around the developing fruit.

COMPANION PLANTING

In the 19th century, roses were planted at the ends of grapevine rows. Roses fall victim to powdery mildew earlier in the season than grapevines, so the roses provided an early warning system for the disease, allowing growers to take action to save the harvest. Today, roses in vineyards are purely decorative.

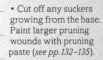

	SPRING	SUMMER	FALL	WINTER
Plant				
Prune				
Harvest				

Time to harvest: **14–18 WEEKS AFTER FLOWERING** • Plant 3ft (90cm) apart

Rotation information: **NOT ROTATED • LIGHT FEEDERS**

Biodynamic prep calendar

		EARLY SPRING	MID-SPRING	LATE SPRING	EARLY SUMMER	MID-SUMMER
Biodynamic sprays	500 Horn manure	Excavate the horns buried in fall				
		Dynamize for 1 hour and apply to soil in large droplets toward the end of the day				
	501 Horn silica		Fill horns with silica, and bury			
		Dynamize for 1 hour and mist the atmosphere above crops—usually early in the morning				
	508 *Equisetum arvense*				Collect and dry *Equisetum arvense*	
		Dilute fresh tea or liquid manure, dynamize for 10–20 minutes, and apply to soil or plants				
Biodynamic compost preps	502 Yarrow					Collect and dry yarrow flowers
			Fill bladder and hang for summer			
		Excavate bladder buried in fall				
	503 Chamomile				Collect and dry chamomile flowers	
		Excavate intestine buried in fall				
	504 Nettle				Collect and bury nettles	
	505 Oak bark	Excavate skulls buried in fall				
	506 Dandelion		Collect and dry dandelion flowers			
		Excavate mesentery buried in fall				
	507 Valerian				Pick, and infuse or juice valerian flowers	
		Dynamize for 10–20 minutes; spray fruit blossoms or soil to guard against frost				
	BC	Make at any time; dynamize for 10–20 minutes and apply in large droplets toward the end of the day on soil or beds where no biodynamic compost was spread				

Your at-a-glance guide shows when to make and apply the biodynamic sprays and the six compost preps.

LATE SUMMER	EARLY FALL	MID-FALL	LATE FALL	EARLY WINTER	MID-WINTER	LATE WINTER
	Fill horns with manure and bury					
	Excavate the horns buried in spring					
		Take down bladder and bury	Apply when making new compost heaps, or when turning compost			
		Fill intestine and bury	Apply when making new compost heaps, or when turning compost			
			Apply when making new compost heaps, or when turning compost			
Excavate nettles after 12–15 months						
Collect oak bark, fill skulls, and bury			Apply when making new compost heaps, or when turning compost			
		Fill mesentery and bury	Apply when making new compost heaps, or when turning compost			
			Dynamize for 10–20 minutes; apply when making new compost heaps, or when turning compost			

Resources

Organizations

Biodynamic organizations offer members resources to make or buy preparations, as well as education and certification.

NORTH AMERICA

Demeter Association, Inc.
P.O. Box 1390
Philomath, OR 97370
www.demeter-usa.org
In charge of Demeter Biodynamic certification in the US. Educates farmers, processors, and consumers on the basic principles of Biodynamic agriculture as outlined in the Demeter Farm and Processing Standard. Can provide details of local Biodynamic farms and gardens. Protects the integrity of Biodynamic agriculture, and the products that will result, in the US marketplace.

Biodynamic Association
661 N. Water Street, Suite 307
Milwaukee, WI 53202
www.biodynamics.com
Association of Biodynamic farmers and growers in the US. Its website provides details of local Biodynamic groups across the US and Canada. Publishes the quarterly journal *Biodynamics*.

Josephine Porter Institute for Applied Bio-Dynamics
201 East Main Street, Suite 14
Floyd, VA 24091
www.jpibiodynamics.org
Source of Biodynamic preparations in the US. Publishes a newsletter called *Applied Biodynamics* for members.

EUROPE

Demeter-International e.V.
Brandschneise 1
64295 Darmstadt
Germany
www.demeter.net
The global umbrella body for the biodynamic movement worldwide. Supervises the Demeter certification mark that is carried by accredited biodynamic produce (food, health and hygiene products, clothes).

Biodynamic Association UK
Painswick Inn Project
Gloucester Street
Stroud,
Gloucestershire
GL5 1QG
United Kingdom
www.biodynamic.org.uk
In charge of Demeter biodynamic certification in the UK and Ireland. Can provide details of local biodynamic farms and gardens. Publishes the *Star & Furrow* journal for members.

Biodynamie Services
Les Crêts
71250 Château
France
www.biodynamie-services.fr
Source of biodynamic preparations in France.

AUSTRALIA & NEW ZEALAND

Bio-Dynamic Research Institute (BDRI)
C/o Post Office
Powelltown
Victoria 3797
Australia
www.demeter.org.au
In charge of Demeter certification in Australia.

Biodynamic Agriculture Australia
PO Box 54
Bellingen, NSW 2454
Australia
www.biodynamics.net.au
Biodynamic farming and gardening association. Sells biodynamic preparations.

Bio Dynamic Farming and Gardening Association
P.O. Box 39045
Wellington
New Zealand
www.biodynamic.org.nz
This New Zealand association offers Demeter certification for farmers, and its website has information on growing various crops using biodynamic methods.

AFRICA

Biodynamic Agricultural Association of Southern Africa
Spier Wine Estate
Stellenbosch 7603
South Africa
www.bdaasa.org.za
This organization is having real success at promoting biodynamic farming, gardening, and education in southern Africa.

Further Reading

The Barefoot Farmer
Jeff Poppen (USA, 2001)
Down-to-earth tips written in an amusing, accessible style by Jeff Poppen, an experienced professional Biodynamic farmer and gardener based in Tennessee. (www.barefootfarmer.org)

The Biodynamic Farm
Herbert Koepf (USA, 1989)
An agronomic text providing a practical view of developing a Biodynamic farm system. Provides an array of research data as well as many helpful details on the core elements of Biodynamic agriculture.

Bio-Dynamic Gardening
John Soper, revised by Barbara Saunders-Davis and K Castelliz (Souvenir Press)
Written from an English garden perspective, this book contains many tips that can be applied to almost any garden worldwide.

The Biodynamic Spray and Compost Preparations Production Methods, Booklet 1
C. von Wistinghausen, W. Scheibe, E. von Wistinghausen, and U. König (Biodynamic Agricultural Association UK)
Contains directions and illustrations explaining the biodynamic preparations.

Biodynamics: Three Introductory Articles
Ehrenfried Pfeiffer (Biodynamic Farming and Gardening Association USA)
A useful primer for the *Agriculture* course by Rudolf Steiner.

The Biodynamic Treatment of Fruit Trees, Berries and Shrubs
Ehrenfried Pfeiffer (Biodynamic Farming and Gardening Association USA)
Useful tips for preparing the ground for planting and maintaining fruit crops.

Companion Plants and How to Use Them
Helen Philbrick and Richard Gregg (USA, 1966)
Profiles of which plants are best friends— and which are not.

Grasp the Nettle
Peter Proctor with Gillian Cole (Random House New Zealand)
New Zealander Peter Proctor has worked extensively in India, helping poor farmers to regenerate their soil using biodynamics. Proctor is a big fan of timing planting to moon–opposition Saturn—in this book he explains why, along with his "brick pit prep."

Monty Waldin's Best Biodynamic Wines
Monty Waldin (Floris Books)
Short profiles of the best Biodynamic wines worldwide, with explanations from winegrowers about how biodynamics works for them.

Monty Waldin's Biodynamic Wine-Growing: Theory & Practice
Monty Waldin (www.lulu.com)
A how-to book for professional winegrowers containing detailed explanations of the biodynamic preps.

Nine Lectures on Bees
Rudolf Steiner, trans. by Marna Pease and Carl Alexander Mier (St. George Publications)
Bees are in crisis. These lectures, written in 1923 by the founder of biodynamics, predicted a crisis would happen "80 years hence" (i.e., around now), and explain why our relationship with bees is so fundamental to us as living, sentient beings.

Grow a Garden and be Self-sufficient
Ehrenfried Pfeiffer (USA, 1942)
Written for Americans in the postwar period, but as relevant today as it was then.

The Omnivore's Dilemma
Michael Pollan (Penguin)
Pollan's message of "Eat food. Not too much. Mostly plants" makes sense and will make a hard day's digging in your biodynamic vegetable garden worthwhile.

Results from the Sowing and Planting Calendar
Maria Thun, trans. by G. Staudenmaier (Floris)
Practical research by the late Maria Thun, whose trials of sowing and planting crops by lunar and celestial cycles provided the basis for the celestial calendar (see Calendars) now written by her son, Matthias.

Sensitive Chaos
Theodor Schwenk, trans. by O. Whicher and J. Weigley (Rudolf Steiner Press)
An in-depth study of why some biodynamic preparations are stirred in water.

Spiritual Foundations for the Renewal of Agriculture
Rudolf Steiner, trans. by C. Creeger and M. Gardner (USA, 1993)
This book contains the reasoning behind biodynamics as outlined by Dr. Rudolf Steiner during his series of lectures in 1924 to concerned farmers. These have become known as the *Agriculture* course.

Weeds and What They Tell
Ehrenfried Pfeiffer (Biodynamic Farming & Gardening Association USA)
Weeds are messengers and this booklet explains what message they are sending gardeners about the health—or otherwise—of their soils.

What is Biodynamics?
Hugh Courtney (Steiner Books USA)
Valuable biodynamic insights from Hugh Courtney, who made the biodynamic preparations when running the Josephine Porter Institute for Applied Bio-Dynamics for over thirty years.

Calendars

Biodynamic Sowing and Planting Calendar (Matthias Thun)
Published annually in English, German, French, and Italian. Used worldwide, this celestial calendar provides guidance of when to sow, plant, and transplant according to all key celestial cycles.

Lunar Organics
www.lunarorganics.com
This UK-based company's "Moon Gardening" wall chart can be used to plan your gardening year according to the celestial calendar.

Stella Natura
www.stellanatura.com
Annual sowing and planting calendar widely used in North America. Contains useful essays and stimulating insights on practical and theoretical aspects of biodynamics.

When Wine Tastes Best (Floris)
Also published in book form, this digital app advises whether it is a root, leaf, flower, or fruit day. Intended for wine lovers (fruit days are best for wine tasting), this app is also useful for gardeners.

Index

About the author

Monty Waldin is an award-winning wine writer specializing in green issues, with firsthand experience of developing biodynamic vineyards in Europe and North America. While living in France, Monty was filmed by Britain's Channel 4 for Château Monty—the first observational TV documentary on biodynamic winemaking (2008). He is the author of several books and contributes to BBC radio and TV, and to British newspapers—including the *Independent*, London's *Evening Standard*, and the *Daily Mail*—and websites, as well as to wine, travel, and environmental publications including *Decanter*, *Harpers Wine & Spirit Trades Review*, *World of Fine Wine*, *The Ecologist*, *Star & Furrow* (the journal of the UK Biodynamic Agricultural Association), and *Biodynamics*, the journal of the North American Biodynamic Farming & Gardening Association.

Author acknowledgments

Reference books are always a team effort, and a groundbreaking book such as this requires both courage—given the esoteric nature of the subject—as well as intricate planning on behalf of the publisher and the team. To create a book illustrated in such fine and coherent detail requires both a biodynamic garden as stage and biodynamic gardeners as protagonists. Photographer Will Heap has captured the essence of the plants, cow horns, and other materials used to make the biodynamic preparations. His photographs reveal the inner vitality of his own biodynamic garden, as well as the intricacies of how biodynamic compost, teas, and, of course, the preparations themselves are made, in this case by experienced biodynamic farmer Briony Young. The choice of images and the way they have been presented in the book in such a clear and thoughtful way is thanks to Sonia Moore. Helen Fewster has edited my explanations of how biodynamic methods can make gardening a more stimulating experience with skill, sensitivity, and, above all, great wisdom.

My career in biodynamic wine really took off when developing a biodynamic garden for a California vineyard in the late 1990s. I learned then that while most gardeners focus solely on the earth beneath their feet, biodynamic gardeners go a few steps further by considering what is going on above their heads—meaning lunar and other celestial cycles—and work toward greater self-sufficiency using animals or animal-based manures for compost. I see biodynamics as a way of growing food that is good for both body and spirit while putting more back into the land than you take out. I hope this book encourages the next generation of gardeners to consider giving biodynamics a try like I did all those years ago.

Publisher's acknowledgments

DK would like to thank Will Heap, Kate Turner, and their children for their dedication, energy, and enthusiasm in creating a biodynamic garden for this book. Thanks also to Michael Fuller for assistance and advice from a biodynamic landscape gardener's perspective; to Dorothea Leber for sharing her expertise and showing us her garden at Michael Hall School; to Peter Brinch for information on seed saving; and to Jessica Standing of the BDA for her help and enthusiasm, particularly at the start of the project. We are immensely grateful to the community at Tablehurst Farm for the loan of Briony Young, who guided us through our photoshoots—and to Briony herself for her generosity and patience throughout the process. Thanks to all at Plaw Hatch Farm, especially Nir Halfon and Liz Charnell for accommodating photography and allowing us to sample their beautiful produce. Thanks also to Sarah Delfas and Sabine Von Szczepanski for the use of their gardens, and to David Josephs and Kamil Demir of Clifton Greens for procuring grocery props.

Designers: Elaine Hewson, Clare Marshall
Editors: Chauney Dunford, Shashwati Tia Sarkar, Annelise Evans, Esther Ripley, Andrea Bagg, Alastair Laing
Additional photography: Gary Ombler
Indexer: Vanessa Bird

Picture credits

The publisher would like to thank the following for their kind permission to reproduce their photographs.
(Key: a-above; b-below/bottom; c-center; f-far; l-left; r-right; t-top)

2 DK: Sonia Moore (cra). **DK:** Kate Turner (fcl, bl). **3 DK:** Kate Turner (c). **9 DK:** Helena Smith/Rough Guides (tr); **Will Heap:** *Biodynamics in Practice*, Rudolf Steiner Press, 2010 (br). **17 DK:** Kate Turner (tr). **22 DK:** Lucy Claxton (bl). **23 DK:** Kate Turner (bl). **30 DK:** RHS Wisley (tr). **32 DK:** Garden designed by Sarah Price/RHS Chelsea Flower Show 2012 (tl). **45 Fotolia:** Alexey Repka. **47 DK:** Paul Whitfield/Rough Guides (br). **57 DK:** Chelsea Flower Show (bc). **73 DK:** RHS Wisley (cr). **140 DK:** Sonia Moore (cla). **143 DK:** Lucy Claxton (ftl); RHS Wisley (fcrb). **149 Getty Images:** (fbl/blackberries); Lauren Nicole/Photodisc (br/cranberries). **150 Fotolia:** Alexey Repka (tl). **156 DK:** RHS Wisley (cr). **157 DK:** Ally Beag (crb). **158 DK:** Luke Anderson (crb). **159 DK:** Sandy Austin (crb). **161 DK:** Moss Doerksen (br). **164 DK:** Peter Warren (br). **166 DK:** Caroline Showell (crb). **167 DK:** Caroline Showell (crb). **171 DK:** Sonia Moore (cr, crb). **172 Fotolia:** Alexey Repka (tl). **175 DK:** Avon Bulbs (tl). **177 DK:** Sonia Moore (crb). **178 DK:** Karen Blakeman (crb). **180 Fotolia:** Alexey Repka (tl).

183 DK: Garden designed by Outerspace Designs/RHS Hampton Court Flower Show 2013 (cl). **186 DK:** RHS Hampton Court Flower Show (cra). **187 DK:** John Stewart (crb). **188 DK:** Sonia Moore (crb). **190 DK:** Drahomira Machackova (cr). **192 DK:** Nikki Mantei—http://gardenpurl.blogspot.co.uk (crb). **194 DK:** Fongshoo Yeh (crb). **195 DK:** Hester Robson (crb). **199 DK:** Amelia Bellamy-Royds (crb). **201 DK:** Wendy Hannan (crb). **203 DK:** Joy Russell (crb). **204 DK:** Olivier Bacquet (crb). **206 Fotolia:** Alexey Repka (tl). **209 DK:** Alan Buckingham (cl). **210 DK:** Sonia Moore (crb). **221 Alamy Images:** Valentyn Volkov (tl). **224 DK:** Joanna Plumb (cr). **225 DK:** Alan Buckingham (cra). **226 DK:** Alan Buckingham (tr). **227 Getty Images:** (tl). **228 DK:** Alan Buckingham (cra). **229 Getty Images:** Creativ Studio Heinemann (bl). **230 DK:** Alan Buckingham (fcra, cr, br). **231 DK:** Alan Buckingham (cr). **232 Getty Images:** Lauren Nicole/Photodisc (ftl, cra). **233 DK:** Alan Buckingham (cra). **234 DK:** Alan Buckingham (cr). **235 DK:** Alan Buckingham (tl, br). **239 DK:** Alan Buckingham (cr). **240 DK:** Airedale (br); Alan Buckingham (cra). **241 DK:** Alan Buckingham/Hampton Court Flower Show 2009 (cr). **242 DK:** Simon Bracken/Rough Guides (br); Alan Buckingham (cr). **243 DK:** RHS Wisley (br).

All other images © Dorling Kindersley.
For further information see: **www.dkimages.com**.